HOW TO BEAT
BOBBY FISCHER

Edmar Mednis

United States Senior Chess Master
International Chess Master

Introduction by
Robert Byrne

DOVER PUBLICATIONS, INC.
Mineola, New York

Published in Canada by General Publishing Company, Ltd., 30 Lesmill Road, Don Mills, Toronto, Ontario.
Published in the United Kingdom by Constable and Company, Ltd., 3 The Lanchesters, 162–164 Fulham Palace Road, London W6 9ER.

Bibliographical Note

This Dover edition, first published in 1997, is a revised and updated edition of the work first published by Quadrangle/The New York Times Book Company in 1974.

Library of Congress Cataloging-in-Publication Data

Mednis, Edmar, 1937–
    How to beat Bobby Fischer / by Edmar Mednis ; introduction by Robert Byrne. — Dover ed., rev. and updated.
        p.   cm.
    Includes index.
    ISBN 0-486-29844-2 (pbk.)
    1. Fischer, Bobby, 1943–   . 2. Chess—Collections of games.
    I. Title.
    GV1439.F5M42   1997
    794.1'59—dc21   97–29737
                                                        CIP

Manufactured in the United States of America
Dover Publications, Inc., 31 East 2nd Street, Mineola, N.Y. 11501

To the Girls in My Life:
My mother, wife, sisters,
and daughter.

ACKNOWLEDGMENTS

The nice thing in writing a book about a famous public figure is that factual information is available regarding his deeds. To go with a considerable amount of personal knowledge I have been able to obtain additional valuable facts and figures from the leading chess magazines of our day, game collections, tournament books and even opening manuals. The complete list of sources is too long to recite here; where appropriate, credits are given in the text. Two books do deserve special mention: *Bobby Fischer's Chess Games* edited by Robert G. Wade and Kevin J. O'Connell and for a look at the thinking of the Champion himself, *My 60 Memorable Games* by Bobby Fischer.

Much assistance, moral as well as physical, is required to bring to fruition such an effort. My thanks to all who helped, with a special personal bouquet to:

—Paul Marshall, Bobby's lawyer in Reykjavik, for his enthusiastic reception of the idea;

—Grandmaster Robert Byrne, editor and friend, for his illuminating introduction;

—My blond wife Baiba, for being my total assistant in all matters non-chessic

—Robert J. Fischer, for being such a great player that even, *maybe especially,* his lost games are a rich source of chess instruction and information for the rest of us.

In such an undertaking some errors of fact and interpretation are almost inevitable. The author accepts responsibility for all of these. Your assistance in bringing them to my attention will be appreciated.

Edmar Mednis

CONTENTS

PART TWO   Hope and Disappointment   **131**

PART THREE   Semi-Retirement   **185**

PART FOUR   Artistry at the Highest Level   247

PART FIVE   1972–1992   281

EPILOGUE: How to Beat Bobby Fischer   288

PREFACE

Scope and Purpose

Although Robert James ("Bobby") Fischer is a great chess champion, perhaps the greatest the world has seen, so far even *he* has lost some chess games. This book contains all 61 tournament and match games that he has lost since achieving Champion status by winning undefeated the 1957–58 U.S. Championship. He was only 14 years old at the time, but such an accomplishment took him out of the "kid" status and established him immediately as a full-grown man in the world of chess.

These 61 losses in 16 years came from a total of 576 games actually played. The number is exceedingly small when compared to the large number of wins: 327, for a win-loss ratio of better than 5 to 1. Also striking is the small number of draws—188—as compared to the large number of wins. At the higher level of championship play a 1 win:1 draw ratio is considered rather good and Bobby is close to a 2:1 ratio. No wonder one of the famous (and only partly jesting) comments about playing against Fischer is that it is easier to defeat him than to draw against him! The total number of points scored is 421 out of 576 for a rather phenomenal 73 percent. Thus it is no surprise that Fischer is the highest-rated player in the history of chess.

Robert J. Fischer also had lost games prior to achieving the top U.S. rung. Records are incomplete, but it appears that he lost about 20 games prior to the 1957–58 U.S. Championship. Even though he was already progressing rapidly, there could be no talk of chess maturity.

Thus, the purpose of this book is to present only the lost games of the Champion Robert J. Fischer. Why should we study such games? For reasons of entertainment and human nature obviously. After all, each of us has lost plenty of games and it is good to know that even the greatest are not invincible. Such knowledge allows us to come back with vigor after our reverses. The major reason, however, is instructional. It is painful, but true, that in chess as in real life we tend to learn more from our defeats. Successes are great for ego and pocket, but not necessarily for the mind. Thus, if we can learn from our defeats, should we not be able to learn much more from carefully studying the reasons, why a great champion loses? The answer is an obvious "yes," but so far no qualified chess master has compiled such a study for the benefit of the public. All analyses have been undertaken in secret, to be used only for an actual combat against Robert J. Fischer.

Misconceptions and the Truth

Many of the conclusions from a study of Bobby's lost games will surprise both the layman and the expert.

From Table 1 we see that Fischer is almost as likely to lose with White as with Black. This is surprising, because it is thought that he takes "inordinate chances" with Black in order to win, and thus should lose much more. The truth is that he wins with Black, regularly as well as White, and because of his active fighting style is just as likely to lose with either color.

Even more surprising are the actual reasons why the games were lost. As Table 2 shows, in almost two thirds of the cases (62 percent), Fischer was simply outplayed. His opponent played better, deserved to win and did win. Another 16 games (26 percent) were lost because of the type of blunders that we all make. I have delicately called this "carelessness." Only 7 games were lost through what can be clearly called "trying too hard to win." This is an exceedingly low number over a period of 16 years. And it demonstrates very convincingly how little Fischer has suffered from overaggressiveness. We have long known how successful this attitude has been for winning purposes.

Every time Bobby loses a game against a non-grandmaster the game is, chessically speaking, front-page news. And well it might be! Despite acknowledged risk-taking, over 16 years he has lost only 9 games to non-grandmasters. However, 52 times he has been forced to congratulate his fellow grandmasters on victories. Thus it is clearly his fellow grandmasters that have given him the hardest time and not the outsiders. (See Table 3.)

Who have been the giant killers? Let us look at the list from Table 4 and the division by nations from Table 5. Thirty-three different players have had the honor of defeating Fischer. By nations, USSR is in first place with 25 wins (41 percent of total). No one else has even 10 and Argentina is in fourth place with only 4 wins. The poor showing by Americans against their champion is striking with only 4 ever being able to defeat him: Benko, Reshevsky, R. Byrne and Mednis. Table 4 is also significant for its omissions. Among the galaxy of international stars we do not see Portisch (Hungary), Hort (Czechoslovakia), Taimanov (USSR), Panno (Argentina), etc. Top American players who don't even have one Fischer scalp include William Lombardy and Larry Evans.

What openings should you select against Fischer for best winning chances? Table 6A shows Bobby's losses with White and Table 6B losses with Black. The first thing to notice is that with White no unusual openings are represented. Thus, don't expect to do well with an off-beat line! He'll kill you! Ruy Lopez and Sicilian Defense are represented at about the level expected. Unusual is the high number of losses against the French (only one less than with the Ruy), a defense not popular with modern masters. The numbers for the Caro-Kann are not significant, because 3 of the 4 losses came with the same unlucky variation at the 1959 Candidates Tournament.

Table 6B shows Bobby's fantastic successes with the Najdorf variation. In 15 years he has lost only 7 times with it. Altogether, his success against the aggressive King's Pawn is fantastic with only 9 games being lost. Two major results stand out from the Closed Games summary. The Samisch variation against the King's Indian has always given him trouble and lately he has become so aware of it that he has not played the King's Indian where he could expect the Samisch. His last matches with Petrosian and Spassky show this. Also striking is the disaster that the Ragosin variation of the Queen's Gambit Declined has been. Despite infrequent usage, Bobby already has 5 losses with it. Even so, he continues its use—including the first match game with Spassky!

A detailed summary of all 61 games appears as Table 7. For those preparing for quiz shows it may be helpful to know that the shortest game Fischer has lost is 22 moves (against Unzicker, Buenos Aires 1960; also carried in some books as 23 moves) and twice Bobby has held out to 73 moves before conceding: Keres in Curaçao 1962 and Mednis in the 1962/3 U.S. Championship.

TABLE 1

Games Lost with White and Black

White—28 (46%)
Black—33 (54%)

TABLE 2

Reasons for Losing Games

Outplayed—38 (62%)
Carelessness—16 (26%)
Trying too hard to Win— 7 (11%)

TABLE 3

Losses Against Type of Competition

Grandmasters—52 (85%)
Non-grandmasters— 9 (15%)

Byrne, R. (USA)	1
Cholmov (USSR)	1
Ciocaltea (Rumania)	1
Donner (Holland)	1
Eliskases (Argentina)	1
Gheorghiu (Rumania)	1
Janosevic (Yugoslavia)	1
Jauregui (Chile)	1
Keller (Switzerland)	1
Kovacevic (Yugoslavia)	1
Letelier (Chile)	1
Matulovic (Yugoslavia)	1
Mednis (USA)	1
Munoz (Ecuador)	1
Najdorf (Argentina)	1
Sanguinetti (Argentina)	1
Smyslov (USSR)	1
Uhlmann (E. Germany)	1
Unzicker (W. Germany)	1
Wexler (Argentina)	1
	61

TABLE 4

Conquerors of Champion Fischer

	number of times
Geller (USSR)	5
Spassky (USSR)	5
Gligoric (Yugoslavia)	4
Petrosian (USSR)	4
Tal (USSR)	4
Benko (USA)	3
Keres (USSR)	3
Reshevsky (USA)	3
Ivkov (Yugoslavia)	2
Korchnoi (USSR)	2
Larsen (Denmark)	2
Olafsson (Iceland)	2
Pachman (Czechoslovakia)	2

TABLE 5

Wins Against Fischer by Nations

USSR	25
Yugoslavia	9
United States	8
Argentina	4
Chile	2
Czechoslovakia	2
Denmark	2
Iceland	2
Rumania	2
East Germany	1
Ecuador	1
Holland	1
Switzerland	1
West Germany	1

TABLE 6 A

Losses by Opening with White

1.	Sicilian Defense	10
	Najdorf	4
	Sozin (6 B-QB4)	4
	Dragon	1
	Scheveningen	1
2.	Ruy Lopez	7
	Closed	5
	Open	1
	Steinitz Deferred	1
3.	French Defense	6
	Winawer	4
	Mac Cutcheon	1
	Tarrasch (Guimard)	1
4.	Caro-Kann	4
	Two Knights (2 N-QB3)	3
	4 ... B-B4	1
5.	Pirc (4 P-B4)	1

Total 28

TABLE 6 B

Losses by Opening with Black

A)	*Closed Games*	24
	1. King's Indian Defense	11
	Samisch	5
	Petrosian	2
	Normal	1
	King's-Fianchetto	1
	Benko	1
	Averbach	1
	2. Queen's Gambit Declined (Ragosin Variation)	5
	3. Nimzo-Indian Defense	4
	Rubinstein	3
	Samisch	1
	4. Gruenfeld Defense	3
	Exchange Variation	2
	4 B-B4	1
	5. English Opening	1
B)	*Open Games* (1 P-K4)	9
	1. Sicilian Defense	8
	Najdorf	7
	Closed	1
	2. King's Gambit	1

Total 33

TABLE 7

Fischer's Lost Games

GAME		PLACE AND TIME	OPENING	REASON FOR LOSS
1	Matulovic–F	Match, Belgrade, Yugoslavia July 1958	King's Indian (Sämisch) 41 moves	Outplayed
2	Benko–F	Portoroz Interzonal August 1958 Round 4	King's Indian (Sämisch) 41 moves	Outplayed

TABLE 7—Continued

Fischer's Lost Games

GAME		PLACE AND TIME	OPENING	REASON FOR LOSS
3	Olafsson–F	Portoroz Interzonal August 1958 Round 11	Queen's Gambit Declined (Ragosin) 44 moves	Outplayed
4	F–Pachman	Mar del Plata March 1959 Round 3	Ruy Lopez (Steinitz Deferred) 56 moves	Trying too hard to win
5	F–Letelier	Mar del Plata March 1959 Round 5	Ruy Lopez (Closed) 59 moves	Carelessness
6	F–Ivkov	Santiago April 1959 Round 3	French (Winawer) 52 moves	Outplayed
7	Sanguinetti–F	Santiago April 1959 Round 4	King's Indian (Sämisch) 55 moves	Outplayed
8	Pachman–F	Santiago April 1959 Round 6	Queen's Gambit Declined (Ragosin) 40 moves	Trying too hard to win
9	Jauregui–F	Santiago April 1959 Round 10	King's Indian (Sämisch) 40 moves	Outplayed
10	Gligoric–F	Zurich June 1959 Round 11	Sicilian (Najdorf) 39 moves	Carelessness
11	F–Keller	Zurich June 1959 Round 14	Ruy Lopez (Closed) 57 moves	Trying too hard to win

TABLE 7—Continued

Fischer's Lost Games

GAME		PLACE AND TIME	OPENING	REASON FOR LOSS
12	F–Petrosian	Candidates Bled Sept 1959 Round 2	Caro-Kann (Two Knights) 68 moves	Outplayed
13	Olafsson–F	Candidates Bled Sept 1959 Round 5	Sicilian (Najdorf) 45 moves	Outplayed
14	Tal–F	Candidates Bled Sept 1959 Round 6	King's Indian (Petrosian) 41 moves	Outplayed
15	F–Keres	Candidates Bled Sept 1959 Round 8	Caro-Kann (Two Knights) 30 moves	Outplayed
16	Petrosian–F	Candidates Bled Sept 1959 Round 9	Nimzo-Indian (Rubinstein) 31 moves	Outplayed
17	Gligoric–F	Candidates Bled Sept 1959 Round 11	Sicilian (Najdorf) 43 moves	Outplayed
18	F-Tal	Candidates Bled Sept 1959 Round 13	Sicilian (Najdorf) 33 moves	Outplayed
19	Tal–F	Candidates Zagreb Oct 1959 Round 20	King's Indian (Petrosian) 34 moves	Outplayed

TABLE 7—Continued

Fischer's Lost Games

GAME		PLACE AND TIME	OPENING	REASON FOR LOSS
20	F–Smyslov	Candidates Zagreb Oct 1959 Round 21	Sicilian (Najdorf) 48 moves	Trying too hard to win
21	F–Keres	Candidates Belgrade Oct 1959 Round 22	Caro-Kann (Two Knights) 55 moves	Outplayed
22	F–Tal	Candidates Belgrade Oct 1959 Round 27	Sicilian (Najdorf) **52 moves**	Carelessness
23	Spassky–F	Mar del Plata March 1960 Round 2	King's Gambit 29 moves	Carelessness
24	Eliskases–F	Buenos Aires June 1960 Round 5	Queen's Gambit Declined (Ragosin) 58 moves	Carelessness
25	Wexler–F	Buenos Aires July 1960 Round 7	English (K-side Symm) 38 moves	Outplayed
26	F–Uhlmann	Buenos Aires July 1960 Round 8	French (Winawer) 42 moves	Outplayed
27	Unzicker–F	Buenos Aires July 1960 Round 11	Sicilian (Najdorf) 22 (or 23) moves	Carelessness
28	Benko–F	Buenos Aires July 1960 Round 19	King's Indian (3 P-KN3) 27 moves	Carelessness

TABLE 7—*Continued*

Fischer's Lost Games

GAME		PLACE AND TIME	OPENING	REASON FOR LOSS
29	F–Munoz	Leipzig Olymp Oct 1960 Prelims vs Ecuador	Sicilian (Dragon, Yug) 36 moves	Outplayed
30	Gligoric–F	Leipzig Olymp Oct 1960 Finals vs Yugoslavia	Queen's Gambit Declined (Ragosin) 33 moves	Outplayed
31	Reshevsky–F	Match July 1961 Game 1 N.Y.	King's Indian (Normal) 60 moves	Outplayed
32	Reshevsky–F	Match Aug 1961 Game 7 Los Angeles	Queen's Gambit Declined (Ragosin) 28 moves	Outplayed
33	Benko–F	Candidates Curaçao May 1962 Round 1	King's Indian (Benko) 40 moves	Outplayed
34	Geller–F	Candidates Curaçao May 1962 Round 2	Sicilian (Najdorf) 40 moves	Outplayed
35	F–Korchnoi	Candidates Curaçao May 1962 Round 5	Pirc (4 P-B4) 33 moves	Carelessness
36	F–Geller	Candidates Curaçao May 1962 Round 9	Sicilian (Sozin) 68 moves	Trying too hard to win

TABLE 7—*Continued*

Fischer's Lost Games

GAME		PLACE AND TIME	OPENING	REASON FOR LOSS
37	F-Petrosian	Candidates Curaçao May 1962 Round 13	French (Mac Cutcheon) 43 moves	Outplayed
38	F-Korchnoi	Candidates Curaçao June 1962 Round 19	Sicilian (Sozin) 45 moves	Carelessness
39	F–Keres	Candidates Curaçao June 1962 Round 21	Ruy Lopez (Closed) 73 moves	Carelessness
40	Ciocaltea–F	Varna Olympiad Oct 1962 Finals, Round 5	Sicilian (Closed) 69 moves	Outplayed
41	F-Donner	Varna Olympiad Oct 1962 Finals, Round 6	Caro-Kann (4 ... B-B4) 45 moves	Carelessness
42	F–Gligoric	Varna Olympiad Oct 1962 Finals, Round 11	Sicilian (Scheveningen) 43 moves	Carelessness
43	F–Mednis	U.S. Champ. Dec 1962 Round 1	French (Winawer) 73 moves	Trying too hard to win
44	F–Ivkov	Havana Sept 1965 Round 10	Ruy Lopez (Closed) 53 moves	Outplayed
45	Geller–F	Havana Sept 1965 Round 17	King's Indian (Sämisch) 57 moves	Outplayed

TABLE 7—*Continued*

Fischer's Lost Games

GAME		PLACE AND TIME	OPENING	REASON FOR LOSS
46	F–Cholmov	Havana Sept 1965 Round 18	Ruy Lopez (Closed) 46 moves	Outplayed
47	F–R. Byrne	U.S. Champ. Dec 1965 Round 8	French (Tarrasch- Guimard) 36 moves	Outplayed
48	Reshevsky– F	U.S. Champ. Dec 1965 Round 9	Nimzo-Indian (Rubinstein) 61 moves	Outplayed
49	F–Larsen	Santa Monica July 1966 Round 6	Ruy Lopez (Open) 30 moves	Carelessness
50	Najdorf–F	Santa Monica July 1966 Round 7	King's Indian (Averbach) 31 moves	Outplayed
51	Spassky–F	Santa Monica July 1966 Round 8	Gruenfeld (Exchange) 50 moves	Outplayed
52	Gheorghiu– F	Havana Olympiad Nov 1966 Finals, Round 12	Nimzo-Indian (Sämisch) 50 moves	Outplayed
53	F–Geller	Monaco April 1967 Round 11	Sicilian (Najdorf) 25 moves	Carelessness
54	F–Geller	Skopje August 1967 Round 2	Sicilian (Sozin) 23 moves	Carelessness
55	Janosevic– F	Skopje August 1967 Round 12	Sicilian (Najdorf) 69 moves	Outplayed

TABLE 7—*Continued*

Fischer's Lost Games

GAME		PLACE AND TIME	OPENING	REASON FOR LOSS
56	F–Kovacevic	Rovinj/Zagreb April 1970 Round 8	French (Winawer) 30 moves	Outplayed
57	Spassky–F	Siegen Olympiad Sept 1970 Finals, Round 6	Gruenfeld (Exchange) 39 moves	Trying too hard to win
58	F–Larsen	Palma Interzonal Nov 1970 Round 9	Sicilian (Sozin) 52 moves	Outplayed
59	Petrosian–F	Candidates Match Buenos Aires Oct 1971, Game 2	Gruenfeld (4 B-B4) 32 moves	Outplayed
60	Spassky–F	World Champ Reykjavik July 1972, Game 1	Nimzo-Indian (Normal) 56 moves	Carelessness
61	Spassky–F	World Champ Reykjavik Aug 1972, Game 11	Sicilian (Najdorf) 31 moves	Outplayed

INTRODUCTION

The patterns of a great player's losses are as fascinating as those of his victories. But the player must be great, the greater the better, and who is greater than Bobby Fischer? While no one would bother with the defeats of a second-rate player, which must simply be taken for granted, one cannot help but wonder, in view of his brilliant play overall, how it is possible for Fischer to drop even so much as a game now and then.

The question is particularly interesting in view of the differences in chess style. In the case of Bent Larsen or Mikhail Tal, who deliberately take risks (the former, "calculated," the latter, "uncalculated"), a number of defeats must be reckoned as part of their tournament style; their losses must, to a considerable extent, be regarded as an investment toward the success of their gambles.

Fischer, however, finds obscure speculation abhorrent. In session after session of post-mortem analysis with him, I learned that he regards a line of play whose outcome is unclear as scarcely a cut above one that loses by force. So if we recognize, as we must, that lucid perfection is Fischer's goal—and that he approaches it more closely than anyone ever has—Fischer's defeats cannot be explained away as rollicking adventures that got out of hand.

This, of course, goes counter to the myth that has sprung up around him—namely, that he is primarily a wild attacking player. Amazingly, the myth has such strength that even some of the renowned theoreticians of the game have swallowed that nonsense. In the press room in Buenos Aires, after Fischer's magnificent victory over Tigran Petrosian in the seventh game of their final Candidates Match in October, 1971, Alexei Suetin,

Petrosian's distraught analyst, stumbled over to me, mumbling incredulously, "*Er spielt so einfach!*"—He plays so simply!

I almost said something like, "You mean to tell me that, after studying Fischer's games night and day, you couldn't discern the Capablanca touch of simplicity that forms their backbone?" Actually, I could not say that, nor anything else. I was grinning from ear to ear and could only nod agreement.

Along with the "wild attacking player" myth goes the belief that Fischer is uncomfortable on defense. Again, nothing could be further from the truth, as confirmed by his marvelous performances in the fourth and nineteenth games of his World Championship match with Boris Spassky. No one "uncomfortable on defense" could possibly have survived Spassky's slashing assaults to achieve two draws.

Neither exclusively an attacker nor primarily a defender, then, Fischer comes closer than anyone who ever played the game to being a man for all seasons. His extraordinarily brilliant attacking play in the game he won from me in the 1963–64 U.S. Championship is the sort of performance which blinds people to the true nature of his well-rounded genius. (It also blinded the grandmaster who was commenting on the game for the spectators in a separate analysis room: when he got the message from the playing room that the game was finished, he assumed that it was Bobby who had resigned, not I. In fact, he quite failed to comprehend that, although a piece ahead, I could not defend against mate.)

Excellence in defensive play makes much less of an impression on the tournament spectator because it does not end the game in a slam-bang checkmate. That is the only reason I can give for the neglect of Fischer's defense virtuosity. No one is harder to beat in an inferior position, as those who have been up against him well know. In the only game in which I defeated him (game 47, from the 1965 U.S. Championship), I jumped him with a surprise piece sacrifice on the Black side of a Tarrasch Variation French Defense and, perhaps flustered, he erred, dooming his resistance. But such failures of analysis are so rare as to be virtually unique.

Moreover, he not only performs brilliantly when the burden of defense is thrust upon him; he will often actively seek the defensive position, if he judges that course the correct one to win. Thus he has from time to time ventured the Taimanov Variation of the Ruy Lopez, in which Black falls behind in development for the sake of acquiring the Bishop pair, and he has gone so far as to resurrect an old line of Wilhelm Steinitz against the Two

Knights' Defense, in which White accepts difficult problems for the sake of maintaining the gambit Pawn.

Fischer's strategy was apparent—and left Fischer open to a very dangerous attack—when he snatched a Pawn against Spassky, a redoubtable attacker if there ever was one, in game 17 of their championship match. As Spassky's analyst, Ivo Nei, explains it in *Both Sides of the Chessboard*, which he wrote with me, "If Fischer does not see a concrete mating continuation, he always takes such pawns." The point is that Fischer will exploit every resource available on the chessboard in order to gain a victory, and voluntarily undertaking defense is no embarrassment to him.

What then is the style of a player who has banished preferences in favor of merciless objectivity? In discussing some of his most exciting games with him, I am struck primarily by his evaluation of the play in predominantly simple positional terms and endgame possibilities, very much in the manner of Capablanca. Even in the midst of mopping up the floor with Miguel Najdorf by smashing through a sacrificial attack in their game at the International Team Tournament in Varna, 1962, he never let the tactical fireworks distract him from envisaging the entire situation in terms of Pawn structure, weak squares, and other solid, positional considerations.

To confirm further Capablanca's heavy influence on his play, it must be pointed out that whenever he is faced with the choice between pursuing a promising middle-game attack and achieving a small but clear and certain endgame advantage, Fischer invariably goes for the endgame. His exploitation of the superiority of Bishop over Knight with Pawns on both wings in the fourth game of his quarter-finals Candidates Match with Mark Taimanov in Vancouver, 1971, is one of the finest performances ever in the realm of endgame play.

I have already mentioned his beautiful victory over Tigran Petrosian in game 7 of their final candidates match in Buenos Aires, 1971. Not only did Bobby cut the position to the bone in order to exploit the disadvantage of an isolated Pawn, but he also succeeded against a man who has been hailed as one of the all-time defensive greats. After 20 moves, Suetin and Yuri Averbach relaxed, confident that their principal could not be beaten in such a position, but nothing could stop Fischer. What he has accomplished in thematic endgames is absolutely enchanting.

While Fischer's basic conception of strategy stems from the lucid classicism of Capablanca, his willingness to defend difficult positions bears the mark of Wilhelm Steinitz, whose games and commentaries he has exhaustively studied. Of course Fischer won't allow himself to become a prisoner of dogmatism, as Steinitz did, in insisting on defending cramped, lost positions, but he does challenge the attacker in Steinitz's style, unfazed by terrific threats if he believes in the ultimate soundness of his position. Quite obviously, Bobby cannot be intimidated by bluff.

There is still another way in which Fischer has followed in the Steinitz mold: until his match with Spassky, he clung stubbornly to his limited favorite opening lines. He did not mind telegraphing his signals to his opponents, letting them know that he would meet 1 P-K4 with the Najdorf Sicilian and 1 P-Q4 with the King's Indian Defense, and that 1 P-K4 would be his only attacking weapon, followed by the Sozin Attack if his opponent offered a Sicilian Defense.

Exhibiting an enormous amount of confidence in his predilections, he turned back prepared analysis time after time with a depth of comprehension and ingenuity his opponents failed to match. An occasional loss with one of his favorite systems did nothing to dampen his courage.

As the book clearly proves, however, one must not take Bobby for granted. Just when it looked as though he might continue ad infinitum with his limited repertoire, he pulled some sensational switches in his match with Spassky. With Alekhine-like guile, he shocked Spassky by undertaking a classical Queen's Gambit for the first time in his life to score a marvelous victory in the sixth game. When his Najdorf Sicilian took a pasting from Boris in the eleventh game and he narrowly escaped disaster with it in the fifteenth, Bobby came up with an array of Alekhine and Pirc–Robatsch Defenses to replace it. In the final game of the match, he wrapped up the championship with a variation of the Sicilian Defense that he had never tried before. Now that he has added the element of surprise to his arsenal, it goes without saying that he is even more formidable.

Fischer wins very heavily with Black as well as with White, but it would nevertheless be wrong to assume that he overextends himself in creating winning chances as second player. He does not indulge in counter-gambits nor plunge headlong into risky complications with the Black pieces. Some years ago, in going over my games, he looked up in surprise whenever he noticed that I was jumping the gun in playing for attack with the Black pieces. Disapprovingly, he advised, "You've got to equalize first with Black before looking for something."

That is precisely what he does in his own games. Taking one problem at a time, he does not try to skip Black's initial task of sapping White's first-move initiative. His play in this phase of the game is realistically logical, once again in the Capablanca style. Even when he has to win this particular game, as in the last round at Skopje, 1967, when only a full point would enable him to seize first prize ahead of Efim Geller, he refused to depart from calm logic. Only after he had neutralized Ratmir Cholmov's threats did he let loose his sharp play to bring home the game.

Whereas most players have great trouble controlling their emotions during an important contest, either overoptimistically evaluating their chances when on the attack, or overpessimistically giving up an inferior position as a certain loss, Fischer somehow manages to remain indefatigably objective. When I first met him as an opponent, in the United States Open Championship in Cleveland, 1957, he was only fourteen years old. Yet, throughout the twists and turns of our bitterly fought battle, he never allowed himself to become deceived about which way the wind was blowing. He knew he had the opening advantage, and he knew precisely when I struggled to equality, as well as the moment when he erred, giving me some winning chances. (The game ended in a draw.) He has never found it necessary to give himself the silly pep talks that players with twice his experience indulge in.

Although he has, in his public utterances, excoriated some of his leading rivals, in private conversations Bobby makes it quite clear that he does not fail to respect them. He has an unlimited appetite for excellent play and, in replaying the performances of his opponents, is keenly aware of their great strengths as well as their weaknesses. I must interject here that not only have I discovered from time to time that he has studied my past productions more carefully than I have, but that he is a veritable gold mine on how I might have finished more elegantly here, or my opponent might have defended better there, etc.

Well then, given his extraordinarily well-rounded game and his excellence in all departments of it, how *do* you beat Bobby Fischer?

The clues are small. The door opens only a crack, but it does open. In his championship match with Boris Spassky, he displayed intermittent carelessness, at times playing so rapidly that it seemed he wanted to dazzle rather than pause to find the best move. Thus he messed up his winning endgames in the seventh and thirteenth encounters (although he recovered to take the latter on a Spassky error). Carelessness can always be turned against a player, and, as Mednis's Table 2 shows, it was responsible for 26 percent of Fischer's losses.

Still, although errors will never be eliminated from anyone's game, counting on Fischer to make them is a thankless task. He sports the most error-free game in chess history. However, the odds in favor of his committing blunders must be on the increase at this writing, because it has been two years since the Spassky match and he has not contested a single game. As Adolf Anderssen observed after his 1857 match with Paul Morphy, "It is impossible to keep one's excellence in a little glass casket, like a jewel, to take it out whenever wanted. On the contrary, it can only be conserved by continuous and good practice."

Although Fischer does not have any real weaknesses, like Morphy he reaches the peak of his genius in open games. The inference is clear: confront him with Queenside openings when you have the White pieces and, when he plays White and opens 1 P-K4, present him with maximal problems by employing the French Defense, preferably the Winawer Variation. If these close openings do not give him trouble, nothing will.

As Mednis counsels, "If the opportunity presents itself, go for a totally wild and unbalanced position." I have already explained that Fischer's forte is the exploitation of simple, lucid strategic ideas in the style of Capablanca, and he must be denied the use of this deadly weapon. Even so, he is a fantastic tactician who is hardly nonplused by combinational complexity.

Despite the valuable analyses in this book, there are decidedly no miracles to be hoped for in playing one or another style against the champion. No miracles, but perhaps—just perhaps—skill, study and determination will do it. They have done it before. Oh yes, good luck! You'll need that, too.

Robert Byrne

How to Beat Bobby Fischer

PART ONE
Youthful Champion

January 1958–August 1961
(Games 1 through 32)

January 1958 was a great date for American and world chess, for in that month 14-year-old Bobby Fischer became U.S. Champion without the loss of a game. His play clearly earned the result expected only by Fischer himself and his hard-driving mother, Regina. It also opened the way toward the world title, as the U.S. Championship served as the zonal qualifying tournament for the 1960 Championship match.

The 1958 Interzonal Tournament at Portoroz, Yugoslavia, became therefore the next logical object. Fischer wisely played no more tournaments in the spring, choosing to prepare for this first international probe. To get used to Yugoslavia, as well as international chess, he arrived in Belgrade early in July and played a two-game (two draws) match against Janosevic before defeating the promising young master Matulovic 2½–1½, despite the loss of the first game. The match progress and result was the first indication of Fischer's iron resolve to succeed and to ignore any immediate roadblocks. Thus in the first game (Game 1), he was simply positionally crushed, but, undaunted, came back to score 2½ points out of the next three games.

This early success put him in fine spirits before the Interzonal. At that time I was returning from the World Student Championship in Varna, Bulgaria, and had to spend the better part of a day in Belgrade waiting for the train to Paris. Wandering onto the streets of Belgrade, I inquired about a chess club. Instead, I was led to the hotel where Fischer was known to be staying and as I entered his room, I found him studying (what else?) chess! His joy was great at seeing the unexpected visitor and he showed me immediately how he had "killed" Matulovic. The afternoon was spent touring the parks of Belgrade with Mr. Fischer as my guide. Already he was a celebrity to the people of Belgrade—everywhere we went he was ogled and stopped. As I bid him good-bye and good luck in the late afternoon at the train station, I felt optimistic about his chances at Portoroz. He had the kind of healthy confidence that is so valuable, but showed no signs of dangerous overconfidence.

The Interzonal at Portoroz was a tough tournament for everyone except the top four qualifiers (Tal, Gligoric, Benko, Petrosian) and only Bobby's iron will and surprisingly strong nerves allowed the now fifteen-year-old Champion to tie for fifth-sixth place and qualify for the Candidates Tournament in 1959. Out of twenty games only two were lost by Fischer. Benko outplayed him in a positional King's Indian (Game 2) and Olafsson did the same in the Ragosin Variation of the Queen's Gambit Declined (Game 3)—the first of too many losses for Fischer with this unlucky opening.

Returning home a hero, he quickly established himself as the premier U.S. player by again winning the U.S. Championship without the loss of a game. In the spring of 1959 came an excursion to South America with mediocre results. At Mar del Plata he tied for third-fourth place. A whole point and thus a clear first place was lost by playing for a win against Pachman when a search for a draw was in order (Game 4), and then by committing a horrible blunder to lose a drawn ending against Letelier (Game 5). Even less satisfactory was the result at Santiago: a tie for 4 through 6 with 7½–4½. Here, a total of four games were lost—much too many for a relatively weak tournament. Ivkov outplayed him on the Black side of a French (Game 6); Sanguinetti did the same as White in a Samisch King's Indian (Game 7); an impetuous attack as Black against Pachman led to another loss (Game 8); and the young Chilean master Jauregui won Fischer's Queen and the game in another Samisch King's Indian (Game 9).

Bobby returned from South America to New York to go on to Zurich for the big international tournament in May-June. He was now sixteen, but his mother, still worried about him, asked me to go along as his second. However, New York University thought that I should take my final exams instead, and Anthony Saidy accompanied him to Zurich. Fischer's high-caliber play at Zurich negated the worries of his admirers after South America. Many fine games resulted (four are annotated by Fischer in *My 60 Memorable Games*) and he ended in a tie for third and fourth with Keres, behind only Tal and Gligoric. Gligoric played well as White in a complicated Najdorf Sicilian (Game 10), but more care on Fischer's part would have saved a half point. The second loss, to Keller of Switzerland (Game 11), also was unnecessary. Rather than accept the indicated equality, Fischer as White decided to attack the young Swiss master, and a painful boomerang resulted.

The next step for Fischer up the world chess ladder was the 1959 Candidates Tournament in Yugoslavia in September and October. Americans had great hopes for their Champion. Obviously, he was a force to be reckoned with; to expect, however, that he would win was unrealistic. In the first place, at 16, he was still too young and inexperienced, and secondly, Tal at that time was simply sweeping everything before him. Fischer, himself, was very confident, however, really overconfident, and this would show very quickly, especially in the nontypical sloppy opening preparation with the White pieces. The immediate start was fine with a win against Keres with the Black pieces in Round 1. But everything was downhill from then, and after Round 9 he was tied for last place with only 3 points scored. Part of the blame goes to his stubborn insistence in playing a doubtful variation against the Caro-Kann (Games 12, 15, 21). His stubbornness was so total that everyone tried to play the Caro-Kann against him, even if they had never played it before! But bad starts never demoralize Fischer. This is one of his great strengths. His confidence in himself is absolute and he just keeps fighting and playing. This endurance accounts for the final Yugoslav result, where he recovered to finish in a tie with Gligoric for fifth and sixth place with a 12½–15½ score. A closer look at his lost games sheds much light on this minus result. In Game 12, Petrosian outplays him as Black in a Caro-Kann. Olafsson then uses Fischer's own 6 B-QB4 against the Najdorf and wins in fine style (Game 13). Tal as White wins a strategic King's Indian (Game 14). Then Fischer plays poorly again against a Caro-Kann, this time against Keres, and loses in 30 moves! (Game 15). Petrosian then wins easily in 31 moves, when Fischer poorly defends a Nimzo-Indian (Game 16). Then it is Gligoric's turn to outplay Fischer as White in a Najdorf Sicilian (Game 17). Tal as Black wins in 33 moves as Fischer plays the opening poorly with his 6 B-QB4 speciality in the Najdorf (Game 18). Throughout, there is no question of bad luck. It is a combination of overconfidence, showing itself in poor and stubborn opening preparation (we can almost say non-preparation) and bad play. In the latter part of the match, the results were better, but losses still came. Tal again won convincingly against the King's Indian (Game 19). Smyslov prepared against the expected 6 B-QB4 against the Najdorf Sicilian and won when Fischer chose an overly sharp variation in his attempt to win (Game 20). Another defeat against the Caro-Kann came in Game 21 against Keres. Only in Game 22 against Tal could the loss be called undeserved. In a wild attacking game, Bobby was careless in thinking that "everything wins"; this was not so and finally came a total reversal.

Of course, objectively speaking, a placing among the top six of the world is still pretty good. Returning to the United States disappointed, but full of interest in further conquests, Bobby again easily won the 1959–60 U.S. Championship, again without the loss of a game.

In the spring of 1960 came another excursion to South America. At Mar del Plata he scored a fantastic 13½–1½, but this was only good enough for a first place tie with Boris Spassky after a painful second-round loss to the Russian (Game 23). As Black in a King's Gambit, Bobby very carelessly turned an opening advantage into a loss. Undismayed, as usual, he went on to score 12½ points out of the next 13 games!

Buenos Aires 1960 was quite different. It was, in fact, a catastrophe. (He got his revenge ten years later!) With a score of 8½–10½ he finished in tie for 13th through 16th, out of a total of 20. Every mortal is entitled to a number of bad tournaments in his life and so far Bobby has had only this one. It is his only "mixed" (masters and grandmasters) tournament with a minus score. Simply nothing went right. He won only three games out of nineteen and lost five. Against Eliskases he committed a horrible, unexplainable blunder right after adjournment to throw away a draw (Game 24). He was unrecognizable in losing to Wexler (Game 25). Then Uhlmann as Black in a French won an outstanding strategic effort (Game 26). Unzicker mated Bobby quickly (Game 27), after a careless "hand error." In the last round Fischer's carelessness allowed Benko to score a full point (Game 28).

The months after Buenos Aires were not happy ones for Fischer or his admirers. Not only had he played poorly, but his number 1 nemesis, Reshevsky, had had an outstanding result, tying for first place with Korchnoi. Still, Bobby continued to work and study, preparing to lead the U.S. team at the Leipzig Olympiad. On the way over to Europe he stopped off in Iceland to win a small tournament against the local masters with a 3½–½ score.

At Leipzig Fischer was a different man, showing none of the indecisiveness of a few months earlier in Buenos Aires. He did create a sensation in the preliminaries by losing a sharp Sicilian Dragon as White against Muñoz of Ecuador (Game 29). This, incidentally, is the only time that the Dragon has eaten him! His play and score in the finals were outstanding, with only one loss: against Gligoric, again with the Ragosin Variation of the Queen's Gambit Declined (Game 30).

Year-end saw Fischer do his usual thing: winning the U.S. Championship for the fourth straight time without the loss of a game and the summer of 1961 finally saw the coming of a greatly anticipated event: a match between Reshevsky and Fischer. The result of it is well known: at a standing of 5½–5½ the match abruptly ended, with Reshevsky apparently receiving the winner's purse in dollars. "Chessically," the match using the "points" system as in boxing should have been Fischer's. Each side won two games and in several others only Reshevsky's great tenacity allowed him to save the games into draws. Both games Fischer lost (Games 31 and 32) were fine efforts on Reshevsky's part.

GAME 1

White: M. Matulovic (Yugoslavia)
Black: R. Fischer

Played in Public Training Match, at Belgrade (Yugoslavia), July 20, 1958, Match Game 1

Young master Matulovic defeats the even younger U.S. Champion when Bobby, in a cramped position, sacrifices a Pawn in an impetuous freeing attempt. Matulovic pockets the Pawn and soon the full point. At the age of 15 Bobby had no psychological hangups, as he scored 2½ out of the next 3 games to win the match. He has not lost since to Grandmaster Matulovic.

*King's Indian Defense
(Samisch Variation)*

1	P-QB4	N-KB3
2	N-QB3	P-KN3
3	P-K4	B-N2
4	P-Q4	P-Q3
5	P-B3	...

This is the Samisch Variation, the positional method of achieving strong center occupancy. The QBP, QP and KP are all advanced two squares and the KBP goes only one square forward so that there is a sound, safe base support. It is difficult for Black to generate active counterplay. The most successful approach is not yet known. Bobby in his career has tried many varia-

tions and we shall see several of them in this book. The superactive central approach, 5 P-B4, forms the Four Pawn attack. In the 1920's this was thought to be the definitive refutation of the King's Indian, but now we know that Black gets fully satisfactory counterplay.

5	...	P-K4

Played usually after castling, but also okay immediately since 6 PxP leads to nothing.

6	P-Q5	N-R4
7	B-K3	P-KB4

In the orthodox Samisch, Black generally attacks on the Kingside by means of the KBP and often KNP, despite having castled there. White's play is usually on the Queenside, no matter where his King is! It would appear that the attack on the King should bring more scalps than Queenside maneuverings, but in modern master play this is no longer true. What determines ultimate success is the fundamental soundness of one's position. Here White's position is just a shade sounder than Black's; thus in master practice White scores more often than Black.

8	Q-Q2	Q-R5 +

A waste of time, since White's Bishop actually stands better on KB2 than on K3. Instead 8 ... O-O 9 O-O-O leads to the Uhlmann subvariation, with tough play and slightly better chances for White.

9	B-B2	Q-K2
10	O-O-O	O-O
11	KN-K2	N-Q2

Possibly better was 11 ... P-QR4 and 12 ... N-R3 as here the Knight turns out to be in the way of his own pieces.

12 N-N3! ...

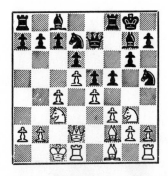

Clearly showing the minus side of Black's 8th move, as this would be impossible (because of ... P-B5) with White's Bishop still on K3.

12 ... NxN

Acquiescing in the early abortion of his Kingside chances. The awkward 12 ... N-B5 would offer greater hope of active play.

13	PxN	P-B5
14	P-KN4!	...

Not 14 PxP? PxP and Black's KB would have a great diagonal and Black's Knight a great square on K4.

White's play continuously keeps those pieces out of meaningful activity.

14	...	P-N3
15	B-Q3	P-QR4
16	B-B2	B-QR3
17	P-QN3	KR-N1
18	Q-K2	B-B3
19	P-R3	K-N2
20	P-N4!	...

At first glance surprising, as it voluntarily opens up the position where the King is located. Actually it is quite thematic to expand on the side where one has the advantage. For White this is the Queenside. His King is quite safe as all the squares in front of him are in White's possession. If only Black didn't have a Pawn on K4!—things then would be different. ...

20 ... PxP

Exchanges are usually in the interest of the passive side.

21 PxP P-QN4?

THE LOSING MOMENT

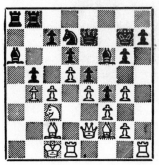

Black stands cramped and without counterplay. However, it is up to White to demonstrate that he can achieve a successful breakthrough. Black's correct strategy was to "pass" by, e.g., playing his Knight back and forth between KB1 and Q2, and seeing what White would do. It is *not* well known that Bobby does not like to defend passive positions and thus has a tendency to look for counterplay even when not justified. Of course, Fischer has had very little experience in defending passive positions, thus his lack of highest expertise in them is quite understandable!

| 22 | PxP | ... |

White has now two additional clear advantages: (1) an extra Pawn (the first QNP will be exchanged for Black's QBP and then White will have an extra Pawn, the passed QNP), and (2) many more open squares and files to infiltrate on.

22	...	B-B1
23	K-N2	N-N3
24	R-R1	RxR

There was nothing better as otherwise White plays 25 R-R5 (only possible because Black no longer has a Pawn on QN3!) and 26 KR-R1.

| 25 | RxR | B-R5 |

Bobby gets a bit of play going on the Kingside, but it is far too little and very late.

26	B-KN1!	P-R4
27	PxP	PxP
28	R-R7	R-N2

This makes White's task of progressing on the Queenside too easy. A better try was 28 ... K-R3.

| 29 | RxR | BxR |
| 30 | N-R4! | ... |

White will now establish a passed QNP.

| 30 | ... | Q-Q1 |
| 31 | Q-B1 | K-N3 |

31 ... N-Q2 would at least force White to see the Pawn sacrifice 32 P-N6!

| 32 | BxN! | PxB |
| 33 | Q-KN1! | ... |

Instead of one passed QNP, White now gets two!

| 33 | ... | Q-B2 |

Bobby makes things as easy as possible for White. Compared to the game, Black would save a move with 33 ... B-K2.

34	QxP	QxQ
35	NxQ	B-K2
36	N-B4	K-N4
37	N-R5	B-QB1
38	P-N6	K-R5
39	B-R4!	...

A pretty deflection/defensive maneuver.

39	...	K-N6
40	B-Q7	B-N2
41	B-R3	...

BLACK RESIGNS

GAME 2

White: P. Benko (now United States
—at that time stateless)
Black: R. Fischer

*Played at Interzonal Tournament,
Portoroz, Yugoslavia, August 10,
1958, Round 4*

A positional masterpiece by Benko.
The young champion accumulates
a number of small weaknesses
and the more experienced Benko
takes advantage of all of them.

*King's Indian Defense
(Samisch Variation)*

1	P-Q4	N-KB3
2	P-QB4	P-KN3
3	N-QB3	B-N2
4	P-K4	P-Q3
5	P-B3	. . .

Two rounds earlier Fischer had
gotten a lost position playing Fuster
of Canada (he won!) against the
Samisch; so Benko decides on a
further testing.

5	. . .	P-K4

Already at that time Bobby was very
confident of his opening preparation.
In some ways, of course, this also
meant a certain degree of stubbornness.

6	KN-K2	O-O
7	B-N5	. . .

Fuster had played the more usual
7 B-K3.

7	. . .	PxP

Giving up the center is very com-
mittal. Subsequently Fischer has
played 7 . . . P-B3. See Game 7.

8	NxP	N-B3
9	N-B2	B-K3

In Evans–Reshevsky, 1972 U.S.
Championship, Black tried 9 . . .
P-KR3, and after 10 B-K3?!, B-K3;
11 Q-Q2, N-K4; 12 P-QN3 (12
BxKRP, NxKP; and 13 . . . Q-R5+),
P-QR4; 13 B-K2, P-R5! got sufficient
counterplay. It was logical to retain
the pin with 10 B-R4.

10	B-K2	P-KR3
11	B-R4!	P-KN4!?
12	B-B2	N-K4?!

Leads to nothing, as White does
not have to weaken his Queenside
with P-QN3. Correct was 12 . . .
N-KR4, with the idea . . . P-KB4
and . . . N-KB5.

13	N-K3!	P-B3?!

One more weakness. Passive
maneuvering with 13 . . . N-N3
was better.

14	O-O	Q-R4
15	Q-Q2	KR-Q1
16	KR-Q1	P-R3
17	P-QR4	Q-B2

There is no future on the Queenside, so the Queen correctly returns.

| 18 | P-R5 | P-B4? |

THE LOSING MOMENT

This additional weakness is the straw that breaks the camel's back. Required was 18 ... Q-K2, and if 19 P-R4, N-R2.

19   P-R4!   . . .

White switches signals and attacks Black's weakened Kingside. Black has to keep his KN on KB3 to prevent White's N-Q5 and thus Black has difficulty with protecting his KNP.

19	. . .	Q-K2
20	PxP	PxP
21	N-B5!	BxN
22	PxB	P-N5

See the previous comment!

| 23 | B-R4 | Q-B1 |
| 24 | PxP! | . . . |

Benko's play is clocklike: it moves forward very accurately.

24	. . .	N4xNP
25	KBxN	NxB
26	Q-N5!	. . .

But not 26 BxR?? B-Q5+ and it is *White's* Kingside that will be seriously weak.

| 26 | . . . | N-B3 |
| 27 | R-Q3 | . . . |

The beginning of the end. White's moves look so clear—in hindsight!

27	. . .	N-R2
28	Q-N4	P-B3
29	N-Q5	Q-B2
30	R-K1	R-K1
31	R3-K3	R-K4
32	B-N3!	RxR
33	RxR	R-K1
34	R-K6	N-N4
35	RxQP	. . .

The first apple.

35	...	R-K5
36	R-Q8+	K-R2
37	B-B4!	B-R3
38	R-Q7!	...

And now comes the steak!

38	...	R-K8+
39	K-B2	N-K5+
40	KxR	QxR
41	Q-N6+	

BLACK RESIGNS

Not much to say about the final position.

GAME 3

White: F. Olafsson (Iceland)
Black: R. Fischer

*Played at Interzonal Tournament,
Portoroz (Yugoslavia), August 22,
1958, Round 11*

In a strategically inferior position
Bobby jumps at the opportunity to
win an exchange. It turns out,
however, that the loss of the
exchange was in fact a deep positional sacrifice by Olafsson. It is
surprising how quickly Black's position becomes untenable.

*Queen's Gambit Declined
(Ragosin Variation)*

1	P-QB4	N-KB3
2	N-QB3	P-K3
3	N-B3	P-Q4
4	P-Q4	B-N5

We have now an unusual position
which can arise from either the
Nimzo-Indian Defense or the
Queen's Gambit Declined. It has
features of both: the KB at QN5 puts
indirect pressure on White's K4 and
the QP at Q4 protected by P-K3
ensures Black's control of his own
Q4. From here the game can transpose into the Nimzo-Indian proper
(e.g., see Game 60). Most of the time
the play is more like the Queen's
Gambit Declined, thus the primary

name I've given it. If the Nimzo-
Indian is good and the Queen's
Gambit Declined is good, isn't a
combination of both even better?
Well, not really. It's something like
a food recipe. Take two excellent
recipes, combine them and the
final product is indigestion. Things
are not quite so severe here, but
the position is very difficult to
handle in a strategically clear way.
Bobby's results have been poorest
with this particular opening;
improvements have come as a result
of practical trial-and-error experience, after much pain and suffering.

5	PxP	. . .

For 5 Q-N3 see Game 24; for 5
P-K3, Games 30 and 32. A position
similar to the Exchange Variation of
the Queen's Gambit Declined now
results, with Black's KB somewhat
misplaced on QN5.

5	. . .	PxP
6	B-N5	P-KR3
7	B-R4	. . .

It would be nice to keep the pin,
but Black could now get sufficient
counterplay by utilizing the fact that
he has not yet castled on the Kingside. Instead, with 7 BxN, White
retains a slight but clear positional
edge.

7	. . .	P-B4
8	P-K3	N-B3
9	R-B1	P-B5?

Correct is 9 ... P-KN4; 10 B-N3, Q-R4 with good counterplay for Black.

10	B-K2	B-K3?!

Here was the last chance for meaningful play with 10 ... P-KN4; 11 B-N3, N-K5; 12 N-Q2, BxN; 13 PxB, NxB; 14 RPxN, Q-R4 followed by castling Queenside.

11	O-O	O-O
12	N-Q2	B-K2

Black had to watch out for an impending P-K4.

13	P-QN3!	P-KN4?

THE LOSING MOMENT

Bobby played this quickly, seeing that he now wins the exchange. Unfortunately, it is the losing move, as Black's Kingside will be weakened beyond repair. The only correct way was 13 ... B-QR6 14 BxN QxB; 15 R-N1, B-QN5!; 16 Q-B1, BxN; 17 QxB, P-QN4; 18 PxP, NPxP; 19 B-B3,

and Black's position is very uncomfortable (weak QP), but may be tenable.

14	B-N3	B-QR6
15	R-B2	N-QN5
16	PxP	NxR
17	QxN	PxP
18	N-N5!	B-QN5
19	N-B7!	BxN
20	NxB!	PxN
21	BxP!	...

White's play has been a model of exactness. Black must protect his KN3 square and thus can't save his Bishop.

21	...	Q-K1
22	QxB	N-K5
23	Q-Q3	NxB
24	RPxN	...

It is somewhat surprising how quickly Black will go under. White only has one Pawn for the exchange and a double one at that! Black even has the Queenside Pawn majority. But White's Bishop is a powerhouse

and Black's King position is so full
of holes that the best Bobby can
achieve is a lost endgame.

24	...	R-B3
25	Q-K4	R-QB1
26	B-N3	Q-Q2
27	R-Q1	...

Threatening 28 P-Q5, PxP 29 RxP.

27	...	R-K1
28	P-B4!	Q-R2
29	Q-K5	Q-B4
30	P-N4!	...

Establishing a Pawn roller for the
endgame.

30	...	QxQ
31	QPxQ	R-B2
32	P-B5	R-B2

32 ... PxP? 33 R-Q7.

| 33 | R-Q6! | ... |

33 BxP+? RxB 34 PxR wins back the
"ox" (the colloquial term for the
exchange) but leaves White with
unbelievably weak Kingside Pawns:
triple, isolated KPs and double,
isolated KNPs and no winning
chances.

33	...	R-B4
34	BxP+	K-B1
35	B-N3!	R4xP
36	RxP	RxKP
37	R-KN6	...

All through the game, White is one
step ahead of Black!

37	...	R1-K5
38	RxP	R-N6
39	R-N8+	K-K2
40	P-N5	...

The passed Pawns win easily.

40	...	R-K7
41	B-Q5	K-Q3
42	B-B3	RxRP
43	P-B6	K-K3
44	R-K8+	...

BLACK RESIGNS

After 44 ... K-B2 it's 45 B-R5 mate!
and otherwise the BP becomes a
Queen.

GAME 4

White: R. Fischer
Black: L. Pachman (Czechoslovakia)

*Played at Mar del Plata (Argentina)
International Tournament, March 25,
1959, Round 3*

Playing White, Bobby gets nothing
out of the opening. When he should
be concerned about keeping
equality, Fischer makes an impetuous
attacking move. Psychologically this
is an interesting moment, since
Bobby had started the tournament
with draws against two relatively
weak players and is hungry for his
first full point. In practice such an
attitude is dangerous, however, and
Pachman with perfect play demonstrates that indeed Black now has
a won game.

Ruy Lopez (Steinitz Deferred)

1	P-K4	P-K4
2	N-KB3	N-QB3
3	B-N5	P-QR3
4	B-R4	P-Q3

The so-called "Steinitz Deferred"
variation which would be more
accurately described "Improved
Steinitz." By interpolation of 3 . . .
P-QR3 4 B-R4 Black does not have
to worry about the cramping effects
of an immediate P-Q4, as after 5
P-Q4, P-QN4; 6 B-N3, NxP; 7 NxN,
PxN; 8 QxP?? would lead to "Noah's
Ark" trap: 8 . . . P-QB4; 9 Q-Q5,

B-K3; 10 Q-B6+, B-Q2; 11 Q-Q5,
P-B5! winning a piece.

5	P-B3	. . .

Fischer's latest opening contribution
to this variation is the demonstration
that 5 O-O is fully playable and
may be most accurate. The
reasoning behind this is that castling
is pretty much always required, but
often P-Q4 does not require the
preparatory P-QB3.

5	. . .	B-Q2
6	P-Q4	KN-K2
7	B-N3	P-R3

Required to prevent 8 N-N5

8	O-O	. . .

A very quiet continuation. Very
sharp is 8 N-KR4. Good and playable
is 8 QN-Q2. Later Bobby recommended and successfully played
8 Q-K2 (with the idea 9 Q-B4).

8	. . .	N-N3
9	QN-Q2	B-K2
10	N-B4	B-N4
11	N-K3	. . .

Modern master practice has shown
that it is more useful for White to
keep the QN and offer to exchange
the QB by playing 11 B-K3. If then
11 . . . BxB; 12 NxB and the Knight
is very well placed here controlling
the Q5, KB5 and KN4 squares.
White also does not have to worry
about 11 . . . P-QN4; 12 N4-Q2,
BxB; 13 PxB, as he will have good
play on the KB file. After the

routine text move Black achieves
full equality.

11	...	BxN!
12	BxB	O-O
13	P-KR3	...

A waste of time, as ... B-N5 was
no threat. 13 N-Q2 was better.

| 13 | ... | R-K1 |
| 14 | N-R2? | ... |

For the chance for a "cheapo"
(14 ... PxP; 15 PxP, RxP?; 16
BxP+!) White completely misplaces
his Knight.

| 14 | ... | Q-K2! |
| 15 | PxP | ... |

Fischer generally likes to liquidate
center tension in the Ruy Lopez,
and we shall see other examples of
this in later games. Here there is
little choice as the KP is under
pressure.

| 15 | ... | PxP |
| 16 | Q-R5? | ... |

THE LOSING MOMENT

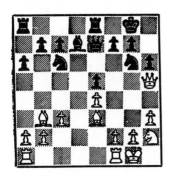

White's position is already somewhat uncomfortable and he should
have been thinking about how to
retain full equality. Indicated in this
regard was 16 B-B2 and if 16 ...
N-R4; 17 P-QN3. The rash "attacking" (threat 17 QXN) text move
turns out to be a further loss of
time. Pachman fully takes advantage
of that.

16	...	N-R4!
17	B-B2	N-QB5
18	B-B1	N-B5
19	Q-B3	...

There should be no doubt regarding
who has been making real progress
lately!

19	...	QR-Q1!
20	BxN	PxB
21	QxP	B-B3
22	N-N4	...

Bobby has no luck with his KN in this
game and it soon even gets lost.
A better practical chance was 22
P-K5 to at least open the diagonal
for his KB.

22	...	P-KR4!
23	N-K3	NxP
24	N-B5	...

Despite appearances, it is Black
who has the attacking chances.
White is still behind in development
(compare the Rooks!).

24	. . .	Q-B3
25	QxP	QxP
26	QR-B1	Q-B3
27	KR-K1	N-Q6
28	BxN	RxB

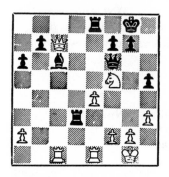

Black has a winning advantage: all of his pieces are very actively placed and he has no weakness. White's pieces stand clumsily, he has a weak QRP and an even weaker KP. Since no satisfactory "normal" continuation exists, Bobby decides to sacrifice his N for some attacking chances.

29	Q-B4	P-KN3
30	R-B5	. . .

30 N-R6+, K-N2 and the Knight is doomed.

30	. . .	R-K3!
31	Q-N8+	R-Q1
32	Q-B4	. . .

32 Q-N3, BxP is hopeless: 33 N-R6+, K-R2, etc.

32	. . .	PxN
33	RxP	Q-N2
34	RxRP	R1-K1
35	P-B3	R-K4!

In attack or defense, Pachman is on the ball.

36	R-R4	. . .

This will lead to a weakening of the Kingside Pawn formation. Therefore, 36 RxR was better, even though White is still lost: 2 Pawns are simply not enough for the piece.

36	. . .	R-KN4!
37	R-N4	RxR
38	RPxR	Q-Q5+
39	R-K3	Q-K4
40	Q-B5	QxQ
41	NPxQ	. . .

White has a 4 against 1 Pawn advantage on the Kingside, but the doubled Pawn devalues the potential offensive punch. Even the advanced KBP that White obtained from the previous exchange is of no help. Black's KBP, being strategically placed, can hold the White Pawns.

41	. . .	R-Q1
42	K-B2	B-N4

The endgame after 42 ... R-Q7+; 43 R-K2, RxR+ should also be won, but Black prefers to keep the Rook for attacking purposes.

43	K-K1	K-N2
44	P-K5	R-Q5
45	P-N4	K-R3!
46	P-K6	P-B3

Black has succeeded in stopping White's Kingside Pawns. White has no defense to Black's offensive, utilizing the Queenside Pawn majority.

47	K-B2	R-Q7+
48	K-N3	K-N2
49	R-B3	B-B3
50	P-R3	R-K7
51	K-B4	P-R4
52	R-Q3	P-R5!
53	R-Q8	R-KB7
54	R-Q3	P-N4
55	R-B3	RxP+!

Accurately prepared.

56	RxR	BxR

WHITE RESIGNS

After 57 KxB, P-N5 Black promotes a new Queen.

GAME 5

White: R. Fischer
Black: R. Letelier (Chile)

*Played at Mar del Plata (Argentina)
International Tournament, March 28,
1959, Round 5*

After a tough opening, middle game and endgame, Letelier is about to receive his just reward: an honorable draw. Then a fairy god-mother appears and presents him with a full point. This game "features" the worst one-move blunder of Bobby's Championship career. Its cause is a blind desire to win when there is no rational possibility of it.

Ruy Lopez (Closed)

1	P-K4	P-K4
2	N-KB3	N-QB3
3	B-N5	P-QR3
4	B-R4	N-B3
5	O-O	B-K2
6	R-K1	P-QN4
7	B-N3	P-Q3
8	P-B3	O-O
9	P-KR3	...

Here for the first time we see the "normal" Ruy Lopez, a very strategic opening. White puts immediate pressure on Black's center and often combines this with attacks on the flanks. What can Black do? Well, not much except to resist and hope for a draw if White plays well. The Ruy is not easy to handle for White either, and Black does have good practical chances for successful counterplay. Fischer is probably the world's leading expert on the Ruy Lopez, but this knowledge has not fallen from heaven; it has been gained from hard study and hard play. Improvements have come from continuations which turned out to be unsatisfactory in over-the-board play. This game is one such precursor.

9	...	N-QR4
10	B-B2	P-B4
11	P-Q4	Q-B2
12	QN-Q2	R-K1

A fairly passive concept, though playable. It is now known that the correct execution of it for Black is to play first 12 ... B-Q2, as now very strong for White is 13 P-QN4!, BPxNP; 14 BPxP, N-B3; 15 B-N2, NxNP; 16 B-N3, and if 16 ... N-Q6; 17 BxP+!

13	N-B1	B-Q2
14	N-K3	...

Most exact is 14 P-QN3!, with the idea of keeping out Black's Knight and then 15 B-KN5.

14	...	B-KB1

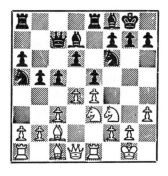

According to theory 14 ... P-N3 is more accurate. Satisfied with his opening here, Letelier repeated it less than a month later at Santiago against Fischer. But Bobby demonstrated the danger of such a repetition against him and obtained a better position with 15 B-Q2, QR-N1?!; 16 P-QN4, N-B3; 17 NPxP. Even stronger is the immediate 15 P-QN4!, BPxNP; 16 BPxP.

15 PxKP ...

This premature liquidation of center tension, though in keeping with Bobby's style, here leads to nothing.

15	...	PxP
16	N-R2	QR-Q1
17	Q-B3	B-K3
18	N2-N4	N-Q2

White's Kingside demonstration leads to nothing because Black has not weakened his KB3 square by playing P-KN3, and thus White has no object to attack.

19	N-Q5	Q-N1

19 ... Q-N2 is more logical.

20	P-KR4	N-B5
21	P-R5	P-R3
22	P-QN3	N-Q3
23	Q-N3	K-R1
24	P-KB4	BxN/Q4
25	PxB	P-K5!
26	N-K5	Q-N2
27	RxP	...

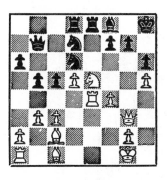

There is nothing better, as otherwise Black puts a stop to everything with 27 ... N-B3.

27	...	NxR

This gives White too many chances. Either 27 ... QxP or 27 ... N-B3 were simpler and better.

28	NxP +	K-N1
29	NxP +	K-R1
30	N-B7 +	K-N1
31	NxR	QxP

Here and during the following moves both sides manage to walk a chess tightrope.

32	Q-Q3!	QxQ
33	BxQ	NxP
34	B-Q2	N-K5
35	R-K1	N2-B3
36	BxN	NxB

White has an extra Pawn, but has weak Kingside Pawns and awkwardly placed pieces. Thus Black just keeps the balance.

37	N-B6	B-Q3
38	B-B1	K-B2
39	B-N2	N-N6!
40	N-K5+	. . .

A better try was 40 RxR, KxR; 41 BxP even though 41 . . . BxP! still leads to a draw with correct play.

40	. . .	BxN
41	RxB	RxR
42	BxR	NxP
43	K-B2	N-B3
44	K-B3	P-N3!
45	BxN	KxB
46	K-K4	K-K3

This is the position that Bobby had in mind. White has significant advantages for the King and Pawn endgame: the more active King and the potential outside passed Pawn on the Kingside. Unfortunately these are insufficient for the win, because: (1) The outside passed Pawn is the KBP which is fairly "inside" and thus cannot deflect Black's King sufficiently far away, (2) Black's Queenside Pawns are quite healthy and the only one that White will win is the QRP and this will be insufficient for the full point.

47	P-R4	. . .

With the idea of getting it to R5.

47	. . .	K-Q3
48	P-B5	. . .

Bobby has seen that the "usual" method is not good enough for the win: 48 P-R5, K-K3; 49 P-N3!, K-Q3; 50 P-KN4, K-K3; 51 P-B5+ PxP; 52 PxP+, K-B3; 53 K-Q5, P-B5; 54 PxP, PxP; 55 KxP, KxP; 56 K-B5, K-K3; 57 K-N6, K-Q2; 58 KxP, K-B1 DRAW. Being hell-bent to win, he tries something else, but objectively speaking this gives even less chances. It is true that White has a "better" outside passed Pawn, but Black has a passed Pawn, too!

48	. . .	PxP+
49	KxP	K-Q4!
50	P-KN4	. . .

Interpolation of 50 PxP is simpler for the draw, but Bobby is only interested in winning.

| 50 | ... | K-Q5! |
| 51 | P-N5 | ... |

51 PxP is simpler.

51	...	P-B5!
52	NPxP	P-N5!
53	P-B5??	...

THE LOSING MOMENT

The single worst move Fischer has made, with absolutely no redeeming features. In his eagerness to win, for a moment he, decided to queen first his *backward* QBP and keep the KNP for a second Queen. A concept that works only in dreams, not in real life. After the obviously correct 53 P-N6, P-N6; 54 P-N7, P-N7; 55 P-N8(Q), P-N8(Q)+; 56 K-K6, Q-N6; the Queen and Pawn endgame is already slightly better for Black, but a draw is still in order. But now ...

53	...	P-N6
54	P-B6	P-N7
55	P-B7	P-N8(Q)+
CHECK!		

56	K-K6	Q-N2
57	K-Q7	K-Q4
58	P-N6	Q-B3+
59	K-Q8	Q-Q3+
WHITE RESIGNS		

A tragedy. Bobby is usually not bothered by previous losses and of course has great comeback qualities. But this game was too much and in the next round he was totally lost against the eventual tailender, Redolfi. That game does not appear in this book, because Fischer *won it!*

GAME 6

White: R. Fischer
Black: B. Ivkov (Yugoslavia)

*Played at Santiago (Chile)
International Tournament, April 1959,
Round 3*

The first of many games where
Bobby presses too hard against the
French. The "attack" yields nothing
but holes in his own position. A
Pawn sacrifice only opens up the
position for the enemy (just as in
Game 1). All swindling attempts in
Ivkov's time pressure only hasten
the end.

French Defense (Winawer)

1	P-K4	P-K3
2	P-Q4	P-Q4
3	N-QB3	...

Only once has Fischer tried 3 N-Q2
—in his loss to R. Byrne (see Game
47).

3	...	B-N5

The Winawer Variation, named after
the 19th-century British master.
Black immediately puts pressure on
White's KP and is willing to part
with his "good" Bishop to obtain
play against the center. It is a strategically very unbalancing variation
which gives good winning chances.
Of course, the absence of the Bishop

from the Kingside also leads to good
losing chances for Black.

4	P-K5	...

There is no other sound way to
prevent the threatened 4 ... PxP.
For 4 P-QR3 see Game 56.

4	...	N-K2
5	P-QR3	BxN+
6	PxB	...

If now 6 ... P-QB4 we get the basic
Winawer position. (See also Game
26.) Apart from a Kingside weakened
by the absence of the Bishop, Black's
other strategic deficiency is his QB
which is locked in by own central
Pawns.

6	...	P-QN3

A marvelously direct method of
handling the problem of the "bad"
QB—Black will play it to QR3 to
exchange it for White's good Bishop!
Its serious side is that it takes time,
something which is of great
importance in open King's Pawn
games. Thus White with exact play
is able to establish clear superiority
on the Kingside. Fischer has tried a
similar strategy, i.e., exchanging a
bad Bishop in the opening, on the
Kingside. However, the results have
also been unsatisfactory—see Games
19 and 31.

7	Q-N4	N-N3
8	B-KN5?!	...

In modern opening practice the key word is timing: not just what to do but *when* to do it. The Bishop eventually should go to KN5 but not quite yet. The correct way of handling this position for White is: 8 P-KR4, P-KR4; 9 Q-Q1! (to protect the QB2 Pawn), B-R3; 10 B-KN5, Q-Q2; 11 BxB, NxB; 12 N-K2, Q-B3 (if 12 . . . Q-R5, White continues his Kingside play with 13 R-R3); 13 P-KB4, N-N1; 14 O-O, N-Q2; 15 Q-Q3, and White gets in P-KB5 with advantage, e.g., Portisch–Ivkov, Zagreb 1965.

8 . . .   Q-Q2

The Queen wants to get here, anyway, but White's QB will be pushed back.

9   P-KR4   P-KR3!
10 B-Q2   P-KR4
11 Q-B3   . . .

Better is 11 Q-Q1!

11 . . .   Q-R5!
12 B-Q3   B-R3

Compared to the variation given above, Black is some tempos ahead and has full equality. White should now play either the quiet 13 N-K2 or the sharp 13 BxN, PxB; 14 K-Q1!

13 P-N4?!   . . .

Such thrusts at the French, before the completion of development,

usually only lead to self-weaknesses. So also here.

13 . . .   PxP
14 QxNP   BxB
15 PxB   N-B3

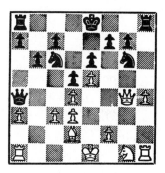

Already threatening 16 . . . N/B3xKP! and if 16 N-B3, O-O-O, renewing the threat. White's next move prevents both this threat and Black's O-O-O.

16 Q-N5   N/B3-K2
17 P-R5   N-B4!
18 N-K2   N3-K2
19 N-N3   O-O-O

White's Kingside sorties have led only to lost time and weaknesses. Black already stands better: his King is safe, his Queen active, he has better Pawn formation and his extra Knight is superior to White's Bishop, which has nothing to attack.

20 Q-N4   QR-B1
21 R-R3   . . .

Hindsight tells us that the Rook is misplaced here. Best was 21 Q-Q1, offering to enter a slightly inferior endgame, as a price of chasing away Black's Queen.

| 21 | ... | K-N1 |
| 22 | B-N5 | ... |

With the logical strategic idea of exchanging the Bishop for one Knight, but Black effectively prevents it.

22	...	Q-B7!
23	R-B1	Q-N7
24	P-R4	Q-R6
25	Q-Q1	...

Forced to protect the QRP. After 25 N-K2, Black first plays 25 ... P-KB3! and then snips off the QRP.

25	...	NxN
26	PxN	N-B3
27	P-R6?	...

THE LOSING MOMENT

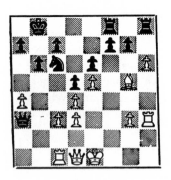

Similar to Game 1, Bobby sacrifices a Pawn for "play," but only makes things easier for Black, who will now have an extra Pawn and the open KN file. White's position is unattractive, but should be tenable after 27 B-Q2!, P-B3; 28 R-QR1, Q-K2; 29 Q-K2.

| 27 | ... | PxP |
| 28 | B-B6 | ... |

28 BxP loses after 28 ... R/B1-N1 threatening 29 ... R-N3; 28 RxP fails in view of 28 ... RxR 29 BxR R-R1. At KB6 the Bishop looks good but is completely out of play (Black has castled Queenside, not Kingside!) The best try was 28 B-Q2, but this would involve swallowing one's pride and confessing the error of 27 P-R6? This is psychologically not easy to do, especially for a Fischer.

28	...	R/R1-N1
29	K-B2	R-N3
30	Q-B2	R1-N1
31	R-QN1	Q-B1

Around here Ivkov was in bad time trouble, which explains the precautionary text (so he won't fall for 30 R-N3, QxRP?? 31 RxNP+) and Bobby's coffeehouse swindling attempts.

32	P-R5?!	NxRP
33	Q-R4	K-R1
34	R-N5	Q-K1
35	P-B4?!	...

The attack has no chance without the KR and the Bishop, but only Houdini could get those pieces into the game.

| 35 | . . . | N-B3! |

So that if 36 PxP, NxQP!

| 36 | Q-R1 | PxP! |
| 37 | PxP | Q-Q2 |

So that if 38 P-Q5, PxP uncovering on the KR. Oh, those misplaced pieces!

| 38 | P-B5 |

Anyone has a better idea?

38	. . .	QxP+
39	QxQ	NxQ
40	R-N4	N-B4

40 . . . N-B3 is more "solid," but this wins very easily, too. Black's time pressure is over and so is White's game. There still followed . . .

41	P-B6	R-N5!
42	RxR	RxR
43	R-R1	P-QR4
44	R-KN1	P-R5
45	R-Q1	R-Q5
46	R-KN1	R-Q7+
47	K-B3	R-Q6+
48	K-B4	RxP
49	R-QB1	R-Q6
50	K-N4	P-R6
51	R-QR1	P-N4
52	R-QN1	P-R7

WHITE RESIGNS

White's Bishop is still on KB6, oblivious to the game of chess just completed.

GAME 7

White: R. Sanguinetti (Argentina)
Black: R. Fischer

*Played at Santiago (Chile)
International Tournament, April
1959, Round 4*

Sanguinetti gets a chess player's
dream position against Fischer: an
endgame with some winning
chances and no danger of losing.
Things continue normally until
Bobby errs by making an
"automatic" recapture and is
surprised by a tactical shot in an
apparently barren Rook and Pawn
endgame.

*King's Indian Defense
(Samisch Variation)*

1	P-Q4	N-KB3
2	P-QB4	P-KN3
3	N-QB3	B-N2
4	P-K4	P-Q3
5	P-B3	P-K4
6	KN-K2	O-O
7	B-N5	P-B3

This is more logical than giving up
the center by 7 ... PxP, as in Game
2. The text move was already
employed by Fischer in a later
round at Portoroz 1958 against
Pachman.

8	Q-Q2	Q-R4

In Round 8 against Romo, Fischer
varied with 8 ... QN-Q2; 9 P-Q5,

N-N3?!. After the correct 10 N-B1!
White stands better, as Black's
Queen is inactive and the QN on
QN3 does not have much of a
future either.

9	P-Q5	...

White must close the center to
complete the development of his
pieces, e.g., 9 N-B1?, PxP and
Black's Queen attacks the Bishop,
thus preventing 10 QxP (10 N-N3?,
PxN!).

9	...	PxP
10	BPxP	...

Also good is 10 NxP QxQ+; 11
KxQ!, NxN; 12 BPxP, and White has
a slightly better endgame.

10	...	B-Q2

Against Pachman Bobby first played
10 ... N-R3. The order in which
theses moves are played does not
seem important.

11	P-KN4!	...

Despite appearances this is actually
a *positional* move rather than an
attacking one. Its major point is to
find a comfortable home for the
KN at KN3 so that White's KB can
control the important QN5 square.
Less exact is 11N-B1, N-R3; 12 B-K2,
N-B4; 13 O-O, KR-B1; 14 N-Q3,
N-R5!; 15 NxN, QxQ; and by
transposition we have the Pachman–

Fischer game with full equality for Black.

| 11 | ... | N-R3 |
| 12 | N-N3 | N-B4 |

More in the spirit of Fischer's fighting style was 12 ... KR-B1! Now White gains a better endgame.

| 13 | R-QN1! | Q-N5 |

Also after 13 ... N-R5 White plays 14 N-N5!

14	N-N5!	QxQ+
15	KxQ	BxN
16	BxB	P-QR3
17	B-K2	KR-B1
18	QR-QB1	...

As is generally true in the Samisch variation, White has play on the Queenside, whereas Black has no play here on the Kingside. Black could prevent White from doubling his Rooks by 18 ... QN-Q2, but after 19 RxR+, RxR; 20 R-QB1, RxR; 21 KxR, White's King has good chances of infiltrating on the Queenside. Black's decision to keep

the Rooks and exchange the black Bishops is a sound one.

18	...	N-K1
19	R-B2	B-B3
20	BxB	NxB
21	R1-QB1	P-QR4

The threat was 22 P-N4 winning the Knight, so that this weakening move is forced.

| 22 | B-N5 | ... |

Black's QN appears well posted on QB4 but actually has no identifiable future. White is still for choice and now starts some Kingside action.

| 22 | ... | K-N2 |
| 23 | P-KR4 | P-R4 |

Bobby typically looks for counter-play opportunities and is willing to absorb additional weaknesses in the process. Safer was 23 ... R-R1.

24	PxP	NxRP
25	NxN+	PxN
26	K-K3	R-KN1

Black is able to contest the KN file just in time.

27	R-KN1ch	K-B3
28	R2-N2	R-N3!
29	P-B4	R1-KN1
30	R-N5	PxP+
31	KxP	RxR
32	PxR+	K-K2
33	R-KR1	...

The situation has clarified somewhat. Both sides now have weak Pawns and Black even has a passed KRP. White still has the advantage based on his more active King.

33	...	R-KR1
34	P-K5	N-Q2
35	BxN	KxB?

THE LOSING MOMENT

This automatic recapture loses. Required was 35 ... PxPch! 36 KxP, KxB, and Black can hold the game as both sides have weak Pawns and Black's KRP cramps White's Rook. One possible continuation is 37 R-R4!, P-N4; 38 P-Q6,

R-R2; and if 39 K-Q5, R-N2!; 40 RxP, R-N3 with a draw.

36	P-K6+!!	...

A perfect example of the need *always* to look out for tactical possibilities. This shot transforms White's KNP into a passed Pawn which, supported by the advanced King, will win.

36	...	PxP

To continue without help from the King is rather hopeless. A better try was 36 ... K-K2.

37	P-N6!	PxP
38	RxP!	RxR

Bobby hopes to set up a successful Rook and Pawn vs Queen blockade. The Rook and Pawn endgame offers no hope at all, e.g., 38 ... R-K1; 39 K-N5!, R-K8; 40 P-N7.

39	P-N7	R-K4

Worthwhile was 39 ... R-R5+ as 40 K-B5?? loses to 40 ... R-R8. To win White must then retreat his King to the third rank.

40	P-N8/Q	K-B2

For a moment it is not clear how White can make progress. At the risk of sounding dogmatic it can be said that where both sides have Pawns, a Queen almost invariably wins against a Rook. The specifics of the win vary, but the result is the same.

| 41 | Q-R7+ | K-B3 |
| 42 | Q-B2+ | K-N3 |

The sealed move.

43	Q-N3+	K-B2
44	Q-QB3+!	K-N3
45	Q-QR3!	...

White's Queen attacks both the QRP and QP and mathematically it is impossible for Black's King to protect both. Also the Rook cannot do it: 45 ... R-K3; 46 K-B5, R-R3; 47 Q-K3+. The game is decided.

45	...	R-K5+
46	K-B5	K-N4
47	QxQP	R-QB5
48	P-N3	R-B3
49	P-R4+!	K-N3
50	Q-Q8+	K-R3
51	QxQP	R-QN3
52	K-K5	R-N5
53	K-Q6	R-N3+
54	K-B7	R-N5
55	K-N8!	...

BLACK RESIGNS

It is mate in short order: 55 ... K-N3; 56 Q-Q6, or 55 ... R-N3; 56 Q-B4+ and 57 QxR mate or 55 ... P-N3; 56 Q-N7.

GAME 8

White: L. Pachman (Czechoslovakia)
Black: R. Fischer

*Played at Santiago (Chile)
International Tournament, April 1959,
Round 6*

The opening is an excellent example of the many opportunities for transposition as exemplified in master chess. Once the middle game starts, Bobby starts an attack even though the position does not call for one. He plays the attack poorly so that even with second-rate moves White wins. A game which Pachman nominally wins, but actually one lost by Fischer, because of a determined but totally impractical insistence on winning.

*Queen's Gambit Declined
(Ragosin Variation)*

| 1 | N-KB3 | N-KB3 |
| 2 | P-B4 | P-K3 |

Starting off as a Reti.

| 3 | P-Q4 | P-Q4 |

Now it's the Queen's Gambit Declined, Orthodox Variation, against which White . . .

| 4 | P-K3 | . . . |

. . . chooses a very tame setup, voluntarily locking in his QB.

| 4 | . . . | N-B3 |

What this is I don't know . . .

| 5 | N-B3 | B-N5 |

. . . but now we have the Ragosin Variation of the Queen's Gambit Declined.

| 6 | B-Q2 | . . . |

Again very tame. Sharper were 6 B-Q3 or 6 Q-B2

| 6 | . . . | O-O |
| 7 | P-QR3 | . . . |

Since Black is quite ready to exchange his KB for White's QN, there is no need to hurry with this move. The flexible 7 Q-B2 was more logical. However, Pachman is not looking for any kind of a big opening advantage: a safe and sound position is his aim.

7	. . .	BxN
8	BxB	N-K5
9	Q-B2	P-QR4
10	P-QN3	. . .

Both to prevent 10 . . . P-R5, fixing White's Queenside and provide a retreat for the QB on the center diagonal.

| 10 | . . . | P-QN3 |

The only, but completely satisfactory, way of bringing the QB into the game.

| 11 | B-N2 | B-R3 |

Apparently playable, even though 11 ... B-N2 putting the Bishop on the center diagonal and giving additional support to Black's important Q4 and K5 points, must be more logical.

12	B-Q3	P-B4
13	R-QB1	R-B1
14	O-O	R-B3?

A complete misjudgment of the position. Since a majority of Black's pieces are on the Queenside, how can a directly brutal Kingside attack succeed? Such attempts must be called "playing to win"; in retrospect, they usually turn out to be "playing for a loss." Correct was 14 ... N-K2 with the idea ... P-B4 and White's advantage, if any, is minimal.

| 15 | KR-Q1 | R-R3 |
| 16 | B-B1 | P-KN4? |

THE LOSING MOMENT

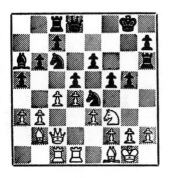

In his eagerness to attack, Black ignores the fact that his QB and QN remain unprotected. Better were 16 ... B-N2 or 16 ... N-K2 or even 16 ... N-N4.

| 17 | PxP | P-N5? |

Attack at all costs! But the costs are too much and the attack is too unsound to have much of a chance of success. A better try was 17 ... BxB and after 18 QxQN, B-K7!, 19 R-K1, P-N5! Black has counterplay. However, 18 PxN!, P-N5; 19 N-K5 keeps the advantage for White: 19 ... B-R3, 20 NxP!

| 18 | BxB | ... |

Around here White's moves are not very difficult to find.

18	...	PxN
19	NPxP	Q-N4+
20	K-B1	RxP

A psychologically interesting moment: Would as fine an attacking player as Fischer sacrifice a whole Rook for nothing?

| 21 | BPxN? | ... |

Pachman has been bluffed. Objectively we can always say "Take off a Rook rather than a Knight," but during an actual game fear rears its ugly head. Here, however, 21 BxR! won rather easily. Both Black Knights remain en prise, and the eventual win of the White Queen will come at too great a material price.

21   ...   R-B1!

Black gets some play now on the KB file which White tries to keep closed.

22	P-K5!	P-B5
23	P-K4	P-B6
24	K-K1	Q-N8+?

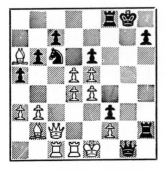

A very obvious yet sloppy continuation from the mind and hand of a top grandmaster. Black voluntarily chases White's King from danger at K1 to safety at QB3. Correct was 24 ... N-K2, saving the Knight with definite practical chances for Black.

25   K-Q2!   ...

Not 25 B-B1?? QxB+! 26 KxQR-R8 mate! This was Bobby's idea, but plans based just on cheapos do not work against top-level competition in tournament games. In 5-minute chess maybe, but not when minutes rather than seconds are available to the master.

25   ...   QxP+

Or 25 ... RxP+ 26 K-Q3.

26	K-B3	Q-N6
27	Q-Q3	PxP
28	R-KN1	R-N7
29	RxR	QxR
30	Q-B1!	...

The correct practical way of playing when you have a material advantage: exchange pieces, especially Queens. This minimizes danger from unexpected counterplay.

30   ...   PxP

There is nothing worthwhile to suggest anymore. The position is simply hopeless.

31	QxQ+	PxQ
32	R-KN1	R-B7
33	B-B4+	K-B1
34	B-Q5	R-B6+
35	K-B4	P-N4+
36	K-B5	...

Of course 36 KxP also wins. In time pressure the "safe" text move is quite logical: White has already more than sufficient material to win and only needs to safely reach the "move 40 harbor."

36...		N-K2
37	RxP	NxB
38	KxN	RxP

A better practical try was 38 ... P-K6, and if 39 K-K4?, R-B7. Of course, 39 B-B3 wins easily.

39	KxP	P-N5
40	PxP	...

BLACK RESIGNS

After 40 ... PxP (40 ... RxP; 41 B-R3); 41 P-Q5, White wins easily enough.

GAME 9

White: C. Jauregui (Chile)
Black: R. Fischer

*Played at Santiago (Chile)
International Tournament, May 1959,
Round 10*

Suspicious of a prepared variation, Bobby tries a new, for him, defense to the Samisch. Jauregui innovates anyway, and Fischer, under the psychological stress of playing against an especially well-prepared opponent, never gets the hang of the variation. Black's game turns into a pretzel and he soon loses his Queen and of course the game. One of the more decisive defeats he has suffered against non-grandmaster opposition.

*King's Indian Defense
(Samisch Variation)*

1	P-Q4	N-KB3
2	P-QB4	P-KN3
3	N-QB3	B-N2
4	P-K4	P-Q3
5	P-B3	O-O

The "normal" move and usually not worth a comment. Here it is noteworthy for two reasons. This is the first time Fischer has employed it, instead of 5 ... P-K4. And thereby

hangs a tale as told by Grandmaster Ludek Pachman, formerly of Czechoslovakia and now living in exile in West Germany. After his defeat of Fischer (see Game 8), Bobby had decided to get even and had specially prepared Colombian master Sanchez for an expected variation that Pachman would play. The result was that Sanchez defeated Pachman with ease and Bobby announced quite openly that it was he, Fischer, who had showed Sanchez everything. On the day that Fischer was to play Jauregui, the latter and Pachman had spent some time together apparently just shooting the breeze. Bobby noticed this and, understandably suspecting revenge, went up to Pachman and said: "So, Mr. Pachman, today you have prepared my opponent," and Pachman without batting an eyelash replied "Yes, Bobby." Thus Bobby was quite suspicious as the game started.

| 6 | B-K3 | QN-Q2 |

A variation popular briefly in the late 1950s and early 1960s as a result of some successes by Tal. The idea is to play ... P-QB4 followed by ... P-QR3 and ... P-QN4 with pressure on the Queenside. Subsequent analysis has shown that at Q2 the Knight is too passively placed, since it exerts no pressure on White's center, and that White keeps an advantage readily enough.

At present the variation is dormant
again.

7	KN-K2	P-QR3
8	Q-Q2	P-B4
9	P-QR3!	...

The theoreticians have paid little
attention to this move—they recommend 9 N-B1 or 9 P-KN4—but I
like it. We have already learned that
in the Samisch, White's play is
usually on the Queenside, so it is
quite logical to expand on the side
where one is stronger.

9	...	R-N1
10	P-QN4	PxQP

The giving up of the center leads
to a clearly superior position for
White. The sharp counter 10 ...
P-QN4 fails after 11 BPxP, BPxNP;
12 RPxP, PxP; 13 N-B1, and Black's
QNP falls. Best was to support
QB4 by means of 10 ... P-N3.

11	NxP	N-K4
12	R-B1	...

White has a very comfortable
"Maroczy bind" position with the
Pawns at QB4 and K4 effectively
stopping Black's counterplay based
on ... P-QN4 or P-Q4.

12	...	B-Q2
13	B-K2	R-B1
14	N-Q5	P-K3

Now the QP will be weak, but no
better was 14 ... NxN; 15 KPxN!
and White has increased his space
control.

15	NxN+	QxN
16	O-O	Q-K2
17	KR-K1	...

A super-safe move, directed against
a potential ... P-KB4. More logical
seems an immediate 17 P-B4. 17
KR-Q1 leads to nothing after 17
... B-R5.

17	...	R-B2

Dreaming of play against the QBP
after 18 ... KR-B1, but it just
remains a dream. However, a con-
structive continuation is nonexistent
as Black's position is rather lifeless.

18	P-B4	N-B3
19	N-B3!	...

Played according to the principle
that exchanges are in the interest
of the side which is cramped.

19	. . .	B-B1
20	KR-Q1	R-Q2
21	P-N5	N-Q1
22	Q-N4	R-K1
23	R-Q2!	. . .

With the apparently obvious plan of doubling on the Queen's file, but with the immediate threat of 24 P-QB5! because after 24 ... QPxP; 25 BxP Black does not have the saving 25 ... RxR *with check.*

23	. . .	P-B4?

THE LOSING MOMENT

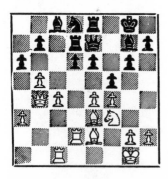

Creates an additional weakness and does nothing about White's major threat—24 P-QB5. Required was 23 ... P-B3. Black's position then is still obviously unpleasant, but the Queen at least has a safe spot at KB2.

24	P-B5!	P-Q4

24 ... QPxP 25 BxP loses the Queen, as in the game. There is no defense, as 24 ... N-B2 is met by 25 BPxP, NxP; 26 B-B5, R1-Q1; 27 P-K5.

25	P-B6!	NPxP

Loses the Queen, but 25 ... QxQ; 26 PxR threatening both 27 PxB(Q) and 27 PxR(Q) gains White a Rook.

26	B-B5!	P-QR4
27	Q-N3	Q-B2
28	N-N5	QPxP

The Queen is trapped: 28 ... Q-B3 29 P-K5, as giving up the KB for nothing with 28 ... B-Q5+ is obviously hopeless.

29	NxQ	. . .

With a Queen ahead there are many ways to win. White's technique is clearly good enough.

29	. . .	RxR
30	N-Q6	N-N2

31	NxN	. . .

White decides to "play it safe." Good enough was also 31 NxR

NxB; 32 Q-B4 PxP; 33 QxNP, e.g.,
33 ... B-QR3; 34 Q-N8!, B-Q5+;
35 K-R1, BxB; 36 N-B6++, K-N2;
37 Q-N8+, KxN; 38 Q-KB8 mate!
Combinations come easy when one
has an extra Queen!

31	...	BxN
32	Q-K3	R1-Q1
33	B-B4	PxP

34	BxNP	P-K4
35	B-N6	PxP
36	QxBP	P-K6
37	BxR	B-Q5
38	B-K2!	B-K5
39	R-K1	B-Q6
40	QxB	...

BLACK RESIGNS

Not too soon!

GAME 10

White: S. Gligoric (Yugoslavia)
Black: R. Fischer

*Played at Zurich (Switzerland)
International Tournament, June 1959,
Round 11*

The second of a series of great
battles between two fighting grandmasters. Black comes out of what
was at that time an avant-garde
opening variation with full equality
and the position remains in balance
deep into the middle game. When all
seems quiet, a careless move leads
to an inherently undeserved loss.

*Sicilian Defense
(Najdorf Variation)*

| 1 | P-K4 | P-QB4 |

Whoever has heard of Bobby Fischer
has heard of the Sicilian Defense.
Except for a few 1 . . . P-K4s in the
early 1960s, the Sicilian has been
Fischer's weapon against the KP
from the start of his serious tournament career and into the Spassky
match. The fact that the first
example of a reversal with it occurs
so late in this book demonstrates
the clear success of the strategy. The
unbalanced nature of the Sicilian
leads to fighting chess and thus is
ideal for Fischer's approach to the
game. Of course there also is the
other side of the coin. White's 1

P-K4 is a very active, sharp move,
yet Black's reply totally ignores it.
This means that White invariably
can build up a strong attacking
position and Black's counterplay
must be well nigh perfect not to
go under. Since we know that Black
gets fine winning chances in practice,
this necessarily must mean that he
also gets excellent losing chances.
Because of Fischer's success with
the Sicilian, many of his legion of
admirers have also become fans of
the Sicilian. But it is a very difficult-
to-play defense and too many of
the non-experts have come to grief
with it.

2	N-KB3	P-Q3
3	P-Q4	PxP
4	NxP	N-KB3
5	N-QB3	P-QR3

And whoever has heard of Fischer
and the Sicilian should also have
heard of the Najdorf Variation,
because to Fischer the Sicilian and
the Najdorf are synonymous. It is
essentially the only Sicilian Variation
that he has played. The variation
is named after Argentinian Grandmaster Miguel ("Moishe") Najdorf
who in the late 1940's was the first
leading master to demonstrate its
playability. It is, however, Fischer
who has been the world's leading
expert and practitioner of it, en-
dowing it with a never-ending
stream of creative ideas. He truly
deserves to be at least the co-name

holder for the variation. I shall have some further comments later regarding the anomaly of not attaching Fischer's name to "his" variations. But what of the move (5 ... P-QR3) itself? The other fully playable continuations here (5 ... P-KN3, 5 ... P-K3, 5 ... N-B3) can be explained readily enough based on the principles of development and central control. It is obvious that 5 ... P-QR3 does very little for either. The move has a defensive point in keeping out White's pieces from Black's QN4 square and an aggressive point in serving as a preparation for an eventual ... P-QN4. These are effective enough but not that powerful against as sharp an opening as 1 P-K4. Yet Fischer has demonstrated through the years that, perfectly handled, the Najdorf gives sufficient counterchances. What is good for a Fischer is not automatically good for everyone else, and many of his followers have been rather less successful with it than the Master. It can be safely stated that the non-experts would have been more successful with the Sicilian if, instead of the Najdorf, they had selected some strategically more straight forward variation.

6   B-KN5   . . .

The most aggressive reply. White clears the back rank for Queenside castling, sets up a potential pin

against the Queen, and keeps in hand the positional threat of BxN, devaluing Black's Kingside Pawn formation. Of course, there are other perfectly playable moves. The quiet 6 B-K2 we meet in Game 34. Another positional continuation is 6 P-B4 (Game 55). Also sharp is Fischer's 6 B-QB4 (Games 13, 18, 20, 22). In the early 1960s Bobby also successfully tried 6 P-KR3 (no losses!) Fischer has had no opportunity yet to play Robert Byrne's move of the 1970s, 6 B-K3.

6   . . .   P-K3

6 ... QN-Q2 is unnecessarily passive and has at present been completely supplanted by the text move.

7   P-B4   B-K2

The "most positional" way of handling this very sharp variation. Games 53 and 61 illustrate 7 ... Q-N3 (Fischer's QNP variation). Other sub-variations start with 7 ... QN-Q2, 7 ... P-KR3, and 7 ... P-N4.

8   Q-B3   QN-Q2

Early in his career, Fischer also played 8 ... P-R3 9 B-R4 P-KN4, the so-called Göteborg Variation. When we talk of Fischer playing for Black "only" the Sicilian Najdorf, it is not as limiting as it sounds, because the Najdorf has many complicated sub-variations and Fischer plays most of them. 8 . . . Q-B2 usually amounts to transposition of moves only: 9 O-O-O, QN-Q2. However, for the faulty 9 . . . O-O? see Game 27.

9 O-O-O   Q-B2

The battle lines are pretty much set as in a typical Sicilian: White will aim at Black's King, often with the help of a central push (P-K5 or P-KB5) and Black will attack on the Queenside.

10 P-KN4   . . .

From about the time of this game through the end of 1972 this move constituted the main variation and tons of literature have been published on it. Because of Spassky's success with the "old" 10 B-Q3 in Match Game 15 against Fischer (he obtained a superior position, but the game ended in a draw), this move has lately been "in." An immediate 10 Q-N3 places the pieces on the Kingside in an awkward position, and in Tal–Fischer, Round 15 (last) Black equalized with 10 . . . P-R3; 11 B-R4, R-KN1; 12 B-K2, P-KN4; 13 PxP, N-K4; 14 P-N6, NxNP. Chess theory in 1973 has shown that with 14 N-B3! White may keep an edge. Thus 10 . . . O-O!? may be Black's best as White now lacks P-KN4. The other reasonable try, 10 B-K2, though

playable, suffers from the twin tactical disadvantages of insufficient support for the KP and taking away a potential retreat square for the QN.

10 . . .   P-N4
11 BxN   . . .

There is no other way to make progress.

11 . . .   PxB

Originally Fischer played this and 11 . . . NxB pretty much interchangeably. In later years he has gravitated to the more positional 11 . . . NxB. For an example with this see Game 17. The third possible capture, 11 . . . BxB?, is inferior because of 12 BxP! PxB 13 N4xNP followed by 14 NxP+ and White has 3 Pawns for the piece and a strong attack.

12 B-N2   . . .

Since this was one of the early games with this variation, we can't be too strict if the players did not yet know all the fine points in it.

The text and the follow-up allows Black easy equality. Sharpest, most modern and probably most difficult for Black to meet is 12 P-B5!. Bad cannot be 12 P-QR3, as in Mednis–Fischer, 1959-60 U.S. Championship.

12	...	B-N2
13	KR- K1	O-O-O
14	P-QR3	N-N3

Black stands well: his King is safe enough, the pieces and pawns control a lot of squares and the two Bishops balance out the inferior Kingside Pawn formation.

15	R-Q3	K-N1
16	KR-Q1	P-Q4

One of Black's main strategic objectives in the Sicilian is to get in ... P-Q4 with no disadvantages. If this is accomplished Black gets full equality. So also here.

17	PxP	NxP
18	NxN	BxN
19	Q-B1	B-B4!

But not the greedy 19 ... BxB?!; 20 QxB, QxKBP+?; 21 K-N1 and Black goes under because of the weakness of his QB3 square.

20	BxB	RxB
21	N-K2	RxR
22	RxR	...

The active present and potential placement of Black's pieces balance the slight weakness in the King position and the KRP. Good now was 22 ... Q-N2 followed by 23 ... R-QB1 and if possible 24 ... Q-K5. Instead ...

22		P-KR4??

THE LOSING MOMENT

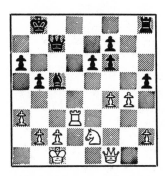

On the face of it quite a logical move: after 23 P-R3, PxP Black exchanges off his weak KRP and opens lines on the Kingside for his Rook. Bobby probably played it because he was proud of its tactical justification: if 23 R-R3?, R-QB1! threatening both 24 ... B-K6ch and 24 ... BxP. A double question mark for it seems harsh yet is quite in order because the move changes an even position into a clearly lost one.

23	PxP!	...

It happens even in master games that the most obvious move is insufficiently heeded. There has now occurred a radical change in the Kingside Pawn configuration: White has a passed RP and White's KBP can hold the three Black Pawns at bay. Gligoric's technically perfect approach of simply pushing the KRP is very instructive.

23	...	RxP
24	Q-N2	R-R1
25	R-QB3	R-QB1

The exchange of Rooks makes White's task easier. A better practical chance was 25 ... Q-N3.

26	P-N4!	B-K6+
27	K-N1	Q-N3
28	RxR+	KxR
29	Q-B3!	...

White is just interested in queening his KRP and thus ignores things such as 29 Q-R8+, K-B2; 30 Q-KB8, Q-Q3!; 31 QxP+, Q-Q2. White has won a doubled KBP, but after 32 QxQ+, KxQ the endgame offers Black good drawing chances. The idea behind the text move is to prevent Black's counterplay via ... Q-Q3 and ... Q-Q7.

29	...	K-Q1
30	P-KR4	K-K2
31	P-R5	P-B4
32	P-R6!	...

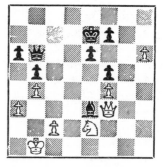

Passed Pawns must be pushed!

| 32 | ... | B-Q5 |

32 ... K-B3 loses to 33 Q-N3 and 32 ... K-B1 to 33 Q-R1! (33 ... K-N1; 34 Q-N2+).

33	NxB	QxB
34	Q-R1!	Q-R1
35	P-R7	K-B1

There is nothing else. If 35 ... K-B3; 36 Q-N1!, Q-N2; (or 36 ... QxP 37 Q-N5 mate); 37 Q-Q4+, K-N3; 38 P-R8(Q). Or 35 ... P-B3; 36 Q-R5, K-B1; 37 Q-N6, P-K4; 38 K-B1! PxP; 39 K-Q2, P-B6; 40 K-K3, P-B5+; 41 KxP/3 and the Queen and Pawn endgame is an easy win.

36	Q-R8+	K-N2
37	QxQ+	KxQ
38	P-B4!	...

Finally the Queenside majority asserts itself.

| 38 | ... | KxP |

If 38 ... PxP; 39 P-R4 P-K4; 40 P-N5! and White queens first with *check!*

| 39 | P-B5 | ... |

BLACK RESIGNS

GAME 11

White: R. Fischer
Black: D. Keller (Switzerland)

*Played at Zurich (Switzerland)
International Tournament, June 1959,
Round 14*

Going into this, the next to last round, Fischer was tied for first with Tal. Thus his selection of a tame opening variation is rather surprising. When the game could be called a draw, Bobby decides to win it by making a series of dubious attacking moves. Keller, basically quite satisfied with a draw, is forced to play for a win, and win he does in good style. A painful and costly loss for Fischer which pushed him all the way down to a tie for third and fourth places.

Ruy Lopez (Closed)

1	P-K4	P-K4
2	N-KB3	N-QB3
3	B-N5	P-QR3
4	B-R4	N-B3
5	O-O	B-K2
6	R-K1	P-QN4
7	B-N3	P-Q3
8	P-B3	O-O
9	P-KR3	N-Q2

A variation quite popular in the late 1950s and up to the middle 1960s. Its main idea is to give support to K4 via B-KB3. However, the clumsy nature of the execution and the removal of pressure on White's KP should make life quite pleasant for the first player. We have had quite a change in fashions in how to defend against the Ruy. After the demise of 9 ... N-Q2 everybody seemed to play Smyslov's 9 ... P-KR3. And in 1972 and 1973 the rage has been Breyer's 50-year-old idea 9 ... N-N1. Only Tchigorin's 9 ... N-QR4, like Old Man River, goes steadily on and on.

10	P-Q4	N-N3
11	PxP?!	...

Despite Fischer's predilection for positions in the Ruy with early removal of central tension, the move is surprising for two reasons. In the first place, the position gets considerably simplified and Fischer definitely felt the need for a full point against his relatively inexperienced opponent. Secondly, in the recently completed Santiago Tournament, Bobby had already twice played thus, without achieving anything noteworthy from the opening. It is, however, rather dangerous, not to say foolhardy, to expect that Bobby will never look for a true improvement. Reshevsky experienced this painfully at the Second Piatigorsky Tournament, (Santa Monica, 1966) when he tried this same variation against Fischer. After the correct 11 QN-Q2!, PxP; 12

PxP, P-Q4; 13 B-B2, B-K3; 14
P-K5, Q-Q2; 15 N-N3, B-KB4; 16
B-N5, KR-K1?!; 17 QBxB, RxB; 18
R-QB1, N-N5; 19 N-B5! White had a
significant advantage and won in 38
moves.

11	...	NxP
12	NxN	PxN
13	Q-R5	...

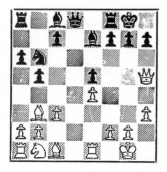

This may *look* active, but it is clear
that by itself the Queen can not
be expected to do much damage to
the Kingside.

13 ... B-B3

Most logical. Flores played 13 ...
Q-Q3 at Santiago 1959 and also
equalized, the game being drawn in
62 moves.

14 N-Q2 Q-K2

Safest. However, 14 ... P-N3 as
played by Sanchez at Santiago 1959
is also okay.

15	N-B1	B-K3
16	N-K3	P-N3
17	Q-B3	BxB
18	PxB	B-N2
19	P-QN4	P-QB3!

It should be pretty obvious that
White has absolutely nothing. In the
spirit of the position was 20 B-Q2
followed by 21 KR-Q1 and a draw
after the exchange of pieces along
the Queen's file. At this moment
it became known that Tal had won
his game and was now a full point
ahead. So Bobby simply decided
that he must win also. But wishing
and doing are quite different, if the
position is juiceless. So ...

20 P-KN3? ...

THE LOSING MOMENT

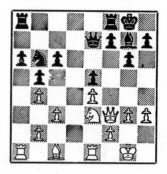

The move is bad enough by itself,
as it provides an attacking object
for Black's KBP after ... P-KB4 and
... KB5. What is even worse is that
it prepares the suicidal advance of
the KRP.

20	...	Q-K3
21	P-R4?	P-KB4!
22	P-R5?	P-B5
23	N-B1	NPxP!
24	QxRP	R-B3
25	N-R2	R-N3
26	N-B3	...

Here Bobby moved from his dream into a nightmare. If 26 K-N2, R-KB1 followed by ... R-R3 and a mating attack. So White tries to exchange off some attacking pieces at the cost of a Pawn. Obviously winning hopes are gone and there are only some fleeting drawing chances.

26	...	PxP
27	PxP	RxP +
28	K-R2	Q-N5
29	QxQ	RxQ
30	R-KN1?	...

The exchange of White's only potentially dangerous piece leads to an easily won endgame for Black. Some chances could only be retained with 30 K-R3, R-N3; 31 N-R4.

30	...	RxR
31	KxR	N-R5!

The extra Pawn is only one trump for Black. The passive position of White's pieces and the fundamental Pawn weaknesses are other reasons why White must lose.

32	K-B1	P-B4!
33	P-N3	...

Desperation. No better is 33 PxP, NxBP/4 and 33 P-B4 losses to the *Zwischenzug* 33 ... R-KB1!

33	...	NxP
34	PxP	NxP
35	P-B6	...

Or 35 P-N4 NxP! 36 PxN P-K5

35	...	N-B4
36	B-K3	NxP

A lovely move to be able to play in time pressure, but faster winning was 36 ... P-K5!

37	R-R2	P-QR4
38	R-KN2	K-R1
39	N-N5	R-KB1 +
40	K-K1	N-Q5
41	BxN	...

Sealed move.

41		PxB
42	N-K6!?	...

A good try!

| 42 | ... | R-K1 |
| 43 | P-B7 | B-K4! |

And not 43 ... RxN+?? 44 R-K2 and it is White who wins! After the text move Black remains three Pawns up. Keller's method is not the only way to win but is fully adequate.

44	K-Q2	R-QB1
45	R-N5	BxP
46	RxP	B-Q3
47	K-Q3	R-R1
48	R-N6	B-N6
49	R-N7	P-R5
50	N-N5	P-R6
51	RxP+	K-N1
52	R-R1	P-R7
53	R-R1	B-K4
54	N-K6	R-R6+
55	K-K4	B-B3
56	K-B5	K-B2
57	N-N5+	BxN

WHITE RESIGNS

GAME 12

White: R. Fischer
Black: T. Petrosian (USSR)

*Played at Bled (Yugoslavia)
Candidates Tournament, September
8, 1959, Round 2*

One of two great Caro-Kann fights between Fischer and Petrosian at the 1959 Candidates. (The second, a draw from Round 16, is annotated in full by Fischer in his book *My 60 Memorable Games*.) This loss is no disgrace: the more mature Petrosian outmaneuvers his opponent in a tough, complicated, unbalanced struggle.

Caro-Kann Defense
(Two Knights Variation)

1 P-K4   P-QB3

A fundamentally sound defense where Black has a somewhat passive yet positionally healthy position. It is beautifully suited to Petrosian's patient style as well as his receptiveness to draws with the Black pieces. The only surprise is that he has not used it more in situations where draws with Black are satisfactory, e.g., against Fischer in the 1962 Candidates and in the 1971 Buenos Aires Match.

2 N-QB3   . . .

The so-called Two Knights Variation, one of several fully satisfactory continuations. At the 1959 Candidates Fischer developed a stubborn streak about it and played it exclusively down to the sub-variations. This made preparation against him very easy. He remained partly true to the variation throughout 1962, but over the last 10 years there has been a total swing in direction. Now he plays almost everything against the Caro-Kann: the quiet 2 P-Q3, the standard 2 P-Q4, 3 N-QB3 and various exchange motifs: 3 PxP, 4 B-Q3 or the Panov with 4 P-QB4.

2 . . .   P-Q4
3 N-B3   B-N5

The usual move in the position. Black is willing to exchange his QB for the KN to set up a sturdy center. Olafsson in Round 26 tried the doubtful 3 . . . N-B3 against Fischer: 4 P-K5, N-K5; 5 N-K2! and Black's Knight is on shaky ground (White won in good style in 42).

4 P-KR3   BxN

The safe continuation. In Round 7 Smyslov played 4 . . . B-R4 against Fischer (a draw). That move may be playable, but leads to wild, open positions, generally unlike those of the Caro-Kann, e.g.: 5 PxP, PxP; 6 B-N5+, N-QB3; 7 P-KN4, etc.

5 QxB   . . .

Is there any other move? Well, in Game 5 of the 1960 match Tal played 5 PxB?! against Botvinnik, got a bad game, but drew.

| 5 | ... | N-B3 |
| 6 | P-Q3 | P-K3 |

Quite an unbalanced and important position for evaluation of the Caro-Kann Defense. White has the potential advantage of the two Bishops, if the position can be opened up for them. With Black's center so firm it is not an easy goal.

7 P-KN3 ...

Fischer remained true to this move all through the 1959 Candidates but in chess terms the move does not deserve such loyalty. The fianchetto of the KB is a reasonable idea but should be executed via the active P-KN4. Also, just a few months earlier at Zurich he had played 7 P-R3 (to prevent a pin via ... B-QN5) against Larsen and obtained a good position (draw in 92!). Later on when his "chess stubbornness" was over, he won with 7 P-R3, QN-Q2; 8 P-KN4 at Netanya 1968 against Kagan. According to 1973 theory, the most promising approach for White is 7 B-Q2 with the idea O-O-O, P-KN4, P-KR4, etc.

7	...	B-N5
8	B-Q2	P-Q5
9	N-N1	BxB +

For 9 ... Q-N3 see Games 15 and 21

| 10 | NxB | P-K4 |

Keeping White's KB as contained as possible.

11	B-N2	P-B4
12	O-O	N-B3
13	Q-K2	P-KN4?!

A reasonable looking idea in a new-for-Petrosian position. (Fischer may well have looked at it in his "home laboratory".) Since Black is planning to castle Queenside he doesn't worry about this weakness and strives to prevent White's P-KB4. Yet the move is both a loss of time *and* a serious weakening. The second time around against Fischer (Round 16), Petrosian had had ample time for reflection and continued simply with 13 ... Q-K2; 14 P-KB4, O-O-O with equality.

14 N-B3? ...

Playing for the wrong break. As Fischer tells it in *My 60 Memorable Games,* he had prepared for any repeaters 14 P-QB3!, Q-K2; 15 N-B3, P-KR3; 16 PxP! and no matter how Black recaptures, White obtains a superior position.

14	...	P-KR3
15	P-KR4	R-KN1
16	P-R3	Q-K2
17	PxP	PxP
18	Q-Q2	N-Q2
19	P-B3	O-O-O

Black has completed his development and has full equality.

20	PxP	KPxP!

Some annotators have criticized this move and suggested instead 20 ... NxP with safe equality. True enough, but the text is a fully justified attempt at winning. Black's pieces now have the important K4 square in their possession.

21	P-QN4	K-N1
22	KR-B1	N3-K4
23	NxN	QxN
24	R-B4	R-QB1
25	QR-QB1	...

This demonstration amounts to nothing. Better is 25 Q-N2 with Black keeping a good position after 25 ... R-B2!; 26 R-N1, R-Q1.

25	...	P-N5!

Sealing off White's Bishop.

26	Q-N2	KR-Q1
27	P-R4	Q-K2
28	R-N1?	...

THE LOSING MOMENT

Incomprehensible. White either ignores or overlooks Black's obvious threat. The correct move was 28 Q-B2 and after 28 ... N-K4! 29 RxBP, RxR 30 PxR, R-QB1!. Black, despite the Pawn minus, has a slight advantage because his Knight just towers over White's Bishop.

28	...	N-K4
29	RxBP	RxR
30	PxR	NxP
31	Q-Q2	NxQBP
32	Q-B4+	...

If 32 P-R5, 32 ... Q-K4 stops everything.

32	...	Q-B2
33	QxNP	NxRP

So Black has won a Pawn and actually has 3 passed Pawns. However, White's Bishop is now back in the game and Black's Queenside Pawns are needed for the protection of the King and therefore rather immobile. Petrosian's winning strategy of first tying down the White Rook with the QP and advancing the RP and NP under support by the King deserves utmost praise.

34	P-K5	N-B4
35	Q-B3	P-Q6
36	Q-K3	P-Q7
37	B-B3	N-R5
38	Q-K4	N-B4
39	Q-K2	P-R3
40	K-N2	K-R2
41	Q-K3	R-Q6

The sealed move. Analysis showed that White can't do anything. But how is Black to make progress?

42	Q-B4	Q-Q2
43	Q-B4	P-N3!
44	R-Q1	...

An attempt for play on the QN file just makes things easier for Black: 44 Q-QN4, Q-N4!; 45 QxQ, PxQ; 46 B-K2, P-N5!; 47 BxR, NxB (threatening 48 ... N-B8); 48 R-Q1, P-N6; 49 RxP, P-N7; 50 R-Q1, N-B8 and the QNP wins. So White has to continue his holding operaiton.

44	...	P-R4
45	Q-B4	R-Q5
46	Q-R6	P-N4!
47	Q-K3	K-N3!
48	Q-R6+	N-K3
49	Q-K3	...

With the threat 50 RxP.

49	...	K-R3
50	B-K2	P-R5
51	Q-QB3	K-N3
52	Q-K3	N-B4
53	B-B3	P-N5
54	Q-R6+	N-K3
55	Q-R8	Q-Q1
56	Q-R7	Q-Q2
57	Q-R8	P-N6!

The second time control is over and Black had time to reassure himself of the safety of the coming King excursion.

58	Q-QN8+	K-R4
59	Q-QR8+	K-N4
60	Q-QN8+	K-B5!

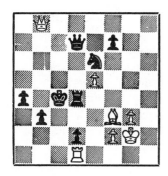

63	B-B3	P-R6
64	Q-B8	K-N7
65	Q-R8	N-K3

65 ... P-R7; 66 RxP+; RxR; 67 P-K6+, Q-Q5; 68 QxQ+, RxQ; 69 P-K7, P-R8(Q) also wins easily enough, but Petrosian does not want to allow any tactics.

To embark *voluntarily* on such King travels requires the strongest of nerves.

61	Q-N8	K-B6!
62	B-R5	N-Q1

Typical Petrosian: no need to rush things.

66	Q-R8	P-R7
67	Q-R5	Q-R5
68	RxP+	K-R6

WHITE RESIGNS

A great fighting performance by Petrosian and no disgrace on Fischer's part.

GAME 13

White: F. Olafsson (Iceland)
Black: R. Fischer

*Played at Bled (Yugoslavia)
Candidates Tournament, September
14, 1959, Round 5*

At the time of the 1959 Candidates, Fischer was already well known both as a practitioner of the Najdorf and for his exclusive use of 6 B-QB4 against it. Thus, surprisingly this is the first time that anyone dared to play "Fischer's 6 B-QB4" against it. Olafsson is well rewarded for his bravery: he scores a full point in a well played game. Incidentally, this is Fischer's first and only loss against "his own variation."

*Sicilian Defense
(Najdorf-Fischer's 6 B-QB4)*

1	P-K4	P-QB4
2	N-KB3	P-Q3
3	P-Q4	PxP
4	NxP	N-KB3
5	N-QB3	P-QR3
6	B-QB4	. . .

A psychologically interesting moment: for the first time ever, Fischer as Black is confronted with the move he always plays with White! Along with 6 B-KN5 this is the other sharp method of attacking the Najdorf. The major strategic difference between the moves is that 6

B-KN5 prepares the attack with White's King castled on the Queenside, whereas after 6 B-QB4 White's King usually goes to the Kingside. Obviously the actual concrete variations are quite different, but the goals are the same: an immediate sharp attack against Black's King. But what about the name of the move? In the 1920s the Russian master Sozin suggested 6 B-QB4 in the position that results if Black plays 5 . . . N-B3. Unfortunately, too many writers, journalists and commentators have attached Sozin's name to this variation also. It is an insult to historical honesty and to our intelligence, and a serious slight of Fischer's contributions. Sozin had never seen or considered the modern-day Najdorf, so what is his name doing here? The move is Fischer's from the beginning of the idea through 15 years of creative play and analysis! It should carry only his name and I hope that in due course (the sooner the better!) other writers will also start calling it the only logical way: Fischer's 6 B-QB4.

6 . . . P-K3

White's Bishop diagonal must be shortened.

7 P-QR3 . . .

It is pretty clear that the Bishop is unsafe on QB4 and will have to retreat. This move prepares such a retreat to QR2. A count of opening tempos tells us that it will have taken three moves to post the Bishop securely on the QR2-KN8 diagonal. This is too much in an inherently open, sharp position and now we know (thanks to Fischer, of course) that with correct play Black at least equalizes. For examples of the sounder 7 B-N3 see Games 18, 20 (by transposition), and 22.

| 7 | ... | B-K2 |
| 8 | O-O | O-O |

The next moves are clear enough: White aims for Black's King via P-KB4 and P-KB5 and Black tries to counter with an attack against White's KP.

9	B-R2	P-QN4
10	P-B4	B-N2
11	P-B5!	P-K4
12	N4-K2	QN-Q2!

Black is too undeveloped to afford 12 ... NxP; 13 NxN, BxN. After 14 N-N3, B-N2; 15 P-B6! BxBP; 16 N-R5 White has a winning attack. This conclusion is reenforced by the fact that in later games Fischer has also refused to take the KP.

| 13 | N-N3 | R-B1 |
| 14 | B-N5 | ... |

Works well this first time around. In later games White successfully played 14 B-K3 with the idea of a grip on Black's Q4 square. It was

Fischer again who showed that after 14 ... N-N3; 15 BxN, QxN+; 16 K-R1, Q-K6! (to prevent 17 N-R5); 17 N-Q5, BxN; 18 BxB, B-Q1!; 19 P-QR4, B-N3 Black has better prospects. (Robatsch–Fischer, Havana 1965—Black won in 33 moves!)

| 14 | ... | N-N3? |

THE LOSING MOMENT

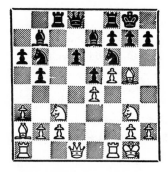

Some time after the game Gligoric showed that with the immediate 14 ... RxN!; 15 PxR, NxP Black gets at least even chances. The difference between this and what happens in the game is that not only is Black a tempo ahead here, but also his Knight is still well placed on Q2 for defense of the Kingside.

| 15 | N-R5! | ... |

Objectively speaking, with the aid of hindsight, we can say that 14 ... N-N3? is the losing move, but it requires some fine play by Olafsson to prove it.

15 ...   RxN

Typical of Fischer's active style: he looks for counterplay. The decision is understandable since the quiet continuations 15 ... NxN or 15 ... N-B5 are not fully satisfactory either.

16 PxN   NxN

About equivalent to 16 ... BxP.

17 BxB   QxB
18 QxN   BxP

Materially Black is not so badly off: he has a valuable KP for the exchange and White's Queenside Pawns are in ruins. The decisive factor is White's attack.

19 Q-N4   P-Q4
20 P-B6   Q-B4+
21 K-R1   P-N3

The KBP remains a pain in Black's side throughout the game, thus 21 ... B-N3 may have been worth a try.

22 QR-K1?   ...

A reasonable-looking move which is a surprising inaccuracy. The correct play is first 22 Q-R4 and only after 22 ... R-K1 23 QR-K1.

22 ...   R-K1?

Black reciprocates. Black can defend with 22 ... QxBP!; 23 Q-N5, N-Q2! and now 24 Q-R6? fails to 24 ... NxP (25 RxN??, QxR+ with mate). We can visualize what has happened: White has wasted an attacking tempo (22 QR-K1? in place of 22 Q-R4) which is just enough time for Black to consolidate.

23 Q-R4   ...

All is well again. Now White threatens 24 RxB followed by 25 BxPch.

23 ...   P-KR4

This Kingside weakening move could have been replaced by the immediate 23 ... N-B5. However, the text move also has a positive side: by giving the King a flight square it prevents back-row mates.

24 Q-N5   N-B5

The threat now was 25 RxB followed by 26 QxNP+.

25 BxN   NPxB
26 R-K3   Q-KB1

There is no time for 26 ... QxRP:
27 R-R3, K-R2; 28 RxP+! wins.

27 R-QN1   R-N1

The exchange of a pair of Rooks
makes things easier for White. Thus
27 ... BxBP should have been tried.

28 R3-K1!   RxR
29 RxR   BxBP

After 29 ... QxP White has a choice
of wins: 30 Q-R6, Q-B1; 31 R-N8
or 30 R-N8ch, K-R2 31 R-KR8+.
These motifs keep reappearing later
on.

30 R-N7   B-B4
31 Q-K3   B-K3

Now 31 ... P-K5 fails to 32 Q-R7,
QxP; 33 Q-N8+!, K-R2 (33 ...
Q-B1 34 QxQ+, KxQ 35 R-N8+
and mate); 34 RxP+, K-R3; 35
P-R4! as White's Queen guards the
KR2-QN8 diagonal, preventing a
perpetual check and the KRP
prevents Black's King from fleeing.
Black therefore protects the KBP,
but there is no way to save the game.

32 QxP   QxP
33 P-R3   Q-B8+
34 K-R2   P-N4
35 R-R7   P-R5
36 RxRP   K-R2
37 R-R1!   ...

An electrifying finish. If now 37 ...
QxR; 38 QxNP and mate on KN7
or 37 ... Q-Q7 then 38 R-Q1!
forces the game continuation.

37 ...   Q-B5+
38 QxQ   PxQ
39 R-KB1   ...

Black's Pawns are so weak that the
win is quite elementary.

39 ...   P-Q5
40 PxP   K-N3
41 RxP   B-B4
42 R-B3   KxP
43 R-K3!   ...

Cutting off the King.

43 ...   K-N4
44 P-N3   B-Q6
45 P-Q5   B-B4
BLACK RESIGNS

Here the game was about to be
adjourned and Fischer resigned
without awaiting White's reply.
Despite the slight slip on move 22,
an outstanding effort by Olafsson.

GAME 14

White: M. Tal (USSR)
Black: R. Fischer

Played at Bled (Yugoslavia)
Candidates Tournament, September
15, 1959 Round 6

Mikhail Tal has always had a fairly broad opening repertoire. Yet he is feared most for his vicious attacks emanating from KP openings. Thus his selection of the White side of the strategic Petrosian variation of the King's Indian against Fischer shows psychological cunning: Young Tal is betting that he can outplay even younger Fischer in a positional struggle. Such an approach of course also may show fine respect for Fischer's tactical abilities. In any case, Tal wins in good style here and again in Round 20.

King's Indian Defense
(Petrosian Variation)

1	P-Q4	N-KB3
2	P-QB4	P-KN3
3	N-QB3	B-N2
4	P-K4	P-Q3
5	B-K2	O-O
6	N-B3	. . .

The beginning of the so-called "Normal Variation," which also has the original names of "Main Line"

and "Orthodox Variation." When the King's Indian came to the fore, in the late 1940s and early 1950s, this was the usual method of meeting it— thus the name. White simply develops his Kingside pieces as quickly as possible to be ready for middle-game action. Depending on Black's play White's chances may be on the Queenside (more often) or in the center aiming in the Kingside direction.

6	. . .	P-K4
7	P-Q5	. . .

The normal Normal Variation continues with 7 O-O—See Game 31 for an example. The text move is Petrosian's idea. In the first place the complications after 7 O-O, N-B3 8 P-Q5, N-K2 are prevented—much in Petrosian's style. Also, since after 7 P-Q5 Black's counterplay must come from a . . . P-KB4 break, White with his next move tries to make that more difficult to achieve. And thirdly, White now has more space on the Queenside which can be used for a Queenside Pawn attack via P-QN4, P-QB5, etc. Sounds great, doesn't it? If Black were not allowed to move, things would be quite clear. The main disadvantage with 7 P-Q5 is that White prematurely closes the center—for no immediate reason and with no immediate gain in sight. We can say that premature center closing for White (with, e.g., P-Q5) or premature center give-up

for Black (with, e.g., KPxP) is not
in the interest of the doer. Of
course, often considerable master
work is required before the word
"premature" can be applied with
confidence. At the present stand
of theory, the Petrosian Variation
is no more a dangerous weapon
against the King's Indian and even
its creator has lately switched over
to the Samisch as his primary choice.

7   ...   QN-Q2

After almost everything else has
also been tried, most experts now
feel that this is the best move. A
tribute to Fischer's fine feel for the
position is the fact that he has
played this move from the very
beginning.

8   B-N5   ...

In the spirit of the original 7 P-Q5
idea. Of course, 8 O-O or 8 Q-B2
are also good.

8   ...   P-KR3
9   B-R4   P-R3

With the idea of ... Q-K1
unpinning the KN, without being
bothered by White's N-QN5. Fischer
had been successful with this plan
against Olafsson at Zurich 1959 and
thus was quite ready for a repeat.
His variation is apparently playable
but has gone out of fashion in favor
of 9 ... P-KN4 10 B-N3, N-R4 with

very sharp tactical play (something
that White supposedly prevents
with 7 P-Q5) and equal chances
for Black with correct play.

10   N-Q2   Q-K1
11   O-O   ...

At Zurich, Olafsson played the sharp
11 P-KN4 and after many ups and
downs Fischer won. Remember that
Tal is planning to outplay Fischer
positionally; thus the quiet text
move.

11   ...   N-R2
12   P-QN4!   ...

As is usual in the Normal Variation
White is going to play on the
Queenside ...

12   ...   N-N4

... and Black on the Kingside. For
the inferior 12 ... B-B3? see
Game 19.

13   P-B3   P-KB4
14   B-B2   ...

With nothing to do any more on
the diagonal, the Bishop retreats to
reenforce P-QB5.

14   ...   Q-K2
15   R-B1   N-B3
16   P-B5   B-Q2
17   Q-B2   N-R4
18   P-N5!   ...

As is to be expected in the early stages, White has made good initial progress on the Queenside. Further progress by normal means is unlikely, so Tal resorts to tactics. If now 18 ... QPxP 19 NPxP, P-N3 (not 19 ... NPxP? and Black's isolated, doubled QBPs will fall like pigeons) 20 N-B4 N-B2 21 P-QR4 and White has a strong grip as 21 ... RxP? loses to 22 NxKP. So Fischer continues playing on the Kingside.

18	...	BPxP
19	N2xP	NxN
20	PxN	...

Black now gets lots of squares on the Kingside and White's QN doesn't get in the game for some time. Thus better seems 20 NxN. This may have been the improvement Fischer was afraid of when facing Tal again —see Game 19.

20	...	N-B5
21	P-B6	Q-N4
22	B-B3	NPxP
23	QPxP	...

After 23 NPxBP?, White has blockaded himself off on the Queenside and Black has free hands on the Kingside.

23	...	B-N5
24	BxB	QxB
25	B-K3	PxP
26	BxN	...

White's interest in getting rid of the annoying Knight is understandable but now the diagonal of Black's Bishop is open again.

| 26 | ... | PxB |
| 27 | NxP | R-B2? |

Black walks into a very annoying pin. The correct move was 27 ... QR-B1 with a very unbalanced position where the chances are equal.

| 28 | Q-B4! | R-QB1?! |

The bizzare unpinning 28 ... K-B1 looks better.

| 29 | R-KB3! | B-K4 |

Last chance for 29 ... K-B1.

| 30 | QR-B1? | ... |

White lets the fruits of his previous fine play slip by. With 30 P-KR3!, Q-N4; 31 Q-K6! he would win a Pawn as Black's counterplay is insufficient after 31 ... R-N1; 32 NxBP, R-N7; 33 Q-K8+, R-B1; 34

QxR+!, KxQ; 35 N-K6+ and White wins.

| 30 | ... | K-N2 |

Now Black is safe.

| 31 | P-QR4 | R-QR1 |
| 32 | K-R1 | Q-N4?? |

THE LOSING MOMENT

With this unmotivated retreat Black walks into a deadly pin. After the logical 32 ... P-N4 the chances would still be level.

| 33 | **P-N3!** | QR-KB1 |

Is not sufficient, but I don't know what else to suggest.

| 34 | PxP | BxP |

Loses but so does 34 ... RxP; 35 NxBP, RxR; 36 N-K6+, K-R1; 37 RxR

35	N-Q4	Q-R5
36	RxB!	RxR
37	N-K6+	K-R1
38	Q-Q4+	...

The deadly check. Obviously 38 ... K-N1 leads to 39 Q-N7 mate, and 38 ... Q-B3 loses a Rook and Knight: 39 RxR, QxQ; 40 RxR+ and 41 NxQ

| 38 | ... | R1-B3 *B/* |
| 39 | NxR *B5* | ... |

39 RxR also wins of course.

39	...	K-R2
40	P-K5!	PxP
41	Q-Q7+	...

BLACK RESIGNS

The win-forcing continuation runs: 41 ... K-N1; 42 Q-Q8+; K-R2; 43 QxP+, K-N1; 44 Q-Q8+, K-R2; 45 Q-K7+, K-N1, 46 P-B7.

GAME 15

White: R. Fischer
Black: P. Keres (USSR)

*Played at Bled (Yugoslavia)
Candidates Tournament, September
18, 1959, Round 8*

A psychologically interesting moment occurs right on move 1: Keres is so sure that Fischer "out of principle" will repeat the variation from Round 2 (Game 12) that for the first time in his life he plays the Caro-Kann. His judgment is rewarded and Keres wins very, very easily as Fischer plays very, very badly.

Caro-Kann Defense
(Two Knights Variation)

1 P-K4   P-QB3!

Quite a challenge and surprise! Against top-level competition Keres has been a consistent 1 . . . P-K4 defender. Sometimes against weaker players he tries something offbeat such as 1 . . . N-QB3. But a Caro-Kann? Never before! Yet Keres is so sure that Fischer will repeat the harmless variation from Round 2 that he is willing to try it here. Being quite proud, determined and stubborn, Fischer accepts the challenge. Bobby is still quite proud and determined, but the stubbornness associated with particular

opening variations is definitely gone. A clear maturing of a great Champion! If Bobby had chosen any other variation, Keres unquestionably would have flipped, as he had to be unprepared for anything else. But . . .

2	N-QB3	P-Q4
3	N-B3	B-N5
4	P-KR3	BxN
5	QxB	N-B3
6	P-Q3	P-K3
7	P-KN3	B-N5
8	B-Q2	P-Q5
9	N-N1	Q-N3

Keres's "improvement" over Petrosian's 9 . . . BxB+ from Round 2, Game 12. Even though he won with it once more in Round 22 (Game 21) it is questionable if it is better or even as good as the simpler Bishop exchange. In any case, Petrosian with an excellent feel for Caro-Kann positions, even after witnessing White's debacle here, stayed with 9 . . . BxB+ in his second cycle game with Fischer in Round 16.

10 P-N3   . . .

Three times did Fischer play this move in this position—twice against Keres and also in Round 24 against Benko. It is quite surprising that not once did he try the centrally oriented 10 P-B3! If then 10 . . . B-B4; 11 B-B1! and White stands very well: Black's outpost on Q5 is shaky and Black's Queen and Bishop are awkwardly placed. If Black tries the interesting 10 ... B-R6!? White gets excellent compensation for a Pawn after 11 NxB, QxP; 12 R-QN1, QxN; 13 PxP, QxRP; 14 Q-Q1!: he has good center influence, open lines for the Bishops and QR and Black's Queen may find herself in an embarrassed situation on White's Queenside. It is even more surprising that Fischer also ignores 10 P-B3! in his *My 60 Memorable Games*.

10	...	P-QR4
11	P-R3	B-K2

For the Bishop exchange see Game 21.

12 B-N2? ...

Very careless. After 12 P-QR4! White would be quite safe on the Queenside and could prepare a slow mobilization of forces on the Kingside. With his Queenside weakened, it would be expected that Black would have to castle on the Kingside and White would have good chances there.

12 ... P-R5!

Ruining White's Queenside Pawn configuration.

13	P-QN4	QN-Q2
14	O-O	P-B4?!

Keres is too eager. Correct was first 14 ... P-K4!

15 R-R2? ...

THE LOSING MOMENT

Simply horrible. The Rook will be out of play for the rest of the game. The correct way was 15 P-K5!, N-Q4 16 P-B4! with excellent counterplay for White. Fischer's usual tactical sharpness is nonexistent in this game.

15	...	O-O
16	PxP	BxP
17	Q-K2	P-K4
18	P-KB4?!	...

White's first objective here should have been getting his Knight back into the game via Q2. For this goal, either 18 B-N5 or 18 B-B1 were indicated.

18 ... KR-B1

The QR is go into the game either via QR3 or QR4.

19 P-R4?   . . .

Just as against Keller (Game 11), Bobby opens up his Kingside for penetration by Black's pieces. He doesn't do those things anymore!

19	. . .	R-B3
20	B-R3	Q-B2
21	PxP	N2xP
22	B-B4	B-Q3
23	P-R5?!	R-R4!

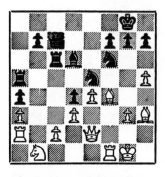

White has serious structural weaknesses on the Queenside and Kingside and White's QR and QN are out of action. With all of Black's artillery swinging into the fray, Fischer's time is counted. He does choose, however, to lose the fastest way.

24	P-R6	N-N3!
25	Q-B3	R-R4
26	B-N4?!	. . .

26 B-N2 must be better.

26	. . .	NxQB
27	BxR	. . .

27 PxN, NxB 30 QxN, RxRP is equally hopeless.

27	. . .	N5xB
28	P-N4	B-R7+
29	K-N2	NxNP

Curtains. If 30 QxN, R-KN3.

30 N-Q2   . . .

The Knight joins the fight a "bit" too late and the QR still sits and waits.

30   . . .   **N-K6+**

WHITE RESIGNS

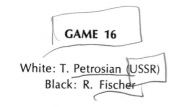

GAME 16

White: T. Petrosian (USSR)
Black: R. Fischer

*Played at Bled (Yugoslavia)
Candidates Tournament, September
21, 1959, Round 9*

Apparently despondent over his loss
to Keres the previous round (see
Game 15), Fischer plays the opening
thoughtlessly and quickly achieves
a hopeless position. It is quite difficult to select the losing moment in
this game: pretty much every one
of Bobby's moves is second-rate, but
where exactly is the point of no
return? In an unorthodox way the
game is an excellent example of
Fischer's great self-confidence and
fighting spirit: in the very next
round he won a brilliant attacking
game against Benko.

*Nimzo-Indian Defense
(Rubinstein Variation)*

1	P-Q4	N-KB3
2	P-QB4	P-K3
3	N-QB3	B-N5

Suggested, analyzed and played
successfully by Latvian-born Danish
grandmaster Aaron Nimzowitsch,
the opening is still considered
hypermodern in some circles despite
the baby's age of some 50 years.
It is modern of course only in

relation to the Queen's Gambit
Declined which Black could enter
here via 3 ... P-Q4. The move's
points are many and logical: indirect
pressure on White's K4 square,
possibility of giving White doubled
QBPs, preparing Black's King for
castling. The opening to this very
moment has a well-deserved good
reputation.

4   P-K3   ...

Rubinstein's continuation and by far
the most popular in modern master
practice. It simply says: there is no
immediate way to refute 3 ... B-N5
so White will complete the development of his Kingside and then
decide what to do next. The move
is good and flexible—the hallmark
of modern opening play.

4   ...   P-Q4

Once the natural rejoinder, it is not
considered best any more, because
it commits Black's QP too soon to
a fixed position. Fischer has not
played it since he obtained a
dubious position with it against
Reshevsky in the 1961 match. For
4 ... P-QN3 see Game 48 and the
normal variation (by transposition)
occurs in Game 60.

5   P-QR3!   ...

Botvinnik's idea which has taken
the fun out of playing 4 ... P-Q4.
If now 5 ... BxN+, White reaches

a favorable variation in the Sämisch (4 P-QR3).

5 ...   B-Q3?!

If Black wants to retreat the Bishop, the correct square is K2 and we have a Queen's Gambit Declined type of position with an extra move for White (P-QR3) and this should be of some value. Fischer's move must be characterized as an unsuccessful opening experiment. If one tries hard enough it is possible to come up with some rational explanations for almost any move, but 5 ... B-Q3?! really doesn't deserve such treatment. You can be sure that Fischer has not played it again!

6 N-B3   O-O
7 P-B5   B-K2
8 P-QN4   ...

White has a clear space superiority on the Queenside and where will Black's play come from?

8 ...   N-K5?!

The wrong idea. In the spirit of the position was 8 ... P-QN3 and if possible ... P-QR4.

9 B-N2   N-Q2?!

This makes ... P-QN3 impossible as White will have the answer P-B6.

10 B-Q3   P-B4?!

The Knight will not be safe on K5. Better 10 ... NxN.

11 N-K2!   B-B3?!

Better 11 ... N-N4. Black seems oblivious of any danger and is only interested in his "own thing."

12 O-O   Q-K2?!

12 ... N-N4.

13 N-K5!   NxN?

THE LOSING MOMENT

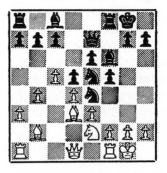

The straw that breaks the camel's back! Black's pieces become hopelessly misplaced on the Kingside. Unexciting, yet best, was still 13 ... N-N4.

14 PxN   B-N4
15 B-Q4!   ...

With the threat 16 P-B3 winning the Knight.

15	. . .	B-R3
16	P-B3	N-N4
17	P-B6!	P-QN3?

Permanently locking in the QB is obviously hopeless. Giving up the exchange was a better practical try.

18	P-N5	P-R3
19	P-QR4	PxP
20	PxP	RxR
21	QxR	N-B2
22	Q-B3	Q-R5
23	R-R1	N-N4
24	Q-K1!	. . .

Typical Petrosian: the only thing that's nicer than a middle game with an extra piece is an endgame with a piece plus.

24	. . .	Q-R4
25	R-R7	Q-N3

With Black's first and last threat: 26 . . . NxBP+.

26	K-R1	Q-R4
27	P-B4	N-K5
28	RxP	P-N4
29	BxP	. . .

White has won the Queenside Pawns and Black's QB is still locked in. The end is imminent.

29	. . .	K-R1
30	BxN	BPxB
31	B-B5	R-N1

BLACK RESIGNS

Fischer resigned without awaiting Petrosian's reply. White has a multitude of wins, two of them being 32 B-K7 and 32 P-N6.

GAME 17

White: S. Gligoric (Yugoslavia)
Black: R. Fischer

Played at Bled (Yugoslavia)
Candidates Tournament, September
24, 1959, Round 11

The contestants continue the
theoretical discussion begun at
Zurich 1959 (Game 10) with Gligoric
the convincing victor. At that time
this was a game of great theoretical
importance.

Sicilian Defense (Najdorf Variation)

1	P-K4	P-QB4
2	N-KB3	P-Q3
3	P-Q4	PxP
4	NxP	N-KB3
5	N-QB3	P-QR3
6	B-KN5	P-K3
7	P-B4	B-K2
8	Q-B3	Q-B2
9	O-O-O	QN-Q2
10	P-KN4	...

Gligoric is basically a 1 P-Q4 player
and essays 1 P-K4 only when he is
quite sure that the opponent will
allow a variation which he, Gligoric,
is interested in playing against. With
the "old" Fischer, Gligoric could
be quite sure of this!

10	...	P-N4
11	BxN	NxB

The "positional" recapture in that
Black does not inherently weaken
his Kingside Pawn structure. For 11
... PxB go back to Game 10. After
the loss here, Fischer reverted to
11 ... PxB for his second cycle
game against Gligoric in Round 25.
After much excitment the game
ended a draw.

12	P-N5	...

A recent try at finessing is 12 P-QR3
leaving White the option of continuing with P-KB5 or P-KN5.

12	...	N-Q2
13	P-QR3	...

Both this and the supersharp 13
P-B5 have been played and analyzed
extensively with complicated
theoretical variations stretching into
the middle 20s the norm. Is 13
P-QR3 or 13 P-B5 better? If anyone
knows the sure answer it is Fischer
and he does all his talking at the
chessboard only!

13	...	B-N2?!

At present this has been completely
replaced by the sharper 13 ...
R-QN1. An example of Fischer's
latest contribution here is 14
P-KR4, P-N5; 15 PxP, RxP; 16 B-R3
and now the dangerous-looking
16 ... O-O! (Minic–Fischer, Rovinj/
Zagreb 1970), where Fischer demonstrated that Black has dynamically

equivalent chances (he won in 34 moves).

14 B-R3! ...

In open positions time is money and White has to strike as quickly as possible against Black's Achilles' heel—the KP on K3. There is no time for the desirable 14 P-KR4.

14 ... O-O-O

The King isn't safe on the Queenside either, but there is no fully satisfactory continuation. After 14 ... N-B4 White retains the better chances with either 15 Q-K3 or 15 KR-K1. Even less satisfactory is 14 ... P-N5?!; 15 PxP, Q-B5; 16 KR-K1!, QxP?!; 17 N-Q5! with a decisive attack.

15 P-B5!? ...

Quite an original and noteworthy idea! It was Tal, however, who took all the fun out of 14 ... O-O-O by playing against Gligoric

(now as Black) in Moscow 1963, 15 BxP!, PxB; 16 NxKP, Q-B5 (after 16 ... Q-N3 White continues as in the game with 17 N-Q5, etc.); 17 N-Q5!, BxN; 18 PxB, K-N2; 19 P-N3, Q-B1; 20 R-Q3 and White had a winning attack.

15 ... BxPch

What else? If 15 ... P-K4 16 P-B6.

16 K-N1 P-K4
17 N4xP! ...

The point.

17 ... PxN
18 NxP Q-B4?!

According to Fischer, correct is 18 ... Q-N3! and roughly even chances after 19 NxP+, K-B2; 20 NxP, B-B3. After 21 NxKR, RxN; 22 R-Q3! White should have a slight plus.

19 NxP+ K-N1
20 NxP?! ...

Later analysis showed that it is in White's interest to exchange Queens. This could have been achieved by either 20 Q-QN3!, Q-N3 or 20 P-N4!, Q-K6.

20 ... Q-K2
21 NxKR RxN
22 KR-K1 B-B5?

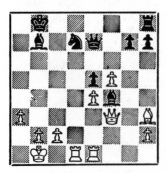

With the unimportant attack on the KRP, Black gives away a crucial tempo for the defense. After 22 ... N-B4 Black would have good prospects for equality. Now White gets his Queen effectively into the game.

23	Q-QN3!	N-B4
24	Q-N5!	...

With the threat of 25 P-N4 followed by 26 R-Q7.

24	...	Q-QB2
25	P-N4	N-R3
26	R-Q7	Q-B1
27	R1-Q1!	...

White decides to keep the bind rather than allow any counter-chances after 27 RxP, N-B2 or 27 P-B6 N-B2!

27	...	Q-B3

Now that White's KP is unprotected, Black offers the exchange of Queens. The results are unsatisfactory, but there is nothing attractive to recommend.

28	QxQ	BxQ
29	RxP	BxKP
30	P-B6	...

The KBP is a terror.

30	...	B-R3
31	R-K7	N-B2
32	P-B7	B-B3

White threatened 33 R1-Q7 followed by 34 R-K8+.

33	B-Q7

Of course there was nothing wrong with 33 RxP.

33	...	K-N2
34	R-Q6	...

The tactical 34 BxB+, KxB; 35 P-N5+!, NxP; 36 R-K6+ also won.

34	...	BxB
35	RxKB	B-N4
36	RxRP	R-KB1
37	R-N7	B-B5

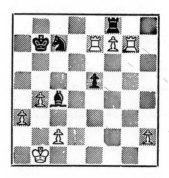

38	RxP	...

White could have quickly queened a Pawn with the immediate 38 P-KR4!: 38 ... K-B3; 39 P-R5, K-Q3; 40 RxN!, KxR; 41 P-R6. But three moves before time control, how can the safe text move be criticized?

38	...	B-K3
39	P-KR4	K-B3

40	P-R5	K-Q3
41	R-K1	BxP
42	P-R6	N-K3
43	R-N4	R-KR1

BLACK RESIGNS

Black had sealed 43 ... R-KR1 but resigned without continuing the game. White plays 44 R-R4 and then pushes the Queenside Pawns to victory.

GAME 18

White: R. Fischer
Black: M. Tal (USSR)

*Played at Bled (Yugoslavia)
Candidates Tournament, September
28, 1959, Round 13*

Fischer handles his own variation
inexactly and Tal plays perfectly to
score the full point. A fine example
of Tal in his prime.

*Sicilian Defense
(Najdorf-Fischer's 6 B-QB4)*

1	P-K4	P-QB4
2	N-KB3	P-Q3
3	P-Q4	PxP
4	NxP	N-KB3
5	N-QB3	P-QR3
6	B-QB4	P-K3
7	B-N3	. . .

The main line of Fischer's 6 B-QB4.
The Bishop is not stable on QB4
and since it must retreat anyway,
White chooses to do so immediately.
This gives White maximum flexibility
later on. With its Master inactive, the
variation experienced an ebb in
interest in the late 1960s but has
come on strong again over the last
two years as a result of discoveries
made by many of the young attacking
players of the world.

7	. . .	B-K2

Recent work has shown that the
immediate goal of Kingside castling
by Black is too passive. For the
sharper and best reply 7 . . . P-QN4,
see Game 22.

8	P-B4	O-O
9	Q-B3	. . .

Much better than the immediate
9 P-B5 PxP! and Black equalizes.

9	. . .	Q-B2
10	O-O?	. . .

But here there is no time to tarry!
The correct move is 10 P-B5!, P-K4
(Soltis suggests 10 . . . N-B3 as
better, but Fischer claims a clear
advantage after 11 B-K3); 11 N4-K2,
P-QN4 and White's position is
better after both 12 P-QR3 (Fischer)
or 12 P-N4 (Soltis).

10	. . .	P-QN4
11	P-B5?	. . .

THE LOSING MOMENT

This finds a convincing refutation. Correct was 11 P-QR3, B-N2 and Black has full equality, but White is in the game.

| 11 | ... | P-N5! |

Shunts the QN to the edge of the board and allows Black to establish full control of the important QR1-KR8 diagonal.

12	N-R4	P-K4
13	N-K2	B-N2
14	N-N3	QN-Q2
15	B-K3	...

If White had realized how badly he stood, he would have tried 15 B-N5 to look for some counter-chances (15 ... P-R3; 16 B-R4!).

| 15 | ... | B-B3! |

Keeps an eye on the Knight and prepares the following Queen maneuver.

16	B-B2	Q-N2
17	KR-K1	P-Q4
18	PxP	NxP
19	N-K4	N-B5
20	P-B4	...

Black was threatening 20 ... N-B3 to which White could now respond with 21 B-B2. However, Tal finds a surprising tactical possibility. Thus a bit better would have been 20 P-B3.

| 20 | ... | P-N3!! |

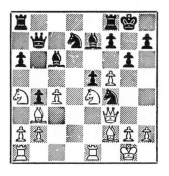

Tal has seen that with the opening of lines on the Kingside, it is Black who will benefit since he has a preponderance of pieces already trained against White's King.

| 21 | PxP | P-B4! |

The point. After 22 PxP+, K-R1! White loses the pinned Knight. With the following maneuver White keeps material equality, but not his King for long.

| 22 | P-N7 | KxP! |

Also playable was 22 ... R-B2, but Tal is the one who wants to do the attacking.

23	Q-N3+	K-R1
24	N/K4-B5	NxN
25	BxN	BxB+

Of course, 25 ... R-KN1 also won.

26	NxB	Q-QB2
27	Q-K3	QR-K1
28	R-K2	...

Resignation to one's fate. 28 P-N3 loses to 28 ... N-R6+ 29 K-B1 P-B5.

28	...	NxR+
29	QxN	BxP!

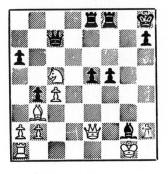

Going for the immediate kill.

30	NxP	Q-R2+!
31	KxB	R-KN1+
32	K-R3	Q-KN2!
33	B-Q1	R-K3

WHITE RESIGNS

34 ... R-KR3+ with an impending mate cannot be stopped.

THE LOSING MOMENT

White: M. Tal (USSR)
Black: R. Fischer

*Played at Zagreb (Yugoslavia)
Candidates Tournament, October 11,
1959, Round 20*

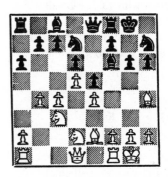

Fischer tries to improve on his previous encounter in the King's Indian against Tal (Game 14) but the cure is considerably worse than the illness. Tal delivers another one of his World Chess Championship-caliber games on the way to the title in 1960.

King's Indian Defense
(Petrosian Variation)

1	P-Q4	N-KB3
2	P-QB4	P-KN3
3	N-QB3	B-N2
4	P-K4	P-Q3
5	B-K2	O-O
6	N-B3	P-K4
7	P-Q5	QN-Q2
8	B-N5	P-KR3
9	B-R4	P-R3
10	O-O	Q-K1
11	N-Q2	N-R2
12	P-QN4	...

So far as in Game 14 where Black played 12 ... N-N4 and obtained a reasonable game. Either dissatisfied with that position or afraid of a potential improvement, Fischer is the first to vary.

| 12 | ... | B-B3? |

According to the tournament scuttle-butt Fischer had spent about ten hours in home analysis to prepare this move. With the help of hindsight we know, of course, that this time expenditure was quite fruitless. The move does have some clear strategic logic: with the blocked center position (White P-Q5, Black P-K4), Black's KB is locked in from his center diagonal and thus has become "bad." What is more logical than exchanging it for White's "good" Bishop? In a static position this would be quite true, but here the idea has dual disadvantages: valuable development time is lost and the King position is seriously weakened. It seems harsh to call this the losing moment, yet Tal plays outstandingly and Black does not miss any significant improvements. It is worth noting that later on Fischer was again unsuccessful with a similar strategic idea—see Game 31.

13	BxB	KNxB

The problem with 13 ... QNxB
is that not only does it allow an
immediate 14 P-B5 but also that it
leaves the KN with no identifiable
future on KR2.

14	N-N3	Q-K2
15	Q-Q2	K-R2
16	Q-K3	...

The Queen was placed well enough
on Q2 and it was more efficient
to prepare P-QB5 via 16 QR-B1.

16	...	N-KN1

What else? 16 ... P-N3 only
weakens the Queenside some more
and with 17 QR-B1 White is sure
of getting in P-QB5 anyway.

17	P-B5	P-B4
18	KPxP	NPxP

18 ... RxP; 19 B-Q3 gives White's
Bishop a strong diagonal against
Black's King and White's QN the
K4 square.

19	P-B4!	...

A thematic move, challenging
Black's King and KB Pawns. With the
KB still on the board Black could
well play 19 ... P-K5 but here the
move would weaken the black
squares and allow White a further
possible undermining action with
an eventual P-KN4. Fischer's next
move at least gives his pieces use
of his K4 square.

19	...	KPxP
20	QxP	PxP?!

Definitely tempting the gods. Fischer
made the move almost instantaneously. He fully realized that
positionally he was busted and felt
that his only hope was that White
would overreach. Objectively better
was 20 ... N-K4 though after 21
QR-B1 followed by 22 N-Q4 White
has a clear advantage on both the
Queenside and Kingside.

21	B-Q3!	...

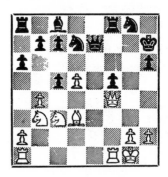

Even though Fischer's last move
caught Tal by surprise he did not
take long on this strong yet fairly
obvious attacking move.

21	...	PxP

Might as well be consistent.

22	QR-K1!	Q-B3

A better try was 22 ... Q-Q3 even
though after 23 BxP+, K-R1; 24
Q-Q4+, Q-KB3!; 25 QxNP, Q-N3+;

26 Q-Q4+!, QxQ; 27 NxQ White still has a very strong attack even with the Queens off.

23 R-K6! ...

It is possible that Fischer had neglected this move when he played 20 ... PxP?!. If instead 23 BxP+, QxQ; 24 QxQ+, RxQ; 25 RxQ, PxN and Black is okay.

| 23 | ... | QxN |
| 24 | BxP+ | RxB |

A direct mate results after 24 ... K-N2; 25 R-N6+, K-R1; 26 RxP+, NxR; 27 QxN+, K-N1; 28 B-K6+; R-B2; 29 BxR mate.

| 25 | QxR+ | K-R1 |
| 26 | R-B3! | ... |

Getting the Rook into the game with a gain of time. It is surprising that Black's Queen doesn't have even one safe check. If now 26 ... Q-N2; 27 R-N3, Q-R2; 28 R-K8!!, so Fischer plays ...

| 26 | ... | Q-N7 |
| 27 | R-K8 | QN-B3 |

Leads to a lost endgame but Black's Queen still has no useful checks and White was threatening mayhem starting with 28 RxN+.

28	QxN+	QxQ
29	RxQ	K-N2
30	R/6-B8!	...

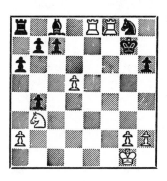

Tying up Black's pieces.

30	...	N-K2
31	N-R5	P-R4
32	P-R4	...

Actually helps to prepare a mating net.

32	...	R-N1
33	N-B4	P-N4
34	N-K5	...

BLACK RESIGNS

35 R-B7+, K-R3; 36 R-R8 mate cannot be prevented in any reasonable way.

GAME 20

White: R. Fischer
Black: V. Smyslov (USSR)

Played at Zagreb (Yugoslavia) Candidates Tournament, October 13, 1959, Round 21

One more example of the disadvantages of choosing an unvarying opening variation. Fischer no doubt expected Smyslov to play 1 . . . P-K4 or 1 . . . P-QB3. Instead Smyslov prepares for Fischer's 6 B-QB4 against the Najdorf and does it better than Bobby. An impetuous attempt at an immediate attack against Black's King is unwarranted, as Smyslov with perfect defense demonstrates. Incidentally, this is Smyslov's only win against Fischer.

*Sicilian Defense
(Najdorf-Fischer's 6 B-QB4 by transposition)*

1 P-K4   P-QB4

Smyslov has a healthy positional style and the potential wild tactics of the Sicilian are of little interest to him. With this rare (for him) selection Smyslov clearly shows that he has something particular in mind.

2 N-KB3   P-K3

One more surprise. Smyslov·is so sure that Fischer will play 6 B-QB4

against anything that he chooses this order of moves to ensure that he gets exactly the variation that he's analyzed. In addition, Black makes sure that he is not surprised by the sharp 6 B-KN5 against the Najdorf—for which he is obviously unprepared.

3	P-Q4	PxP
4	NxP	N-KB3
5	N-QB3	P-Q3
6	B-QB4	B-K2
7	O-O	P-QR3
8	B-N3	P-QN4
9	P-B4	. . .

We now have via transposition a 100 percent genuine position from Fischer's 6 B-QB4 against the Najdorf.

9 . . .   O-O?!

The years 1972-73 have taught us that correct is 9 . . . B-N2; 10 P-K5, PxP; 11 PxP, B-B4! with wild play and equal chances. I don't guarantee that this is still true today! Evaluations of complicated, popular variations can change suddenly, and then again sometimes there are no further significant discoveries to make.

10 P-B5?   . . .

In the early days of all B-QB4 variations it was pretty axiomatic that the correct strategic aim is P-KB5 for White to open up the

Bishop's diagonal. Today we know that there is no real basis for such rigidity of thought. Very good here is 10 P-K5!, PxP; 11 PxP, KN-Q2; 12 Q-R5! with a very strong attack for White. White gets his KB powerfully into the game quite often with sacrifices such as RxKBP, NxKP, or BxKP.

| 10 | ... | P-N5 |
| 11 | QN-K2 | ... |

No better is 11 N-R4, P-K4; 12 N-K2, B-N2; 13 N-N3, QN-Q2; 14 Q-B3, B-B3; 15 B-K3, Q-B2; 16 P-B3, P-QR4 with advantage for Black in Janosevic-Polugajevsky, Skopje 1971.

| 11 | ... | P-K4 |
| 12 | N-KB3 | B-N2 |

Even stronger is 12 ... NxP! as 13 B-Q5 is met by 13 ... B-N2!; 14 B-K3 (or 14 BxB Q-N3+), Q-B2 followed by ... N-KB3. The exchange of the white-square Bishops is in Black's interests because White's attacking power is lessened.

13	N-N3	NxP
14	NxN	BxN
15	Q-K1	...

With a double attack on the Bishop and QNP, forcing Black to decide whether to give up the Bishop or give back the Pawn.

| 15 | ... | BxN!? |

A surprising decision again by Smyslov. More in his positional style was 15 ... P-Q4. After 16 NxP White has recovered the Pawn, but Black has a lovely risk-free position.

| 16 | RxB | N-B3 |
| 17 | Q-K4? | ... |

THE LOSING MOMENT

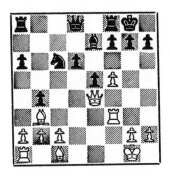

With some fine defensive play Smyslov turns back this overeager attacking try. The right way was first 17 P-B3! to keep out the Knight. The resulting position is very difficult to judge, but seems to give *dynamically* equal chances.

| 17 | ... | N-Q5 |

Rather obvious, but still strong.

| 18 | R-R3 | B-B3! |

Fischer didn't really expect Black to overlook the threat of 19 P-B6!? Or maybe at that moment in his career he did?

19	B-Q5	R-B1
20	P-B3	PxP
21	PxP	N-N4
22	B-Q2	R-B4!
23	K-R1	Q-Q2
24	B-N3	...

The Bishop is poorly placed at Q5 and requires protection by the Queen. Of course 24 P-B4 allows 24 ... N-Q5.

24	...	P-Q4
25	Q-B3	N-Q3!
26	R-KB1	...

26 BxP? loses a piece after 26 ... P-K5; 27 BxKP, NxB; 28 QxN, QxB.

26	...	N-K5!
27	Q-R5	P-R3
28	BxRP!?	...

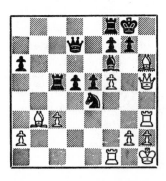

Not good enough, yet still a better try than the hopeless retreat to QB1.

28	...	PxB
29	B-B2	...

The Knight prevents R-KN3. Equivalent is 29 QxRP, KR-B1 (or to QN1);

30 B-B2, B-N2; 31 Q-R7+, K-R1; 32 BxN, PxB and 33 P-B6? fails to 33 ... BxP (34 RxB?, Q-Q8+ and mate).

29	...	B-N4

29 ... R-N1 was also playable, but Smyslov decided to hold on to the KRP.

30	P-B6	R-N1
31	BxN	PxB
32	R-N3	...

Threatening 33 RxB+ as well as 33 P-KR4, and if 32 ... K-B1?; 33 RxB! anyway (33 ... PxR; 34 Q-R8 mate).

32	...	Q-B4!!

Combining defense and attack: 33 RxQ?? R-N8+ and mate. White wins the piece back, but remains down the Pawn sacrificed in the opening. This fact will be decisive.

33	K-N1	Q-N3
34	Q-K2	R-B3!
35	P-KR4	RxKBP
36	RxR	QxR
37	Q-R5	...

Best chance. Faster losing is 37 PxB, Q-B5!; 38 Q-N4, P-KR4!

37	...	Q-B5
38	K-R2	K-N2
39	PxB	PxP
40	QxNP+	QxQ
41	RxQ+	K-B3

Blacks wins the endgame easily, because White's King is shut off and Black's advanced KP is too strong.

| 42 | R-R5 | R-N8 |
| 43 | K-N3 | R-KB8! |

Exactness to the very end. White's King remains cut off.

44	R-R4	K-B4
45	R-R5+	K-K3
46	R-R6+	P-B3
47	R-R4	P-K6!
48	R-K4	P-B4!

WHITE RESIGNS

A fine finish. If 49 RxKP/3, P-B5+ wins the Rook and otherwise the KP promotes.

GAME 21

White: R. Fischer
Black: P. Keres (USSR)

*Played at Belgrade (Yugoslavia)
Candidates Tournament, October 18,
1959, Round 22*

For the third time Fischer goes under against the Caro-Kann. He did gain a bit of revenge by scoring in Rounds 24 and 26 against the Caro-Kanns set up by the tournament tailenders Benko and Olafsson. With the win here Keres equalized the mini-match against Fischer 2 to 2. It is interesting that Black won all four games! What is there to say about this game? Simply that Keres played better and won deservedly.

*Caro-Kann Defense
(Two Knights Variation)*

1	P-K4	P-QB3
2	N-QB3	P-Q4
3	N-B3	B-N5
4	P-KR3	BxN
5	QxB	N-B3
6	P-Q3	P-K3
7	P-KN3	B-N5
8	B-Q2	P-Q5
9	N-N1	Q-N3
10	P-N3	QN-Q2

A small yet significant improvement over 10 ... P-QR4 played in Game

15. It is clear that the QN must be developed to Q2 and the need for ... P-QR4 is not certain.

11	B-N2	P-QR4

The value of this move is open to question. It clearly weakens Black's Queenside and thus makes castling there unattractive; and what does it accomplish?

12	P-QR3	BxB+

More logical than the retreat to K2 as in Game 15. Now White has definite weaknesses on the black squares on the Queenside.

13	NxB	Q-B4
14	Q-Q1	...

At first glance it may appear that Black has achieved something with his Q-Q1-QN3-QB4 maneuver but this is not so. White's Queen on KB3 was blocking the Bishop and KBP so she is quite content to go back to Q1. We can now clearly appreciate the wisdom of Petrosian in sticking to 9 ... BxB+ in Round 16 rather than indulging in fruitless Queen maneuvers. Black should now play 14 ... P-K4 followed by 15 ... O-O and an approximately even position.

14	...	P-R4?!

A sharp Kingside thrust in keeping with Keres's style but of dubious strategic merit.

15 N-B3?! . . .

A silly idea. An even stronger epithet would be used, except that after this move the position still remains in balance. It was two rounds later that Fischer demonstrated the right concept against Benko: 15 P-KR4! Suddenly it was apparent that Black's King could expect no safety on either flank, while White's turned out to be quite safe on the Kingside. Fischer opened lines against Black's King and won convincingly.

15 . . . Q-B6+
16 K-K2 . . .

Nowadays it is well known that Fischer is an admirer of the first official World Champion, Wilhelm Steinitz. One of Steinitz's trademarks was to go on early King walks in the center of the board. I'm not sure that Fischer at the time of the 1959 Candidates was yet a student of Steinitz's, perhaps this is Bobby's own idea!

16 . . . Q-B4

The Queen has no future on QB6 so it is quite in order to go back.

17 Q-Q2 N-K4
18 P-QN4? . . .

Quite a thoughtless move. White seriously weakens his Queenside while losing time on the Kingside. Correct was 18 NxN, QxN; 19 P-KB4 with an unbalanced position and equal chances.

18 . . . NxN!

Did Fischer overlook this *Zwischenzug*?

19 BxN Q-K4
20 Q-B4 . . .

It is indicative of Bobby's unsure play at the 1959 Candidates that he voluntarily enters an unpromising endgame. From the "real Fischer" we would rather expect 20 B-N2 and 21 P-KB4.

20 . . . N-Q2
21 QxQ NxQ
22 PxP? . . .

Opens the gates on the Queen-side for Black. Fischer apparently missed the tactical trick on move 25. The required move was 22 P-KR4! with the idea 23 B-N2 and 24 P-KB4. Black still stands better, but it is quite far for the win.

22	...	K-Q2!
23	KR-QN1	K-B2
24	R-N4	...

24 P-KR4 was better.

| 24 | ... | RxP! |
| 25 | B-N2 | ... |

White can't play 25 RxQP because after 25 ... P-QB4! the Rook is trapped! Even so, 25 P-KR4 was better.

| 25 | ... | P-KN4! |

From now on Keres gives a masterful

demonstration of play with a Knight against an inferior Bishop.

26	P-KB4	PxP
27	PxP	N-N3
28	K-B3	...

There is nothing to cheer about either after 28 RxQP, NxP+; 29 K-B3, P-K4; 30 R-N4, R-KN1.

| 28 | ... | R-KN1 |

Threatening to win the B after 29 ... N-R5+.

29	B-B1	P-K4!
30	PxP	NxP+
31	K-K2	P-QB4
32	R-N3	P-N3
33	R1-N1	R-N3

33 ... R-R3 was a bit more accurate.

| 34 | P-KR4 | ... |

Prevents an immediate ... P-R5 by Black, all right, but exposes the Pawn to sure death. However, I don't have any good suggestions for White. Mainly because of the superiority of the Knight over the Bishop, Black has a strategically won game.

| 34 | ... | R-QR3! |

Freeing the KR for action on the Kingside.

| 35 | B-R3 | R-N6 |

36 B-B1   . . .

Worse was 36 B-B5, R-N7+ and no better was 36 R-KR1, R-K6+ and 37 . . . P-B5!

36	. . .	R-N5
37	B-R3	RxKRP
38	R-KR1	R-R1
39	R3-QN1	R-KN1
40	QR-KB1	. . .

Bobby keeps on playing, yet there can be no doubt about the result. For his minus Pawn, White has a lost position.

40	. . .	R-N6
41	B-B5	R-N7+
42	K-Q1	R5-R7
43	RxR	RxR
44	R-N1	P-B5!

Pushing the RP was good enough. Keres's move, by taking advantage of the insecure position of White's King, is even more decisive.

45	PxP	NxP
46	R-N7	K-Q3
47	RxP	N-K6+
48	K-B1	RxP+
49	K-N1	R-KR7
50	R-Q7+	K-K4
51	R-K7+	K-B5
52	R-Q7	N-Q8!

A very pretty finish. If now 53 RxP, N-B6+; 54 K-B1, N-K7+ and 55 . . . NxR or 54 K-R1, R-R7 mate! What an economical use of the remaining material!

53	K-B1	N-B6
54	B-R7	P-R5

Black also has a passed KRP!

55 R-KB7+   K-K6
WHITE RESIGNS

56 . . . P-Q6 will cost White a piece.

GAME 22

White: R. Fischer
Black: M. Tal (USSR)

*Played at Belgrade (Yugoslavia)
Candidates Tournament, October 26,
1959, Round 27*

After three straight defeats by Tal,
Fischer was gung ho for revenge.
After employing an extremely sharp
variation, he built up a very
promising attack. But the decisive
stroke never came, and Tal by an
inspired defense started to turn the
tables. Bobby was psychologically
unprepared for such a development
and for the rest of the game put up
a very dispirited defense. Thus the
mini-match Fischer–Tal ended in a
0–4 disaster! Bobby must have said
to himself "Never again," and he
hasn't lost to Tal since! This game
was "memorable enough" to be one
of three lost games to be included
in Fischer's *My 60 Memorable
Games.*

*Sicilian Defense
(Najdorf-Fischer's 6 B-QB4)*

1	P-K4	P-QB4
2	N-KB3	P-Q3
3	P-Q4	PxP
4	NxP	N-KB3
5	N-QB3	P-QR3
6	B-QB4	P-K3
7	B-N3	P-QN4

According to the most modern
opening theory, the most exact
continuation.

8   P-B4   . . .

More popular now is 8 O-O, which
keeps some added options in
White's arsenal. Thus Kingside
castling is required anyway, but in
certain variations P-KB4 may be
replaced by e.g., R-K1.

8   . . .   P-N5?!

It requires much intestinal fortitude
to play such a move, especially
against Fischer, and even more so
in this situation for Tal, where a
draw was fully satisfactory toward
clinching first place while a loss
could be quite painful. Yet, in chess
at least, the brave inherit the world!
This has been one of the main
reasons for Fischer's successes and
also for Tal's whenever his health
hasn't been an overriding handicap.
The normal, safer, "sane" move is
8 . . . B-N2

9   N-R4   NxP

Obviously the point of 8 . . . P-N5?!
Why play . . . P-N5 if you aren't
going to take the Pawn?

10   O-O!   P-N3

How should Black defend? There
has been very little actual experience
with this position as very few players

have dared to follow in Tal's footsteps. After the game Fischer suggested as better 10 ... B-N2 but Vukovic has shown that 11 P-B5, P-K4; 12 N-K6!, PxN; 13 Q-R5+ is very strong then. If the KN retreats by 10 ... N-KB3 White has 11 Q-B3, P-Q4; 12 P-B5, P-K4; 13 R-K1, P-K5; 14 Q-N3 with strong pressure, and if now 14 ... B-Q3; 15 QxP, BxP+; 16 KxB, R-N1; 17 RxP+! wins (Keres). Since White is threatening 11 P-B5, anyway, Tal's response is as logical as any. It is clear that White will have a strong attack in any case, thus Black's best hope is that White will become careless or overreach himself.

11 P-B5!!   . . .

Anyway!

11 . . .   NPxP
12 NxBP!!

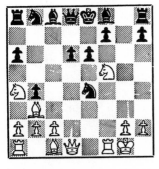

The point of the previous move. If now 12 ... PxN White wins with 13 Q-Q5, R-R2; 14 Q-Q4 with an attack on both Rooks. Fischer now suggests as best for Black 12 ... P-Q4; 13 N-R6, BxN; 14 BxB, but it is difficult to understand why this should be any better for Black than the game continuation.

12 . . .   R-N1
13 B-Q5!   . . .

One more shot, yet curiously enough it also signifies the last pinch of powder in Fischer's barrel, as his game inexplicably goes down from here on, move by move. White's position here is already strong enough to do without fireworks and the simple 13 Q-R5 also was very good, e.g., 13 ... N-KB3; 14 Q-B3, R-R2; 15 N-N3 followed by 16 B-K3, etc.

13 . . .   R-R2
14 BxN   . . .

This move is okay, but much more in the spirit of the previous one (13 B-Q5) was 14 B-K3, as pointed out by Kevitz. After 14 ... N-B4; 15 Q-R5, R-N3; 16 QR-K1 White has a very strong attacking position where all the pieces are still on the board. You may have noted that in none of the variations is there yet a clear forced win, White "only" has a very strong attack.

14 . . .   PxN
15 BxP?   . . .

But this is clearly off the mark. White exchanges off a second piece, this time against Black's undeveloped QB. White's KB has been moved *five* times to do this and it just can't be right. In addition White's KNP will experience some weakness with Black's KR pointed against it. After the consistent 15 B-Q5! White still would have a very strong attacking position.

15 ...   R-K2!

From now on Tal beautifully demonstrates the resilience of the Sicilian.

16 BxB   ...

Otherwise 16 ... B-QN2.

16 ...   QxB
17 B-B4?   ...

Going for exchanges just can't be the right way of playing for an attack in an open position. Fischer has correctly pointed out that 17 P-B3! was in order, both protecting the QN and trying to get it back into action. White then would still have some advantage. After the text move he has nothing.

17 ...   Q-B3!
18 Q-B3   QxN!

As Fischer relates it, this move really floored him. He had expected that the exchange of Queens was forced, giving White a slightly superior endgame.

19 BxP   Q-B3!
20 BxN   Q-N3+
21 K-R1   QxB

Unbalanced, wild, crazy attacking positions are very difficult to judge correctly during the progress of the game. Wisdom and clarity often appear only after exhaustive post-mortems. Fischer, incorrectly, thought that White had a winning attack here and Tal, incorrectly, thought that Black was lost. Why then did not Tal exchange Queens on move 18? Well, reason number 1 is that he is a very brave person, and number two is that he felt that Fischer could easily misplay the attack.

22 Q-B6+?   ...

Psychologically speaking, the losing move. White's attack now runs into the ground and he is unprepared for a long defense to hold the draw. 22 QR-K1! was required to keep the game in dynamic balance. Fischer then gives 22 ... K-Q1!; 23 R-Q1+,

K-B2; 24 Q-B4+, K-N2; 25 R-Q6, Q-B2; 26 QxNP+, K-B1; 27 RxRP, Q-N2!; 28 QxQ+, KxQ; 29 R6-KB6, R-N2 with material and positional equality.

22	...	R-Q2.
23	QR-K1+	...

23 QR-Q1 is met by 23 ... B-Q3!; 24 RxP, Q-B2!; 25 QxQ, RxQ!

23	...	B-K2
24	RxP	KxR
25	Q-K6+	K-B1

Here Bobby had expected only 25 ... K-N2 which loses to 26 QxR/Q7 as the Bishop can't be protected. This kind of underestimation of "the Russians" was not only costly at the 1959 Candidates, but would be even more costly and painful in 1962.

26	QxR/Q7	...

This is simply one of those crazy positions where Black always has a defense. Thus 26 R-KB1+, K-N2; 27 R-B7+, K-R1; 28 QxR, and now 28 ... R-Q1; 29 Q-N4 (29 QxB??, R-Q8+ and mate), Q-K4.

26	...	Q-Q3
27	Q-N7	R-N3
28	P-B3!	...

White's attack is gone and he is left with a material disadvantage of only two Pawns for Black's Bishop. Thus the dream of a win is gone. Well, how about a draw? The chances for this are excellent, mainly because of the inadvertent situation on the Kingside where Black has the wrong Bishop for his RP. Thus an endgame, with the Queenside Pawns off the board would be drawn. Because of the exposed nature of Black's King it is also very questionable if Black can mount a decisive attack in the middle game. With the text move White starts on the right plan for exchanging Queenside Pawns.

28	...	P-QR4?!

In a sense thematic in that it keeps White's Queenside Pawns more contained, but it runs also much greater danger of leading to a wholesale liquidation there. Thus for strategic reasons the correct idea was 28 ... PxP.

29	Q-B8+?	...

THE LOSING MOMENT

Very inconsistent play. The obvious 29 PxP was correct: if then 29 ... PxP; 30 P-QR3! immediately exchanges everything and after 29 ... QxNP; 30 Q-B3+, R-KB3; 31 Q-K2, Black's now advanced QRP will also be an attractive exchange target.

29	...	K-N2
30	Q-B4	B-Q1
31	PxP	PxP

Here probably better than 31 ... QxP as White has already lost some two tempos with his foolish check.

32 P-KN3? ...

Allows a clearly lost endgame. A better try was 32 Q-K4 with some chances for a defense. It was already too late for 32 P-QR3 because of 32 ... B-B2; 33 P-KN3, P-N6! 34 QxP, Q-QB3+; 35 K-N1, B-N3+; 36 K-B1, R-KB3+; 37 K-K2, Q-K5+ and wins.

32	...	Q-QB3+
33	R-K4	QxQ
34	RxQ	R-N3

The endgame is won for Black, that's all. He keeps his QNP and the extra piece pushes White back step by step. Care is required of course and Tal makes it look simple. The general public thinks of Tal as an attacking player only, but he is fully versed in all the technical aspects of the game.

35	K-N2	K-B3
36	K-B3	K-K4
37	K-K3	B-N4+
38	K-K2	K-Q4
39	K-Q3	B-B3
40	R-B2	...

Very passive, but 40 P-N3 is positionally hopeless as White then has no chance for P-QR3.

40	...	B-K4
41	R-K2	R-KB3
42	R-QB2	R-B6+
43	K-K2	R-B2
44	K-Q3	B-Q5
45	P-QR3	...

Gets the same reply as on any of the previous 10 moves, but what is White to do?

| 45 | ... | P-N6 |
| 46 | R-B8 | ... |

If 46 R-Q2, R-B6+; 47 K-K2,
R-B7+; and after the exchange of
Rooks Black again picks off the QNP.

46	...	BxP
47	R-Q8+	K-B3
48	R-QN8	R-B6+
49	K-B4	R-B6+
50	K-N4	K-B2
51	R-N5	B-R8!
52	P-QR4	P-N7!

WHITE RESIGNS

A pretty finish. If 53 KxR, P-N8(Q)+
or P-N8(R)+, but not the double
check after P-N8(N)!

GAME 23

White: B. Spassky (USSR)
Black: R. Fischer

*Played at Mar del Plata (Argentina)
International Tournament, March 30,
1960, Round 2*

A game of great historical interest as
it was the first meeting between
two future World Champions.
Looked at from the standpoint of
chess quality, however, the evaluation is quite disappointing.
Apparently both players were quite
nervous, with resulting poor play.
Unfortunately for Bobby, he made
his errors at the end of the game
and thus had to absorb an undeserved loss. Despite the rather
indifferent play, the game was
memorable enough for Fischer to
be included in his *My 60 Memorable
Games.*

King's Gambit
(Kieseritzky Variation)

1   P-K4   P-K4

As mentioned earlier, Fischer played
some 1 ... P-K4's in the early 1960s
and this was the starting point.
As a matter of fact, for a brief
time he even claimed to have
"refuted the Ruy Lopez." Such
talk is of course long gone and it is
noteworthy that in his 1972 match

with Spassky, where he for the first
time demonstrated a broadened
opening repertoire against the KP,
his new choices were the Alekhine
and the Pirc, rather than 1 ... P-K4.
Fischer's 1 ... P-K4 here came as
both a complete surprise to Spassky
as well as a challenge.

2   P-KB4   . . .

Accepted! It was well known that
Spassky periodically ventured into
the King's Gambit and Fischer
wanted to dare him "to try it against
me." From the game continuation
it is apparent that neither player
was prepared for this opening.
Spassky hadn't expected to encounter 1 ... P-K4, and even if
he had expected it, would've had
no idea what defense Fischer would
choose and Bobby was simply offering a challenge. Who was the
psychological winner here? Fischer
obtained a superior game out of the
opening, yet Spassky scored the full
point! Everybody knows that Fischer
is one of the world's leading authori-
ties, if not *the* leading authority
on the Ruy Lopez, but how many
know that he has a perfect score
with the King's Gambit? With it,
he has defeated Evans, Wade and
Minic—three out of three!

2   . . .   PxP

The only way to try to refute a true
gambit is to accept it! Surprised by

Fischer, Wade at Vinkovci 1968
declined via the dubious 2 . . .
N-KB3.

3   N-KB3   . . .

The N move is the most common
one. Fischer, however, has played
3 B-B4 in the other two King's
Gambits: against Evans in the
1963-64 U.S. Championship and
Minic at Vinkovci 1968.

3   . . .   P-KN4

Unquestionably the most consistent
continuation but, because of its
Kingside weakening nature, a very
rare guest in modern opening
practice. Some time after this game
Bobby published an analysis claiming
that 3 . . . P-Q3 is the definite
refutation of the Gambit.

4   P-KR4   P-N5
5   N-K5   N-KB3
6   P-Q4   P-Q3
7   N-Q3   NxP
8   BxP   B-N2

There is nothing unique to say about
the previous moves, beyond noting
that it was one logical way of
handling a complicated variation.
Usually 8 . . . Q-K2 is played, but
most often it only amounts to a
transposition of moves.

9   N-B3??   . . .

A kind of move that masters of the
19th century used to play: quick
development and who cares about
things like the center or Pawn
weaknesses! But Boris, this is 1960,
not 1860! One additional disadvantage of the move is that White's
King will no longer be safe anywhere, as the Queenside now gets
defoliated. The obvious 9 P-B3 is
the correct way and after 9 . . .
Q-K2; 10 Q-K2, B-B4; 11 N-Q2,
NxN; 12 QxQ+; KxQ; 13 KxN, we
get an interesting position where
White has full compensation for the
Pawn, but no more.

9   . . .   NxN
10   PxN   P-QB4!

The simple 10 . . . O-O is good
too, but the sharper text move is
much to be recommended.

11   B-K2   . . .

11 Q-K2+ is met by 11 . . . B-K3!
as 12 P-Q5 fails after 12 . . . BxP+,
etc.—the first example of White's
weaknesses.

11	...	PxP!
12	O-O	...

What else?

12	...	N-B3

Quite playable was 12 ... P-KR4; 13 B-N5, Q-B2; but being already up material but behind in development, there is no reason for Black to be greedy.

13	BxNP	O-O
14	BxB	RxB
15	Q-N4	...

What else?

15	...	P-B4

Fischer suggests 15 ... K-R1, but there is nothing wrong with the text move either.

16	Q-N3	PxP
17	QR-K1	...

The best try. If 17 BxP, R-B3 followed by R-KN3 is devastating.

17	...	K-R1?

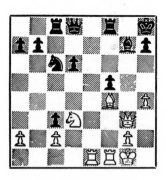

From now on Black gets so hypnotized by attacking chances on the KN file that he forgets about other aspects, such as the center. Correct was 17 ... Q-Q2! 18 BxP, KR-K1 and White has no compensation for his minus Pawn.

18	K-R1?	...

Horrible. White loses a tempo and misplaces the King (see, e.g., move 22). The obvious 18 BxP was the right way, with some chances for White.

18	...	R-KN1
19	BxP	B-B1

The active 19 ... B-Q5 leads to nothing special after 20 Q-R2, R-N5; 21 B-K5+!

20	B-K5+	NxB
21	QxN+	R-N2!
22	RxP	...

22 QxKBP QxP+ 23 K-N1, Q-KN5 leads to play similar to the game.

22	...	QxP+

The error in 18 K-R1? is now obvious.

23	K-N1	Q-KN5?

Fischer saw that 23 ... Q-N6!; 24 QxQ (24 Q-K2, B-Q3!), RxQ leads to a superior endgame with a Pawn advantage, but decided to go for mate. Here too greed did not pay!

24	R-B2!	B-K2
25	R-K4	Q-N4?!

White has such a complete domination of the center squares that Black has no more winning chances and the clearest road to a draw was move repetition via 25 ... Q-Q8+; 26 R-K1 (or 26 K-R2, R-B3; 27 Q-N8+, R-N1; 28 Q-K5+, R-N2 etc.), 26 ... Q-N5 etc.

26	Q-Q4	...

Now 26 ... B-B4?? loses to 27 NxB, QxN; 28 R-K8+. The only defense is 26 ... B-B1! and after 27 QxRP, B-Q3! with now material equality and even chances.

26	...	R-KB1??

THE LOSING MOMENT

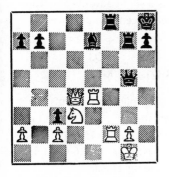

Blinded by his own threats, Black fails to notice that White also has some. As Fischer tells it, he only expected 27 N-K5?? and after 27 ... RxR; 28 QxR, B-B4 Black wins. One more example of inability to give his opponents any credit for seeing anything.

27	R-K5!	...

This strong yet fairly obvious move wins immediately. Black can't protect his Bishop, since his Queen can't remain on the diagonal (27 ... Q-R5 28 RxR+ or even 28 QxQ followed by 29 RxR+ wins) and the Rook at N2 is pinned. If 27 ... B-B3; 28 Q-Q6 spells curtains. So ...

27	...	R-Q1
28	Q-K4	Q-R5
29	R-B4	...

BLACK RESIGNS

Next move White plays RxB.

GAME 24

White: E. Eliskases (Argentina)
Black: R. Fischer

*Played at Buenos Aires (Argentina)
International Tournament, June 28,
1960, Round 5*

Bobby loses a completely even
endgame by a horribly careless
move—his worst single move since
Game 5. It will take another 12
years, until Game 60, to see a
similar blunder. The psychological
explanation of the defeat would
have to focus on a relentless urge to
win, yet it appears simply as an act
of chess blindness committed by a
human being.

Queen's Gambit Declined
(Ragosin Variation)

1	P-QB4	N-KB3
2	N-QB3	P-K3
3	N-B3	P-Q4
4	P-Q4	B-N5
5	Q-N3	...

Since his youth in the 1930s in
Austria/Germany, Eliskases had been
noted as a fine positional player
and after his emigration to Argentina
in 1939, he added a strong dose of
caution which led to invariable
satisfaction with draws against the

top players. The text move is quite
solid: it protects the QBP and the
pinned Knight, while attacking the
Bishop. Additionally it prevents the
possible complications after 5
Q-R4+, N-B3; 6 B-N5, PxP.

5	...	N-B3
6	B-N5	P-KR3
7	BxN	QxB
8	P-K3	...

Eliskases continues with good sound
moves. If instead 8 PxP then 8
... NxP (9 QxB??, N-B7+).

8	...	PxP
9	BxP	O-O
10	O-O	Q-K2
11	Q-B2	...

White has a slight advantage because
of his greater central influence.

11	...	B-Q3
12	QR-Q1	K-R1

Prepares the following move since
an immediate 12 ... P-K4? can be
met by 13 N-Q5, Q-K1; 14 N-B6+!,
PxN; 15 Q-N6+, K-R1; 16 QxRP+
with a winning attack.

13	P-QR3	P-K4
14	N-Q5	Q-K1
15	PxP	NxP
16	NxN	QxN
17	P-B4	...

Despite Black's two Bishops, White as a result of his control of more center squares still has a slight advantage. However, neither side has any fundamental weaknesses, so that with reasonable play the game must end a draw.

17	...	Q-K1
18	P-K4	P-QB3
19	N-B3	B-B2
20	Q-K2	B-K3
21	P-K5	Q-K2
22	N-K4	QR-Q1
23	K-R1	KR-K1
24	BxB	QxB
25	N-B5	Q-B1
26	Q-R5	...

Now the game *should* deteriorate into a draw. More aggressive was 26 Q-B4! and if 26 ... RxR; 27 RxR, Q-N5; 28 R-QB1!

26	...	RxR
27	RxR	R-Q1
28	P-R3	...

It is silly here to give up the Queen's file by 28 RxR+, QxR as 29 NxP?? loses after 29 ... Q-Q7.

28	...	K-N1
29	RxR+	...

The game would have ended a draw on any move through 41 N-B8 by the simple act of *Fischer's* offering it. He continues to play, meaning playing to win, but even though fundamentally there is no danger in this, it is quite fruitless from a practical point of view. The position is just too even in a static way to do anything with. Despite somewhat indifferent play, Bobby's start in the tournament was good enough with one win and three draws, so there also was no tournament standing reason for not agreeing to a draw.

29	...	QxR
30	P-K6	...

Draw?!

30 ...   **Q-K2**

Not yet! 30 ... PxP would guarantee that result.

31	Q-B5	P-QN3
32	PxP+	QxP
33	Q-B8+	K-R2
34	N-K6	B-Q3

34 ... BxP would allow the perpetual check with 35 N-B8+, K-N1; 36 N-K6+ etc. Horrors, Bobby!

35	P-KN4	Q-B3
36	Q-Q7	Q-K2
37	QxQ	BxQ
38	N-Q4	P-B4

"Everything" leads to a draw and there is no win. Thus 38 ... B-B3; 39 NxP, BxP; 40 NxP, BxP; 41 N-N5, and material is even and the QNP blockaded.

39   **N-B6**   **B-Q3**

Also playable for a draw, but no better for a win was 39 ... B-B3; 40 P-N3, P-R3.

40   **NxP**   **P-B5**

On the last move before time control Bobby continues pressing for the win. Of course 40 ... BxP was also playable.

41   **N-B8!**   ...

White sealed this, the best yet fairly obvious move. Usually adjourned games are played off the following morning or on a special free day for adjourned games. At Buenos Aires there was only a 1½-hour break for "dinner" before the games had to be resumed. On its face, this is a reasonable idea, yet who can enjoy a leisurely dinner when there is a crucial unfinished game to analyze?

41   ...   **B-B4??**

THE LOSING MOMENT

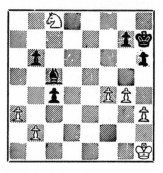

Coming immediately after adjournment this move is chessically totally incomprehensible. It was high time to grab the draw with 41 ... BxRP!; 42 NxP! (not 42 PxB??, P-B6 and the Pawn queens), 42 ... BxP; 43 NxP, B-B8!; 44 P-B5, P-R4!, with a theoretically very easy draw, as Black will exchange off all his Pawns.

42   **P-QR4!**   ...

White now remains a Pawn ahead. Even though Eliskases was unprepared for this position since in his wildest dreams he couldn't have expected 41 ... B-B4??, he is a fine endgame player and wins the game with careful and instructive maneuvers.

| 42 | ... | K-N3 |

42 ... B-Q5; 43 N-Q6! wins for White.

43	K-N2	K-B3
44	K-B3	K-K3
45	K-K4	B-B7

In his "quickie home analysis" Bobby had expected to trap the Knight with 45 ... P-QN4; 46 PxP, K-Q2 and only now noticed that White has the winning 47 K-Q5!. A "legal" explanation, yet still incomprehensible from a world title aspirant!

46	P-B5+	K-Q2
47	N-R7	K-Q3
48	N-N5+	K-B4
49	N-B7!	...

The weakness of White's QNP gives Black some chances; however, Black has a NP weakness too (the KNP!) and with fine play White simply wins.

| 49 | ... | B-R5 |
| 50 | N-K8 | K-N5 |

If 50 ... B-B3; 51 NxB, PxN; 52 P-R4, and White's extra Pawn on the Kingside decides.

51	K-Q5!	B-K2
52	NxP	B-B3
53	N-K8	BxP
54	P-B6	BxP

(Position after 54 P-B6)

Equally dramatic would have been 54 ... P-B6; 55 P-B7, P-B7; 56 P-B8(Q)+, KxP (56 ... K-R4; 57 Q-B1!, threatening 58 Q-N5 mate) and the best White has is a won endgame after 57 Q-B4+, K-R6; 58 Q-K3+, K-R7; 59 QxRP!, P-B8(Q); 60 QxQ, with an easy win as the passed Pawns on the Kingside are unstoppable.

| 55 | NxB | P-B6 |
| 56 | N-R5! | ... |

The Knight just gets back.

| 56 | ... | KxP |

Black could get into a lost Knight and Pawn endgame with 56 ...

P-B7; 57 N-B4, K-B6; 58 N-K2+,
K-Q7; 59 N-Q4!, P-B8 (N)! (59 . . .
P-B8(Q); 60 N-N3+).

57	**N-B4**	**P-N4**
58	**N-K2**	**P-B7**

BLACK RESIGNS

The game was adjourned again and
Fischer resigned without continuing.
The win is simple, e.g., 59 K-B5,
P-N5; 60 K-B4, K-R6; 61 P-R4, P-N6;
62 K-B3, P-N7 (or 62 . . . K-R7; 63
N-B1+ and 64 NxP); 63 KxP, K-R7;
64 N-B3+.

GAME 25

White: B. Wexler (Argentina)
Black: R. Fischer

Played at Buenos Aires (Argentina) International Tournament, July 1, 1960, Round 7

The only game Fischer has lost against an English-type opening. His play, especially in the opening, is incomprehensible.

English Opening

1	P-QB4	N-KB3
2	N-QB3	P-KN3
3	P-KN3	B-N2
4	B-N2	O-O
5	P-Q3	. . .

When this game was played, Wexler had already lost twice and decisively on the White side of a King's Indian against Fischer, so his interest in a change of pace is quite understandable.

5	. . .	P-Q3
6	B-Q2	N-B3

More usual is 6 . . . P-B4 and only then 7 . . . N-B3 but the text is okay also.

7	Q-B1	P-K3??

Looks ugly, feels ugly, and is ugly! The idea behind 6 . . . N-B3 is 7 . . . P-K4, Bobby! Of course,

Fischer was fully aware of this and the only explanation for the text move is that masters sometimes get a sudden urge to "try something different"—usually with disastrous results!

8	N-B3	P-Q4?

The "idea" behind 7 . . . P-K3?? The result is that Black is playing a bad idea a tempo behind! Correct was still 7 . . . P-K4 when Black would be playing the right idea a move behind. Because of the closed nature of the position such a loss of time need not be overly serious. After all, White's Queen on QB1 is not ideally posted either.

9	O-O	P-Q5?

Better 9 . . . R-K1. With the text move, Black allows White an advantageous regrouping, while at the same time weakening his own central squares. Maybe I've been too harsh with the question marks, but such a total lack of understanding of the principles of an opening, coming from Robert J. Fischer, must raise questions.

10	N-K4	N-Q2?!

Not too many wars are won by retreating and this is not even a strategic retreat. More logical was 10 . . . NxN and Black at least has the practical benefit of an unbalanced position.

11	P-QN4!	P-B4
12	N4-N5	Q-K2
13	P-N5	N-Q1
14	R-N1	...

With the threat 15 B-N4, N-B4; 16 Q-R3, thus Black's counter is best.

14	...	P-QR4
15	P-KR4!	P-K4

White is preparing to play P-K3 so that a strengthening of Black's outpost on Q5 is required. Worse would be 15 ... P-B4 as after 16 PxP e.p. White's QR and KB would have the benefit of additional open lines.

16	P-K3	PxP??

THE LOSING MOMENT

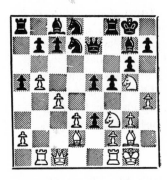

Opening lines for the better-developed opponent is suicide! Black's position is unpleasant after 16 ... P-R3; 17 N-R3, N-B4, but for a Bobby Fischer probably tenable!

17	BxKP	P-R3
18	N-R3	K-R2
19	P-B5!	...

White is rolling already! Black's Queenside is undeveloped and weakened, center is shaky and Kingside weakened—small wonder that the position is indefensible!

19	...	N-KB3
20	R-K1!	N-N5?!

Leads to a direct loss of the KP. Therefore 20 ... P-K5 had to be better.

21	B-B4	N-B2
22	NxP!	N5xN
23	P-Q4	B-K3
24	PxN	...

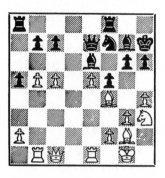

White not only is a Pawn ahead but also has a completely won position. When Bobby has positions such as this for *White* he states that the "rest is a crunch." So also here, but for the "wrong guy"!

24	...	QR-QN1
25	P-R4	KR-Q1
26	Q-K3!	...

Keeping the bind. 26 Q-B3 would allow some counterplay after 26 ... P-N4.

26	...	B-B5
27	P-N6!	...

More lines open, please!

27	...	R-Q6

27 ... PxP 28 P-K6! is devastating.

28	Q-B1	B-K3
29	PxP!	QxBP/2
30	R-N6	B-Q4

If 30 ... Q-Q2 or 30 ... Q-K2 31 P-B6! (crunch!).

31	P-K6	N-K4
32	R-Q6!	...

Wins more material. The rest is a mop-up.

32	...	BxB
33	RxR	BxN
34	BxN	Q-B3

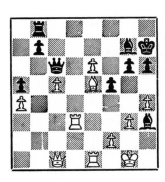

If 34 ... BxB; 35 R-Q7+ wins the Queen—a perfect example of the weaknesses on the Kingside.

35	P-B3	...

He saw the threat!

35	...	R-Q1?!

Anyone have a better idea?

36	RxR	QxKBP
37	Q-Q2	BxB
38	Q-KB2	...

BLACK RESIGNS

Too much is too much!

GAME 26

White: R. Fischer
Black: W. Uhlmann (East Germany)

*Played at Buenos Aires (Argentina)
International Tournament, July 2,
1960, Round 8*

This game is a perfect example of
Fischer's lack of patience in the first
half of his career when meeting the
French Defense. Before he realizes
it he has drifted from a superior
position into a lost one. Uhlmann's
play is exemplary throughout.

*French Defense
(Winawer Variation)*

1 P-K4   P-K3

Throughout his tournament career
spanning over twenty years, Uhlmann
has played nothing but the French
against the KP. He is unquestionably
the world's leading expert on the
French. This fact, coupled with
Bobby's relative difficulties with the
French should remove our surprise
that Uhlmann has done better with
the Black pieces than with White
against Fischer!

2	P-Q4	P-Q4
3	N-QB3	B-N5
4	P-K5	N-K2
5	P-QR3	BxNch
6	PxB	P-QB4

Here we have the normal position
in the Winawer. Black's opportunities for play are against White's
center and Queenside via ... P-QB4
and center by way of a later ...
P-KB3. However, great care must be
used in the execution so as not to
open the position in a way favorable
to White's Bishops.

7 P-QR4   ...

Bobby has never been interested in
the complications resulting from
7 Q-N4, PxP etc. He has made the
text move, originally an idea of
Smyslov's his favorite weapon. It
may well be, however, that the
developmental 7 N-B3 is more
accurate.

7	...	QN-B3
8	N-B3	B-Q2
9	Q-Q2	Q-R4

Through a rather unusual order of
moves a well-known position has
been reached.

10 B-Q3   ...

Also playable is 10 B-K2, after
which the most accurate move is
10 ... R-QB1 with immediate play
against the Queenside.

10 ...   P-B5

Seems perfectly okay. However, in
later games Uhlmann has preferred
the immediate 10 ... P-B3!, so I

guess that move must be rated as a shade better. One example: 11 O-O, PxKP; 12 NxP, NxN; 13 PxN, O-O; 14 P-QB4, QxQ (or 14 . . . Q-B2!, Tringov–Korchnoi, Skopje 1972); 15 BxQ, B-B3 with an even endgame and a draw on move 32: Fischer–Uhlmann, Stockholm Interzonal, 1962.

11	B-K2	P-B3
12	B-R3	N-N3?

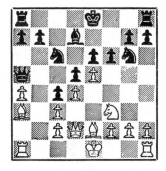

An error. The Knight accomplishes nothing here and actually stands considerably worse than on K2 from where it can also go to KB4, if required (e.g., after White's B-Q6). An immediate 12 . . . O-O-O was correct.

13 O-O! O-O-O

With the King in the center it is too dangerous to grab the KP, e.g., 13 . . . PxKP; 14 NxP, KNxN; 15 PxN, NxP; 16 Q-N5!, N-N3; 17 B-R5.

14	B-Q6	QN-K2
15	N-R4!	. . .

With this and the following series of fine moves, White ensures an excellent diagonal for his QB and paralyzes any hopes Black may have for meaningful counterplay.

15	. . .	QR-K1
16	NxN!	PxN
17	PxP!	PxP
18	P-KR3!	N-B4
19	B-R2	P-KN4
20	P-B4?	. . .

But this brute force attempt at an immediate win spoils everything. Correct was the positional 20 KR-K1! and White has a marvelous position: pressure on Black's somewhat shaky center, open diagonals for both Bishops, while Black's King can find himself uncomfortably open soon.

20	. . .	N-Q3

It is rather clear that Bobby overlooked this obvious response.

21	B-B3	. . .

And now he also overlooks the following move. This is quite understandable, however. Had he seen what comes he may have preferred the complications after 21 PxP, N-K5; 22 Q-K3, QxBP; 23 QxQ, NxQ; 24 B-B3, PxP; 25 P-R5.

21	. . .	P-N5!!

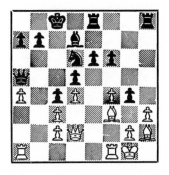

A move and idea which anyone can be proud of! Black sacrifices a Pawn and allows a protected passed Pawn, to boot, for the strategic objective of locking in White's QB. The damage done by White's 20 P-B4? is now very obvious.

22	PxP	P-B4!
23	P-N5	R-K2
24	B-N3	B-K1
25	Q-K3	N-K5
26	BxN	...

Pretty much forced.

| 26 | ... | QPxB |
| 27 | K-B2 | ... |

Fischer evaluates this position much too optimistically and plans to husband the extra Pawn to victory. The blocked nature of the position makes winning attempts for either side less than fruitful. Thus a sharp move like 27 P-Q5!? was in order if White hopes to go for the full point.

| 27 | ... | R2-R2 |

Safer was 27 ... Q-Q4 as after the text move White could again try 28 P-Q5!?

| 28 | KR-QN1 | Q-Q4 |

Now we have a rather full blockade and the game could well be called a draw here.

| 29 | Q-B1? | ... |

With the idea of 30 K-K3 but tactically careless. The required move for this purpose was 29 Q-Q2. For keeping the status quo 29 P-R5 was ideal.

| 29 | ... | R-R8! |
| 30 | QxR?? | ... |

THE LOSING MOMENT

This move illustrates Fischer's bad form in the tournament, as it is obviously played without noticing Black's *Zwischenzug*. The required move was 30 Q-K3. After 30 ... RxR; 31 RxR, BxP; 32 R-QR1, BxP; 33 RxP, K-N1!; 34 R-R1, B-Q6 Black only has a slight advantage.

| 30 | ... | P-K6 + ! |
| 31 | K-N1 | ... |

There is nothing better. If 31 KxP
Q-K5+ 32 K-B2 (32 K-Q2?, RxQ;
33 RxR, QxNP+ wins the Bishop)
32 ... RxQ; 33 RxR, B-B3!; 34
R-KR2, QxQBP+; 35 K-N1, QxBP
wins.

31	...	RxQ +
32	KxR	P-K7!
33	R-N5	...

Bobby finally realized that he must
be lost and thus characteristically
goes for active counterplay. It is not
good enough, but is as good a try
as any. With the passive 33 R-K1 or
33 R-N1 White could hold out
longer but there would be no
question about the outcome. Black
plays 33 ... Q-K5, walks his King
over to the Kingside to stop the
KNP, then the Bishop goes to QB3
and the powerful Queen and Bishop
combination starts chopping off
White's Queenside Pawns.

| 33 | ... | BxR |
| 34 | PxB | QxQNP! |

Now Black's QRP is passed!

| 35 | R-K1 | ... |

So White wins the advanced KP, but
Black's QRP is the winner now.

| 35 | ... | P-R4 |
| 36 | RxP | P-R5! |

Passed Pawns must be pushed!

| 37 | RxP | P-R6 |
| 38 | P-N6 | ... |

If 38 R-K5, simply 38 ... QxR.

| 38 | ... | Q-Q2 |

But not 38 ... P-R7??; 39 P-N7
P-R8(Q)+; 40 K-R2, and White has
at least a draw.

39	R-K5	P-N3
40	B-R4	P-R7
41	R-K1	...

White wins the QRP all right, but
has to give up the passed KNP after
which Black is simply a Queen
ahead.

| 41 | ... | Q-KN2 |
| 42 | R-QR1 | QxNP |

WHITE RESIGNS

After 43 RxP, Q-R4; 44 P-N3,
Q-B6+; 45 K-R2, QxQBP; 46 B-B6,
P-N4 the win is elementary.

GAME 27

White: W. Unzicker (West Germany)
Black: R. Fischer

*Played at Buenos Aires (Argentina)
International Tournament, July 7,
1960, Round 11*

Fischer chooses an opening variation
known to be dubious at that time.
A "touch piece" happening on move
12 seals his fate and soon thereafter resignation is forced.

Sicilian Defense (Najdorf Variation)

1	P-K4	P-QB4
2	N-KB3	P-Q3
3	P-Q4	PxP
4	NxP	N-KB3
5	N-QB3	P-QR3
6	B-KN5	P-K3
7	P-B4	B-K2
8	Q-B3	Q-B2
9	O-O-O	...

So far as in Games 10 and 17, in
both of which Fischer played 9 ...
QN-Q2. The 1959 Candidates
Tournament had showed that to be
fully playable.

9	...	O-O?

This continuation was already
thought to be dubious at the time
the game was played, thus Bobby's
choice of it is difficult to explain.
In any case, he has not played it

since. There are two major faults
with it: (1) Black should start
immediately his play on the Queen-
side; therefore logical is 9 ...
QN-Q2 and 10... P-QN4 and (2)
Black's King is less safe on the
Kingside than in the center or
Queenside.

10	B-Q3!	...

Training his sights on Black's KR2.

10	...	N-B3
11	NxN	PxN

11 ... QxN; 12 P-K5 also leads to
advantage for White.

12	Q-N3!	...

Threatening 13 P-K5 and positioning
the Queen against the King. Black's
best defense now was probably
12 ... P-K4.

12	...	P-KR4??

THE LOSING MOMENT

An unbelievable move and yet all commentators have tried to explain it in normal chess terms. Here's what actually happened: Bobby had touched the KRP to move it to KR3. With shock he noted that White can reply 13 BxKRP. Thus there was no choice but to push the KRP two squares. 12 ... P-KR4?? is horrible, but 12 ... P-KR3??? would be even worse.

13 P-K5!   ...

White breaks through in the center and moves in for the King kill.

13	...	PxP
14	PxP	N-N5
15	BxB	QxB
16	N-K4!	Q-B2
17	P-KR3!	NxP

White's Knight protects his Queen so that 17 ... QxP is refuted by 18 PxN. 17 ... N-R3; 18 N-B6+, K-R1; 19 Q-N5, is obviously hope-

less, so that there was nothing better than the text move.

18	N-B6+	K-R1
19	Q-N5!	NxB+
20	RxN	PxN
21	QxRP+	K-N2
22	Q-N4+	...

BLACK RESIGNS

After 22 ... K-R2; 23 Q-R4+, K-N2; 24 R-KN3+ White wins Black's Queen on the way to the King. Fischer's shortest loss ever.

GAME 28

White: P. Benko (United States)
Black: R. Fischer

*Played at Buenos Aires (Argentina)
International Tournament, July 21,
1960, Round 19*

Going into the last round, Fischer
needed a win to finish with an even
score. Benko selects an innocuous
variation in the hope that Bobby
will overreach himself in trying to
win. Benko wins the game, all right,
when Fischer in a perfectly good
middle-game position makes a
careless move. An undeserved loss
for Bobby.

*King's Indian Defense
(KB Fianchetto)*

1	P-Q4	N-KB3
2	P-QB4	P-KN3
3	P-KN3	B-N2
4	B-N2	O-O
5	N-QB3	P-Q3
6	N-B3	N-B3
7	P-KR3	. . .

At this moment a rather obvious
"nothing" move and this was fully
realized as far back as 1960. The
explanation for it is based strictly
on psychological factors. Fischer
needed a win in this last round to
finish with an even score. Thus

Benko selects a variation which is
fundamentally sound yet objectively
innocuous in the hope that Black
will overreach in storming a safe
bastion.

7	. . .	P-K4
8	O-O	. . .

We can get a better appreciation of
this position if we select the normal
way that it could have arisen in
the Uhlmann variation: 7 O-O,
P-K4. The theoretical continuations
now are the simplifying 8 PxP or
the very complicated 8 P-Q5.
Instead, White has played 8 P-KR3,
which really does not have much
to do with the position.

8	. . .	PxP

The thematic way to "punish"
White for the lost tempo (7 P-KR3).
It is fully playable, yet more in the
spirit of playing for a win is the
good development move 8 . . . B-Q2.

9	NxP	NxN
10	QxN	B-K3
11	Q-R4	. . .

Rather double-edged and thus
surprising in combination with 7
P-KR3. Safer and probably better
was 11 Q-Q3.

11	. . .	N-Q2!
12	B-N5	. . .

After the exchange of Queens, Black's Bishops would rake White's Queenside. With this maneuver White tries to upset the coordination of the Bishops, yet this, of course, costs time.

| 12 | ... | P-KB3 |

After 12 ... B-B3? 13 N-K4! White has a huge advantage.

13	B-K3	P-KN4!
14	Q-Q4	P-KB4
15	Q-Q2	P-B5!

Black has obtained by means of some sharp play an excellent position. The sacrificed Pawn can be readily regained as White has potentially loose Pawns on both sides of the board. White's negligent development has given Black these chances.

| 16 | PxP | PxP |
| 17 | BxBP | N-N3! |

White has no direct means of protecting the QNP (18 P-N3??, RxB wins material, but not 18 ... BxN?; 19 QxB, RxB?; 20 Q-N3+), so he tries tactics.

| 18 | Q-K3 | Q-B3 |

Black is interested in taking off the QBP with the Knight rather than the Bishop.

| 19 | B-N5 | ... |

And now 19 P-N3? is refuted by 19 ... QR-K1!

| 19 | ... | Q-N3 |
| 20 | Q-N3 | NxP?? |

THE LOSING MOMENT

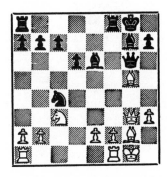

Sloppy, careless, greedy! Black is so preoccupied with *his* threats that he neglects to look if in such an open position White might also have some tactical shots. Correct was the simple 20 ... P-KR3! After the forced 21 B-B4, Black has at least equality in the endgame after 21

... QxQ; 22 BxQ, NxP; 23 BxNP, QR-N1; 24 B-Q5, BxB; 25 NxB, RxNP. Or he may prefer a complicated middle game after 21 ... Q-B3 22 P-K3, K-R1!

21 N-Q5!   ...

Turns the tables completely. There is no satisfactory way of preventing a devastating Knight incursion either to K7 or QB7.

| 21 | ... | **Q-B2** |
| **22** | **B-R6!** | **P-B3** |

Or 22 ... QR-B1; 23 BxB, QxB; 24 N-K7+ wins the exchange and then the game.

23	**BxB**	**QxB**
24	**QxQ+**	**KxQ**
25	**N-B7**	**K-B3**
26	**NxR**	**RxN**
27	**P-N3**	...

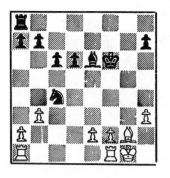

BLACK RESIGNS

He is a clear exchange down and must lose readily enough. It is quite understandable that Fischer was in no mood to continue playing on in this position.

GAME 29

White: R. Fischer
Black: C. Muñoz (Ecuador)

*Played at Leipzig (East Germany)
Olympiad, October 18, 1960,
Preliminaries, Round 2*

Fischer has been the most successful Dragon slayer of all time. He's lost exactly one game, this one, but what a game! The unheralded Equadorian simply outplays the great Bobby in middle game complications. Psychologically speaking, Fischer's loss is caused by an overestimation of his position and an underestimation of his opponent. Yet, except for the dubious 9 ... P-QR3, Fischer himself couldn't have improved on Black's play.

Sicilian Defense (Dragon-Yugoslav)

1	P-K4	P-QB4
2	N-KB3	P-Q3
3	P-Q4	PxP
4	NxP	N-KB3
5	N-QB3	P-KN3

Defining the variation as the Dragon, a strategically logical and sound continuation. The fianchetto KB will bear down rather directly on the center and from a longer-range viewpoint also against White's QN and Queenside. In addition Black is ready for quick Kingside castling.

| 6 | B-K3 | B-N2 |
| 7 | P-B3 | ... |

The modern approach, called the Yugoslav, leads to castling on opposite sides and sharp tactical play. In the 1930s when the Dragon came to the fore, the continuation invariably was 7B-K2 and 8 O-O leading to a positional type of game. Over the last 15 years the Yugoslav Attack has pretty much displaced the "old" Kingside castling.

7	...	O-O
8	Q-Q2	N-B3
9	B-QB4	...

The straightforward 9 O-O-O allows potentially great complications after 9 ... P-Q4!? Thus since 1958 or so the theoretical and popular move has been 9 B-QB4. The pluses are clear enough: ... P-Q4 is prevented and the Bishop puts pressure on Black's KB2 square. However, there are also minuses: the Bishop won't be able to remain on QB4, and retreat to QN3 will take additional time. Thus the whole maneuver is rather time-wasting and contributes little to the Kingside attack.

| 9 | ... | P-QR3?! |

At the time of this game the variation was still in its infancy and the correct method for Black was not yet established. However, the text move was thought to be too slow even then. The late 1960s and the 1970s

have shown that quick mobilization
of the Queenside is in order with
9 ... B-Q2 and then either 10 ...
R-B1 and 11 ... N-K4 or 10 ...
Q-R4 and 11 ... KR-B1.

10	B-N3	Q-R4
11	O-O-O	B-Q2
12	K-N1	...

The greatest danger to an accurate
analysis of a game is a superficial
assumption that the loser had a
lost game from the very beginning.
This is illustrated much too well by
the treatment that this understandably famous game has received.
Invariably the text move has been
labeled "too slow" and has been
blamed, at least by inference, for
White's loss. Yet in the modern
treatment starting with 9 ... B-Q2
for White, on move 12 K-N1 is
given an excellent rating. So how on
earth can the same move here, in
effect with an extra tempo for White,
be suddenly inferior? In fact, the
move is quite good and playable.
However, White does have an even
sharper continuation: 12 P-KR4! If
then 12 ... KR-B1; 13 P-N4, N-K4;
14 B-R6, N-B5; 15 BxN, RxB; 16
BxB, KxB; 17 P-R5, with a very
strong attack for White.

12	...	QR-B1

More logical is 12 ... KR-B1 so
that: a) The King has a flight square
on KB1, b) Black can respond to

White's B-KR6 with B-R1, and c) The
QR may have something to do on
the QR or QN files.

13	P-N4	...

Now we know that the attack can
be started more efficiently via 13
P-KR4, as White often is able to
play the Pawn sacrifice P-KR5.

13	...	N-K4
14	B-R6?!	...

This is a serious inaccuracy. Correct
was 14 P-KR4, and if now 14 ...
N-B5; 15 BxN, RxB; 16 N-N3!, as
16 ... Q-K4 can be met with the
positionally strong 17 B-Q4!.

14	...	N-B5
15	BxN	RxB
16	N-N3	Q-K4!!

Because of some wild tactical stuff,
the Queen is safe here. It is clear
that 17 B-B4, Q-K3 leads to nothing
since 18 N-Q4? is refuted by 18 ...

NxKP! After 17 P-B4 Black has the choice between the "quiet" 17 ... BxB; 18 PxQ, BxQ; 19 NxB, RxN with good compensation for the exchange or the crazy 17 ... Q-K3; 18 P-B5, Q-K4; 19 B-B4, QxN!!; 20 PxN, NxKP; 21 Q-K3, KR-B1, with a position impossible to evaluate: Black has a very strong attack, yet White has an extra Queen.

17 P-KR4   . . .

A logical, "safe" continuation of the attack.

17 . . .   KR-B1
18 B-B4?   . . .

Rather pointless. Fischer apparently overvalues his position and wastes valuable time here. The simple 18 BxB, KxB; 19 P-R5 was also the best. If Black then plays 19 ... P-KN4 White has 20 P-R6+, K-N1; 21 N-Q4, with a tough position and chances for both sides.

18 . . .   Q-K3
19 P-R5   . . .

Again 19 N-Q4? is refuted by 19 ... NxKP!

19 . . .   P-QN4!
20 PxP   BPxP
21 B-R6   B-R1!
22 P-K5??   . . .

This coffeehouse move is the definitive loss factor. No good for Black were 22 ... PxP?; 23 P-N5, winning a piece and 22 ... QxKP?; 23 KR-K1! with a winning attack. Bobby didn't bother to consider Black's rather obvious reply. Either 22 R-QB1 or 22 R-R2 was correct. Black already stands somewhat better, but the game is still full of fight. But now ...

22 . . .   P-N5!

If now 23 N-K2, then 23 ... QxKP is quite playable *and strong*. Yet this was better for White than the suicidal text move.

23 PxN?!   PxN
24 Q-R2   QxBP!

White has nothing on the Kingside while his Queenside will be in shreds. Black's game plays by itself—quite a rare situation against Bobby!

25	B-N5	Q-B2
26	Q-K2	...

There is absolutely nothing to suggest for White anywhere; his position is beyond hope and salvation.

26	...	PxP
27	QxP	QxQ
28	BxQ	RxBP
29	RxQP	B-R5
30	B-N5	R-B7!

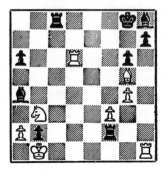

31	B-K3	...

If 31 RxQRP, B-QB3! is the strongest.

31	...	RxP
32	B-Q4	BxN
33	PxB	BxB
34	RxB	RxP
35	R-Q2	...

35 R-Q7 doesn't even have a threat as 36 RxP (either Rook) loses to 36 ... R-B8+.

35	...	R1-N1
36	R-Q7	R-QR6

WHITE RESIGNS

Not much to say about the final position!

GAME 30

White: S. Gligoric (Yugoslavia)
Black: R. Fischer

*Played at Leipzig (East Germany)
Olympiad, October 31, 1960, Finals,
Round 4*

During the first half of Fischer's
career, among his most difficult
opponents was Gligoric. Here we
see why. Playing sound positional
moves, Gligoric retains a small
advantage and then refutes an
unfounded attacking attempt by
well-calculated tactics.

*Queen's Gambit Declined
(Ragosin Variation)*

1   P-Q4   . . .

As discussed earlier, Gligoric is
basically a QP player who ventures
1 P-K4 only if he is quite sure of
his opponent's reply. Already at
Buenos Aires 1960 Fischer surprised
"Gliga" with 1 . . . P-K4. Not being
in the mood for any such surprises,
Gligoric has since played nothing
but 1 P-Q4 against Fischer—up to
this very day!

1	. . .	N-KB3
2	P-QB4	P-K3
3	N-QB3	B-N5
4	P-K3	O-O
5	B-Q3	P-Q4
6	N-B3	N-B3

From a normal Nimzo-Indian
we finally have the Ragosin which
was first discussed under Game 3.

7   O-O   . . .

Noncommittal, safe and sound.
For 7 P-QR3 see Game 32.

7   . . .   PxP

Also reasonable is the "tempo
move" 7 . . . P-QR3 after which
White's best is the "super tempo
move" 8 P-KR3! (so that after an
eventual . . . P-K4 by Black, White
doesn't have to worry about a . . .
B-KN5).

8	BxBP	B-Q3
9	N-QN5	. . .

Gligoric was already familiar with
this move from the game Taimanov–
Fischer, Buenos Aires 1960, when
White obtained a small yet clear
advantage. Thus his interest in
repeating the variation is understandable. Objectively more forcing
for White is 9 B-N5! and after 9
. . . P-K4!?; 10 BxN, PxP; 11 PxP,
PxB; 12 B-N5! White has the
advantage, which, however, did not
prevent Ghitescu (Rumania) from
losing almost instantaneously
against Fischer (Black) in the Preliminaries, thus: 12 . . . R-K1; 13
Q-Q3?!, P-B4; 14 PxP??, BxRP+
White resigns!

9	. . .	B-K2

It is true that 9 ... P-QR3; 10 NxB, PxN; 11 B-Q2, P-Q4 is playable for Black from a theoretical point of view, but in practice the somewhat passive symmetrical position is unpleasant to play and is completely unsuited to Fischer's active style.

| 10 | P-KR3 | P-QR3 |
| 11 | N-B3 | P-QN4 |

An improvement over 11 ... B-Q3; 12 P-K4, P-K4; 13 B-K3! as in the Taimanov–Fischer game cited above.

| 12 | B-Q3 | B-N2 |
| 13 | Q-K2 | ... |

Better chances for an initiative were to be obtained by the sharper 13 P-QR4!

13	...	B-Q3
14	R-Q1	Q-K2
15	B-N1	...

An immediate 15 P-K4 can be met by 15 ... P-K4; 16 P-Q5, N-Q5! so White has to make this clumsy preparatory move.

15	...	P-K4
16	P-Q5	N-Q1
17	N-N5!	P-R3

Instead 17 ... P-B3? loses a Pawn after 18 PxP, NxP; 19 NxRP, NxN; 20 BxN+, KxB; 21 Q-Q3+ and 22 QxB.

18	KN-K4	NxN
19	NxN	P-KB4
20	NxB	PxN
21	P-QR4!	...

Despite the closed character of the position, White still has some pull as a result of the inactive placement of Black's minor pieces, especially the QB.

| 21 | ... | PxP |

Pretty much forced as after 21 ... P-N5; 22 P-R5!, Black's QNP is a goner.

| 22 | RxP | R-B3 |

To keep the KBP protected and thus allow ... N-B2 to be played.

| 23 | R-QB4 | ... |

The Rook doesn't have much to do here and even gets in the way. Much better was 23 B-R2! protecting the QP and preparing for an attack on the QRP with B-B4.

23	...	P-K5
24	P-QN4	N-B2
25	B-N2	R-N3?

Just as in Game 8 against Pachman, this attempt at an unfounded Kingside attack meets quick punishment. With Black's Queenside pieces, especially the Bishop, out of play there can be no reasonable chance for success. The obvious move, 25 ... N-K4, was also the correct move, with, for practical purposes, an even position.

26 P-B4! ...

The refutation. Black has the unenviable choice of leaving the Rook out of play or allowing a murderous opening of lines for White's Bishops. He chooses quick death via the second possibility.

26 ... PxP *e.p.*
27 QxP R-KB1

Or 27 ... N-K4 28 QxP, NxR 29 QxR, NxB 30 R-KB1! with mate to follow.

28 BxP ...

Also playable was 28 QxP, e.g., 28 ... N-K4; 29 Q-K4, N-B6+; 30 K-R1 and wins.

28 ... N-N4
29 Q-R5! RxB
30 QxR NxP +
31 K-R2! ...

Gligoric is not about to fall for 31 PxN??, QxP+ (even stronger than 31 ... R-N4ch) and it is Black who wins!

31 ... R-N4

32 R-K4! ...

And not 32 Q-K6+?, QxQ; 33 PxQ, N-B7 and Black again is okay.

32 ... Q-B1
33 Q-K8! ...
BLACK RESIGNS

The Knight is trapped and lost after, e.g., 33 ... BxP; 34 QxQ+, KxQ; 35 R-KB1+ (35 RxB, RxR 36 KxN should also win), 35 ... K-N1; 36 R-K8+, K-R2; 37 P-K4, B-B5; 38 R1-KB8! and Black will be down a Rook.

GAME 31

White: S. Reshevsky (United States)
Black: R. Fischer

*Played in Public Match,
New York City, July 16, 1961,
Game 1*

An inauspicious start for the young
Champion. Repeating a strategically
inferior variation, Fischer is on the
defensive the whole game through
and after missing a drawing chance
following adjournment must soon
concede. A great example of
Reshevsky at his best.

*King's Indian Defense
(Normal Variation)*

1	P-Q4	N-KB3
2	P-QB4	P-KN3
3	N-QB3	B-N2
4	P-K4	P-Q3
5	B-K2	O-O
6	N-B3	P-K4
7	O-O	...

The "Normal Variation" has long
been Reshevsky's favorite. The
normal, sound piece deployment
suits his healthy, positional style
very well.

7	...	N-B3
8	B-K3	...

Keeping the central tension thus is
Reshevsky's idea and the variation

justly carries his name. Equalizing
methods have been found for Black,
however, and thus 8 P-Q5 must be
played instead, if White hopes to
achieve more than a draw.

8	...	N-KN5

Safer is 8 ... R-K1! and as Fischer
himself has subsequently (starting
with Game 9 in this match!) demonstrated, White achieves nothing in
the endgame after 9 PxP, PxP! Also
if 9 P-Q5, N-Q5!; 10 NxN, PxN;
11 BxP, NxKP (the point of 8 ...
R-K1), with full equality.

9	B-N5	B-B3?

The same questionable strategic idea
as in Game 19 with the same disadvantages: loss of time and
weakening of the Kingside. Fischer
hasn't tried it since. The correct
move is 9 ... P-B3 with complicated
play and good chances for full
equality.

10	BxB	NxB
11	P-Q5	N-K2
12	N-K1	N-Q2

About seven months earlier in the
1960-61 U.S. Championship, Fischer
had tried 12 ... N-K1, also against
Reshevsky. But it was clear that after
13 P-B4!, PxP; 14 RxP, P-KB4; 15
PxP, NxBP; 16 Q-Q2, Q-K2; 17
N-B2, B-Q2; 18 QR-KB1 White was
much better off, as Black's Kingside
very much misses the KB. Even

though that game was eventually drawn, Fischer obviously isn't interested in a repeat of the above position. But the text move is only a marginal improvement. The fault simply lies in 9 ... B-B3? From then on, up to move 50 Bobby defends perfectly, but oh, what a thankless task!

13	N-Q3	P-KB4
14	PxP!	...

As Black's Kingside is weakened it is obviously in White's interest to open lines there.

14	...	PxP

It is easy to criticize this move and suggest 14 ... NxBP instead, yet the truth of the matter is that after the latter move White has an easier time in getting at Black's King, since he also has use of White's K4 square.

15	P-B4!	N-KN3

Here or subsequently ... P-K5 is bad for Black as White's Knights will find ideal spots on Q4 and K3

and at his leisure White will prepare the undermining of Black's center via P-KN4.

16	Q-Q2	R-K1
17	PxP	N2xP
18	NxN	RxN

After 18 ... PxN 19 P-B5 White gets a strong passed QP. Now, however, Black has a different problem: a chronically weak KBP. Reshevsky immediately goes after it.

19	N-N5!?	...

There is little basis for objectively criticizing this move and the idea behind it. Yet, thanks to hindsight, we know that the resulting position is extremely difficult, if at all possible, to win. Thus, possibly the straightforward attack via 19 B-Q3 and 20 QR-K1 may be more effective. The advantage of this approach, of course, is that White's center and Queenside Pawns are not weakened.

19	...	B-Q2
20	B-Q3	BxN
21	PxB	Q-Q2
22	Q-KB2	...

Now 22 ... R-KB1 loses to 23 QxRP and 22 ... N-K2 is totally unsatisfactory after 23 QR-K1. Fischer finds the best practical chance.

22	...	P-B5!
23	BxN	PxB
24	QxBP	QR-K1!

And not 24 ... RxP? 25 Q-B6!
(25 ... Q-N2 26 Q-K6+ wins the
Rook). The point of Fischer's idea is
now clear: With only heavy artillery
left on the board Black can defend
his Kingside well. Also White's extra
Pawn is on the Kingside, along with
his own King, so that there is no
safe way of realizing this advantage.
In addition, White's QP is chronically weak and the doubled QNPs
are no beauties either. Thus the
technical problems facing Reshevsky
in the realization of his material
advantage are considerable.

25	QR-Q1	Q-N2
26	P-KR3	R4-K2
27	R-Q2	R-K5
28	Q-B2	P-N3
29	P-QR3!	R1-K4

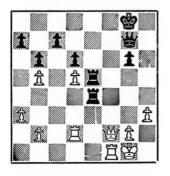

White has consolidated his material
advantage, but how to make
progress? Reshevsky decides to try
a double Rook endgame.

30	Q-B6	QxQ
31	RxQ	K-N2
32	R6-KB2	K-R3
33	K-R2	R-QB5

This active defense (threat 34 ...
R-QB4) allows White to exchange a
pair of Rooks and some of the weak
Pawns on the Queenside. It does
not seem that this can be ultimately
prevented, anyway, since White will
otherwise at the proper moment
double Rooks on the QB file.

34	R-B2!	RxR
35	RxR	RxP
36	P-QR4!	...

The 34th and 36th moves are master
strokes on Reshevsky's part and he
now wins the QBP and QRP, thus
remaining the Kingside Pawn ahead.
The point of the maneuver is that
Black cannot offer to exchange
Rooks with 36 ... R-QB4 because
White wins the King and Pawn
endgame after: 37 RxR, NPxR (37
... QPxR is hopeless because Black
then has no passed Pawn); 38 K-N3,
P-Q4; 39 K-B4, P-Q5; 40 P-QN3!,
K-R4; 41 P-N3, K-R3; 42 K-K4, K-N4;
43 P-R5, K-R4; 44 P-QN4!, PxP;
45 KxP, K-N4; 46 K-B4, K-B4; 47
KxP, K-K5; 48 K-B5, K-B6; 49 K-B6,
KxP; 50 KxP, KxP; 51 P-N6, and
White queens first. This may appear
long and farfetched but for the
master is just a careful execution of
the principle that in King and Pawn
endgames the side with the outside

passed Pawn (in this case White's two Kingside Pawns vs one Black Pawn there) wins.

36	...	R-Q5
37	P-QN3	R-Q6
38	RxP	RxNP
39	RxP	P-Q4!

Passed Pawns must be pushed!

40	R-Q7	R-Q6
41	R-Q6	R-Q5
42	RxQNP	RxP
43	K-N3	R-QN5

In Rook and Pawn endgames, Rooks belong *behind* passed Pawns, no matter whose Pawns they are. Thus Black has here the superior-placed Rook. The game was adjourned at this point and White sealed his move. Both players had ample time for home analysis. Reshevsky's play upon resumption is perfect, but Fischer soon thereafter makes a serious error.

44	R-N8	P-Q5
45	K-B3	R-N6+
46	K-K4	P-Q6
47	K-K3	...

Black's Rook is now tied to the protection of the QP, but the Pawn also ties down White's King. Thus a "stalemate"!

| 47 | ... | P-N4 |
| 48 | R-N6ch | K-N2! |

Black avoids the *Zugzwang* position which would arise after 48 ... K-R4?; 49 P-N4+, K-R5; 50 R-KR6+, K-N6; 51 P-N6. If then 51 ... K-N7, White wins with 52 P-R4!, PxP; 53 P-N5, P-R6; 54 P-N6!, RxP; 55 P-N7, RxR; 56 P-N8(Q)+ and White wins at least both Pawns with appropriate checks and then the win is elementary.

| 49 | K-Q2 | K-B2 |

Or 49 ... K-R2.

| 50 | P-N3 | R-N7+? |

THE LOSING MOMENT

Reshevsky now demonstrates an instructive win. However, after the waiting 50 ... K-N2 I don't see a win for White! White can get many attractive-looking positions, but they don't turn out to be wins. E.g., after the exchange of Pawns on the Kingside White can get what looks like a *Zugzwang* position: White: K-K3 R-QN7 P-QN6 P-KR7 Black: K-KR1

R-QN6 P-Q6. With Black to move
he must lose something, but there
is a draw after 1 . . . P-Q7+!; 2
KxP, R-Q6+!!; 3 KxR stalemate!

51	KxP	R-N6+
52	K-B4	RxKNP
53	R-KR6	K-N2
54	R-QB6!	. . .

But not first 54 R-R5?, K-N3, draw.
The whole point of Reshevsky's
maneuver is to keep Black's King
away from his third rank, thus all the
White Rook vs Black Pawn endgames are easy wins since Black's
King can't help his Pawn advance.

54	. . .	RxP
55	P-N6	R-R8
56	K-N5	R-QN8+

If 56 . . . P-N5; 57 R-B4, R-KN8; 58
P-N7, R-N8+; 59 R-N4 wins.

57	K-R6	R-QR8+
58	K-N7	P-N5
59	K-B8	R-R3

Or 59 . . . P-N6; 60 R-B3, R-KN8;
61 P-N7 wins.

60	K-B7	. . .

BLACK RESIGNS

The threat of 61 P-N7 can't be
prevented as 60 . . . P-N6 loses the
Pawn after 61 R-B3. A masterwork
of technical accuracy by Reshevsky.
Yet a tough game for Fischer to
lose, especially after having put
up such a terrific resistance.

GAME 32

White: S. Reshevsky (United States)
Black: R. Fischer

*Played in Public Match, Los Angeles,
August 1, 1961, Game 7*

One more unsatisfactory result with the Ragosin. The whole game is a strange precursor of what also happens in Game 52. Here too, Bobby is never in the game and Reshevsky wins very decisively.

*Queen's Gambit Declined
(Ragosin Variation)*

1	P-Q4	P-Q4
2	N-KB3	N-KB3
3	P-B4	P-K3
4	N-B3	B-N5
5	P-K3	O-O
6	B-Q3	N-B3
7	P-QR3	...

Obviously a more forcing move than the 7 O-O of Game 30. More importantly a clever psychological challenge to Fischer: will you be man enough to play for a win by accepting a complicated unbalanced position?

7 ...   BxN + ?!

Reshevsky's psychological ploy has worked. Even though a point ahead in the match at this stage, Fischer felt "honor bound" to try for a win here. Yet the text move is strategically quite inferior: Black accepts an inferior-for-him variation in the Samisch Nimzo-Indian. Correct was 7 ... PxP! 8 BxBP (the "combinational" 8 BxP+, NxB; 9 PxB, NxNP leads to less than nothing for White), 8 ... B-Q3 and compared to Game 30, Black is a full tempo ahead which ensures him clear equality.

8 PxB   N-QR4

Black already has to resort to clumsy maneuvers to get in ... P-QB4.

9	N-Q2!	P-B4
10	O-O	P-QN3
11	BPxP!	KPxP

At the time this game was played, it had been more than 20 years since Botvinnik had showed that this type of position is very favorable for White. Black's center Pawns, though seemingly well placed, have no prospect for future usefulness, as they are pretty much fixed on their present squares. On the other hand, White after proper preparation always gets in P-K4 and after establishing central superiority and opening the position for the two Bishops has excellent winning chances. Reshevsky demonstrates a model performance of how to do this. Instead of 11 ... KPxP Black already didn't have anything better, because with the QN off the center, a recapture such as 11 ... NxP just completely cedes central control to White. Black's fundamental strategic error already occurred on move 7.

| 12 | P-B3 | R-K1 |
| 13 | R-K1 | B-K3 |

The Bishop would have a more useful diagonal on QN2.

| 14 | R-R2 | R-QB1 |
| 15 | N-B1 | PxP |

For the type of position resulting after 15 ... P-B5 see Game 52.

| 16 | BPxP | P-R4? |

THE LOSING MOMENT

Not an attacking move (as some commentators have suggested), but a defensive move to contain White's planned positional Kingside attack starting with P-KN4. But Black is in no position to afford such a serious Kingside weakness. Black's position is unsatisfactory already, yet there was no need for suicidal actions;

16 ... Q-Q2 seems as logical a move as any.

| 17 | P-R3! | ... |

Preparing for the following Rook and central maneuver.

| 17 | ... | P-R5? |

Spreading oil on troubled waters! The move does prevent White's Knight from going to KN3, but the Pawn now is hopelessly weak.

18	R-KB2	Q-Q2
19	P-K4!	PxP
20	PxP	B-N6

White's central Pawn advance is based on some sharp tactics. If 20 ... QxP?; 21 P-K5 R-Q1 (either Rook) (21 ... KN moves loses the Queen after 22 B-R7+); 22 PxN, QxB; 23 R-Q2! winning a Rook!

| 21 | Q-Q2 | B-B5 |

The QP is still taboo: 21 ... QxP?; 22 P-K5, KR-Q1; 23 PxN, QxB; 24 R-K8+! wins the Queen or QR.

22	B-B2	N-N6
23	BxN	BxB
24	P-K5	N-Q4
25	Q-N5	...

The weakness of Black's KRP is now obviously apparent.

25	...	Q-K2
26	Q-N4	R-B3
27	B-N5	...

A blunder caused by a combination of carelessness and disgust with the position. Necessary was 27 ... Q-K3, yet after 28 QxP there can be no doubt about the outcome.

28   Q-Q7   . . .
BLACK RESIGNS

If Black protects his Rooks with, e.g., 28 ... R3-K3; 29 RxP leads to things too gruesome to contemplate!

27   . . .   QxRP?

PART TWO

Hope and Disappointment

September 1961—January 1963

(Games 33 through 43)

The match with Reshevsky was unquestionably good for Fischer's chess. Eleven games in close combat against an outstanding opponent are sure to sharpen any player. This became readily apparent next month (September 1961) at Bled where a powerful international tournament was organized. Despite the bitter aftertaste of his match with Reshevsky, Bobby's play at Bled was outstanding in every respect. Many people feel that his hard negotiating and shenanigans must unfavorably affect his play. Nothing could be further from the truth. When he sits down to play, Bobby enters a completely different world: a world of nobility consisting only of Kings and Queens, Bishops and Knights, of which he is the supreme ruler. His concentration during the game is absolute, and personal factors that bother him greatly before and after the game simply evaporate from his conciousness during play. At Bled he got his revenge against Tal and was the only undefeated player. Tal won the tournament with 14½ points and Fischer was a clear second with 13½–5½.

In the winter, he skipped for the first time the U.S. Championship to concentrate on the coming World Championship cycle. The first step was the Interzonal at Stockholm from late January through early March 1962. He achieved this in grand style, being undefeated and with a 17½–4½ score to finish 2½ points ahead of the field. Only in the game against Geller was he in serious danger of losing.

From this great play and result came an unexpected, unwelcome, and very serious aftereffect. Many commentators, journalists and even players started talking about the Fischer syndrome or cult. It isn't Fischer's moves, it is Fischer himself that so overawes his opponent as to make reasonable resistance impossible. A superficially attractive theory, but wide of the mark! Bobby's moves, so simple, clear and obvious in *hindsight,* in reality were the result of the outstanding opening preparation of a Fischer (there is no one else to compare him to), the iron logic of a Capablanca, and the great fighting qualities of an Alekhine. It was not the gods, but Fischer's search for the truth and his ability to find it on the chessboard that brought his outstanding results. Unfortunately, however, Bobby took this cult talk seriously and started believing in it. His thinking was exemplified by the kind of statement: "I can play anything—they'll just fall apart!" The consequences of this were disastrous at the Candidates Tournament at Curaçao, May–June 1962 and almost tragic for his chess future.

The American public and Bobby himself had great hopes and expectations at Curaçao. After all, his recent play had been outstanding. But the very start showed that something was inherently wrong. In Round 1, Benko defeated him in a positional K-Indian (Game 33) and in Round 2 Geller did the same as White in a positional Najdorf Sicilian (Game 34). In neither game did Fischer get the thread of the position. A further defeat followed in Round 5 against Korchnoi (Game 35), the immediate cause of the loss being a rare carelessness with the White pieces in the opening.

For practical purposes this sealed his hopes, but as always Bobby fought on. His great combative qualities would still have given him a chance, if only his chess quality had improved. He tried too hard to win against Geller and lost an instructive Rook and Pawn ending (Game 36). As White against Petrosian's French Defense, he tried an incomprehensible Bishop maneuver in the opening and lost again (Game 37). Next came another loss to Korchnoi, with carelessness again the cause (Game 38). Round 21 saw Fischer's last defeat. As White against Keres he had long defended a slightly inferior position, and then when he finally stood well, a careless Knight's tour ended with the loss of the Knight and the game (Game 39).

On the face of it, Fischer's Curaçao result was not that bad. He had finished fourth, ahead of Korchnoi, Benko, Tal and Filip and even had a plus score (14–13). The result could well have been worse, however, since included is a totally lost game against Korchnoi which he still managed to win. Bobby took the Curaçao result very badly and blamed it all on "Russian collusion." There may or may not have been certain types of "collusion," but the only reason for Bobby's disappointing showing was bad play. An unusual but meaningful measure of the quality of his play is the number of games deemed worth including in Fischer's own *My 60 Memorable Games*. From the 1959 Candidates Tournament, where Bobby obtained 12½ points out of 28, we see seven games, but from the 27 games of Curaçao only two! At Curaçao he had temporarily stopped being the searcher for ultimate truth on the chessboard. To hope to achieve great results against the top players of the world by playing second-rate moves is unrealistic and impossible. Robert J. Fischer should have learned this at Curaçao 1962.

Bobby continued to complain about "Russian collusion" all through the summer and did nothing to improve his newly found unhealthy approach to chess. Small wonder that his form crisis continued at the 1962 Varna Olympiad. Despite some fine individual efforts (his wins against Najdorf, Robatsch and Unzicker are included in *My 60 Memorable Games*), in the Finals he only achieved a 50 percent score. The Rumanian master Ciocaltea, whom Bobby had easily beaten in the Preliminaries, outplayed him in the Finals (Game 40). An uncharacteristic sacrifice, followed by a sloppy continuation, led to a loss against Donner (Game 41). And in the last round, carelessness botched a better game against Gligoric into a painful loss both for Fischer and the U.S. Team, which as a result finished fourth (Game 42).

Fischer returned home to participate in the 1962-63 U.S. Championship. He had won the previous four without the loss of a game, but here disaster struck in Round 1. Trying to force a semiblocked position against Mednis, he overreached and was forced to concede after the second adjournment (Game 43). Still despite his international reverses, he was the best U.S. player and went on to cop his fifth straight U.S. title.

A look at his losses according to color clearly shows the effect of his "unscientific play." Out of 11 losses, eight were with the White pieces! Such a result can only be traced to problems with bad moves.

Thus 1962 was a year which started with hopes for the World Championship and ended with a mere regaining of the U.S. Championship. Not a bad year for anyone else, but with Robert J. Fischer's hopes and talent, a distinct disappointment.

GAME 33

White: P. Benko (United States)
Black: R. Fischer

*Played at Curaçao (Netherlands
Antilles) Candidates Tournament,
May 2, 1962 Round 1*

After being undefeated in the great
international tournaments of Bled
1961 and Stockholm 1962, here
Fischer gets a shock in Round 1.
Benko just completely crushes him
in a positional masterpiece—a
portent of bad things to come for
Bobby.

King's Indian Defense (Benko System)

1 P-KN3   . . .

A great moment in the development
of modern chess theory. In this
game, and against Tal in Round 3,
Benko clearly demonstrated that 1
P-KN3 is fully sound and playable
as an opening move.

1	. . .	N-KB3
2	B-N2	P-KN3
3	P-K4	P-Q3

Black has decided to set up a King's
Indian type of formation—a completely logical approach.

4	P-Q4	B-N2
5	N-K2	O-O
6	O-O	P-K4
7	QN-B3	. . .

The idea behind the Benko System.
White chooses a sound, noncommittal piece development approach
and avoids possible weaknesses
resulting from an active P-QB4.
Such strategy was successful for
Benko in earlier games against
Fischer (see games 2 and 28) and
succeeds here. For opening con-
noisseurs it can be pointed out that
this position can also arise from the
Pirc Defense if White chooses the
unusual approach of KB fianchetto.

7 . . .   P-B3?

Unfortunately, information is lacking
on how much time Bobby spent on
this move. I assume that he took
little time because the move is a
cardinal opening error. This was
the start of his disastrous "system"
of grossly underestimating his
opponent. Bobby was already
recognized as one of the great
experts of the King's Indian and it
is inconceivable that he would have
played this move if he had looked
coldly at the merits of the position.
The philosophy of the King's Indian
is to accept a somewhat cramped
position to be able eventually to
strike at White's, the defender
hopes, overextended center. Fischer
here voluntarily accepts the cramped
position, but White's central buildup
has been so cautious that he has
nothing extended (much less over-
extended) for Black to later attack.
Meanwhile White simply retains

and builds on his natural space advantage.

The fundamental disadvantage of White's setup is that it is slow and innocuous and thus Black has an immediate opportunity for central pressure with 7 ... N-B3! This threatens the combinational 8 ... PxP; 9 NxP, NxP! And after 8 P-Q5, N-K2 we get the type of position where White's chances are on the Queenside and for that he needs his QBP on B4 rather than hemmed in on B2 by his Knight.

8   P-QR4!   QN-Q2?

THE LOSING MOMENT

Yes, Virginia, at the higher level of master play, apparently insignificant opening inaccuracies can take on gigantic proportions. In the so-called "long variation" of the King's Indian (Black plays ... QN-Q2 and P-QB3 against White's KB fianchetto), Black's play is on the Queenside via ... Q-R4 or P-QR4, P-R5 and Q-R4. After White's next move all these possibilities are closed off and White together with his usual central superiority achieves a bind against Black's Queenside. Benko's play in demonstrating these advantages is exemplary. Black's only correct response, as Tal played under similar circumstances in Round 3, is 8 ... P-QR4. Black's position is still bad, but he has significantly more breathing room than he gets here.

9   P-R5!   PxP?!

Opening of the position allows White to accentuate his positives with greater ease. Black should try to keep the position closed as long as possible and play 9 ... R-K1.

10   NxP   N-B4
11   P-KR3!   ...

Taking away as many squares as possible from Black's pieces. Development of the QB becomes a special problem.

11   ...   R-K1
12   R-K1   KN-Q2

Starting here, I don't have any more recommendations for improving Black's play. He suffers from chronic weakness of his QP and has absolutely no play anywhere.

13   B-K3   Q-B2
14   P-B4   R-N1
15   Q-Q2   P-QN4
16   PxP *e.p.*   **PxP**

Grandmaster Kotov of Russia recommends here 16 ... NxNP as better. That is like locking the barn after the horse has been stolen. True enough, it prevents White's next move, but at the cost of a new fundamental weakness: the isolated QRP.

| 17 | P-QN4! | N-K3 |
| 18 | P-N5! | NxN |

Even worse is 18 ... PxP; 19 N3xP, Q-B4; 20 NxN, QxN; 21 N-B7.

19	BxN	BxB
20	QxB	P-QB4
21	Q-Q2	B-N2

Leads to the forced loss of the QP, yet there is nothing worth suggesting. After 21 ... N-B3; 22 QR-Q1, R-K3; 23 P-N4!, Black's survival time is also measured.

22	QR-Q1	R-K3
23	P-K5!	BxB
24	KxB	Q-N2+
25	K-B2!	...

It is impossible to be overly generous with exclamation points for Benko's play in this game. His play is outstanding in every respect and the text move is a mark of a real grandmaster. Instead of routine "safe" 25 K-R2, White centralizes his King to exert control over the important KB3 square. White sees that Black is in no position to start any kind of an attack.

25	...	R-Q1
26	PxP	N-B3
27	RxR	PxR
28	Q-K3	K-B2
29	Q-B3!	...

When you are ahead in material, exchange pieces—that's the first principle of good technique.

29	...	Q-N1
30	N-K4!	NxN
31	QxN	...

Benko crowns his fine positional play with some sharp tactics. If now 31 ... RxP; 32 Q-K5, R-Q1; 33 R-Q7+! and Black has a choice of losing his King or Queen.

31	...	R-Q2
32	Q-B6	Q-Q1
33	K-B3	K-N2
34	P-N4	...

Safer was 34 Q-K4.

| 34 | ... | P-K4 |

A valiant attempt at a counterattack while White is in time pressure. It must fail, however, as Black just doesn't have enough attacking material left.

35	PxP!	R-KB2 +
36	K-N2	Q-R5
37	R-KB1	. . .

Puts a stop to everything, after which White's passed center Pawns must win.

37	. . .	RxR
38	KxR	QxRP +
39	Q-N2	Q-K6
40	Q-K2	Q-KR6 +

BLACK RESIGNS

Here the game was adjourned and Bobby resigned without even bothering to find out Benko's sealed move. After 41 K-K1, Q-R8+; 42 K-Q2, Q-R3+; 43 Q-K3, Q-R7+; 44 K-B3, the checks are at an end and so is the game.

GAME 34

White: E. Geller (USSR)
Black: R. Fischer

Played at Curaçao (Netherlands Antilles) Candidates Tournament, May 3, 1962, Round 2

The start of an impressive series of successes by Geller against Fischer. As of today, of the leading masters only Geller and Tal (thanks solely to the 1959 Candidates!) have a plus score against Bobby. Earlier, at the 1962 Stockholm Interzonal, using this same variation, Geller had established a winning position against Bobby, only to have him escape with a draw. But there is no escape here, as Geller holds on to his opening advantage all the way through. Just as against Benko in Round 1, so also here Fischer is never in the game.

Sicilian Defense (Najdorf Variation)

1	P-K4	P-QB4
2	N-KB3	P-Q3
3	P-Q4	PxP
4	NxP	N-KB3
5	N-QB3	P-QR3
6	B-K2	...

A deceptively quiet continuation, originally introduced by Smyslov and worked into a powerful weapon by Geller. White simply continues his development and is neutral about the Najdorf: neither trying to refute it nor being afraid.

6 ...   P-K4

The consistent Najdorf continuation to which Fischer has remained forever true. At the cost of a backward QP and especially of weakening his Q4 square, Black gets more center influence and opportunity for Queenside play. For those disliking such a Pawn formation, a safe alternative is the Scheveningen with 6 ... P-K3.

7 N-N3   B-K2

After the disaster here, in his next game with Black against Geller (in Round 16) Bobby tried 7 ... B-K3 and just managed to draw a lost position.

8 O-O   O-O

While White's castling is part of his development, Black must first get his Queenside pieces into play with 8 ... B-K3, 9 ... QN-Q2 and 10 ... R-QB1.

9 B-K3   Q-B2?!

Things now get more serious. Development of the Queenside by 9 ... B-K3; 10 .. QN-Q2; 11 ... R-QB1 is still correct. At the moment Black's Queen actually stands better on Q1 as she then doesn't have to worry about White's N-Q5.

10 P-QR4 B-K3

In Stockholm 1962 Fischer had played against Geller 10 ... P-QN3, but after 11 Q-Q2, B-N2; 12 P-B3, B-B3?!; 13 KR-Q1, QN-Q2; 14 Q-K1, P-R3; 15 Q-B1! White had a big advantage.

11 P-R5 QN-Q2

No better is 11 ... Q-B3; 12 B-B3, QN-Q2; 13 N-Q5! with advantage for White in Smyslov–Tal, 1959 Candidates.

12 N-Q5! NxN

Even worse is 12 ... BxN; 13 PxB, P-QN4; 14 PxP e.p., NxNP; 15 P-QB4!, QN-Q2; 16 N-R5! KR-B1; 17 P-QN4, and White's Queenside Pawns rolled forward decisively in Kostro–Pokojowczyk, Poland 1972.

13 PxN B-B4
14 P-QB4 B-N3?

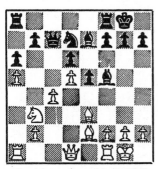

(Position after 14 P-QB4)

With his optimistic nature Fischer looks forward to starting Kingside play with ... P-KB4. Yet there is no time for that nor meaning in it. Thus, at best the text move is a loss of time. Correct was 14 ... QR-B1 (or 14 ... KR-B1) followed by ... Q-Q1 and an attempt at exchanging the black Bishops via ... B-KN4 (if White plays Q-Q2 then first ... P-R3).

15 R-B1 N-B4?!

When playing this Fischer overlooked Geller's 17th move. Better would be 15 ... QR-B1 or 15 ... KR-Q1. Pointless is 15 ... P-B4. Apart from the preventive 16 P-B3 or 16 P-B4, White also has the sharp 16 P-B5! If then 16 ... PxP; 17 NxP, NxN; 18 P-QN4, KR-Q1; 19 PxN, QxRP; 20 P-Q6, with the threat 21 Q-N3+ (as pointed out by Yugoslav I.M. Rabar).

16 NxN PxN
17 P-QN4! ...

White opens up the Queenside and this coupled with the protected passed QP gives a significant advantage. All the way through Black has no hope for anything else than protracted passive resistance. The tactical justification for the move is 17 ... PxP; 18 B-N6, Q-Q2; 19 P-B5, and the Pawns have become unblocked.

17	...	QR-B1
18	Q-N3	B-Q3
19	KR-Q1!	...

Keeping the bind rather than allowing the complications after 19 PxP, BxP; 20 BxB, QxB; 21 QxP, R-N1; 22 QxRP, R-N7; 23 QR-K1 (23 KR-K1?, B-Q6), R-R7 and Black has good practical chances for a draw.

19	...	Q-K2
20	PxP	BxP
21	BxB	RxB

Now after 21 ... QxB White has 22 P-Q6.

22	R-R1!	...

A great strategic idea: the Rook goes to QN4 to attack the QNP.

22	...	R-Q1
23	R-R4	B-B4

The error of Black's 14th move is now clearly apparent.

24	R-N4	B-B1
25	R-N6!	R-Q3

Black's only hope for resistance is a successful blockade. Unsatisfactory was 25 ... RxRP because of 26 P-Q6.

26	Q-N4	Q-B2
27	RxR	QxR
28	R-N1	Q-B2?

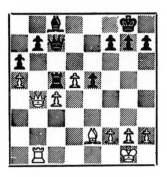

Allows White a successful regrouping. The required move was 28 ... P-KN3 preventing back-rank mates, and with the tactical point that 29 Q-R3? is unplayable because of 29 ... RxQP! Black's position after 28 ... P-KN3 is obviously unattractive yet may be barely tenable.

29	Q-R4!	B-Q2
30	Q-R3	RxRP

Obviously hopeless is 30 ... B-B1 31 R-N6, etc. Capturing with the Queen is worse: 30 ... QxP; 31 QxQ, RxQ; 32 RxP, and because of the mate threat Black loses his Bishop.

31	RxP!	...

White's QBP and QP are now connected passed Pawns and the win must be near.

31	...	QxR

No better is 31 ... RxQ; 32 RxQ, R-R8+; 33 B-B1, B-B4; 34 P-B3, and the Pawns reach the eighth rank.

| 32 | QxR | P-N3 |

Four moves too late!

| 33 | P-R3 | Q-N8+ |
| 34 | K-R2 | B-B4 |

The alternative is a clearly lost Queen and Pawn endgame after 34 ... Q-B7; 35 Q-Q8+, K-N2; 36 QxB, QxB; 37 Q-B7!, P-QR4; 38 P-B4!, e.g., 38 ... P-R5; 39 PxP, P-R6; 40 P-K6, P-R7; 41 QxP+, K-R3; 42 Q-B6, etc. (Rabar).

| 35 | Q-B3! | ... |

Centralization and support for pushing the QBP.

| 35 | ... | Q-K5 |
| 36 | B-B3 | Q-Q5 |

Loses, as does everything else.

| 37 | QxQ | PxQ |
| 38 | P-N4! | B-B1 |

If 38 ... P-QR4; 39 PxB, P-R5; 40 P-Q6, K-B1; 41 P-B6! (threatening 42 P-Q7), K-K1; 42 B-B6+ wins.

| 39 | P-B5 | P-QR4 |
| 40 | P-B6 | K-B1 |

BLACK RESIGNS

Here White sealed his move (obviously 41 P-Q6) and Bobby later resigned without waiting to find out. Indeed after 41 P-Q6 Black's only choice is *how* he wants to lose a piece. Either by 41 ... P-Q6; 42 P-Q7, BxP; 43 PxB, K-K2; 44 B-B6, P-Q7; 45 B-R4, or via 41 ... P-R5; 42 P-B7, P-R6; 43 B-B6, P-R7; 44 P-Q7, BxP; 45 BxP, P-R8(Q); 46 P-B8(Q)+ etc.

GAME 35

White: R. Fischer
Black: V. Korchnoi (USSR)

Played at Curaçao (Netherlands Antilles) Candidates Tournament, May 9, 1962, Round 5

The only game Fischer has lost against the Pirc. Also the only time that Fischer has fallen into an opening trap. After that, the rest of the game is slaughter. A very easy win for Korchnoi.

Pirc Defense (4P-B4)

1   P-K4   P-Q3

The Pirc Defense, named after Yugoslavian Grandmaster Vasja Pirc who was the first grandmaster to play it actively, can be looked upon as a KP counterpart to the King's Indian Defense against the QP. The basic strategy of both is the same: at the appropriate time to launch a counterattack against White's center, while in the beginning retaining some central Pawn influence by . . . P-Q3. The major difference is that in the Pirc, White's QBP remains back at QB2, while in the King's Indian the QBP invariably goes to QB4. This means that in the Pirc, White has a less imposing center (but therefore also one which is more difficult to annihilate) but is a move ahead for developmental purposes.

2   P-Q4   N-KB3
3   N-QB3   P-KN3
4   P-B4   . . .

This active centrally oriented Pawn move has been Fischer's favorite over the last ten years. Earlier in his career he played 4 B-KN5. The text move, called by some writers the "Austrian Attack," could also be named the "Three Pawns Variation" to illustrate the comparison with the "Four Pawn Attack" (5 P-KB4) against the King's Indian. Compared to the "Four Pawn Attack," the "Three Pawns Variation" is much superior, since by keeping the QBP back home at the start, White's center does not become over-extended and this extra tempo can be profitably used for piece development.

4   . . .   B-N2
5   N-B3   O-O
6   B-K2   . . .

Immediately after this game, Fischer switched to 6 B-Q3 which he has played with great success ever since; that move has also become the main variation of the whole opening. At the present time the Pirc has become one of the popular defenses against the KP, but when this game was played the full theoretical development was still in the early stages.

6   . . .   P-B4

As soon as possible Black strikes at White's center. If now 7 P-Q5, 7 ... P-K3! continues the undermining process and if 7 B-K3, PxP; 8 NxP, N-B3 and we have a position from the "old" Dragon Variation in the Sicilian Defense where White has played a premature P-KB4. So—

7 PxP   Q-R4

And not 7 ... PxP?; 8 QxQ, RxQ; 9 P-K5, where Black has a horribly cramped endgame.

8 O-O   ...

The point of Black's maneuver is that 8 PxP is bad because of 8 ... NxP; 9 PxP, R-K1 and Black wins back the sacrificed material, with interest. Note that this tactical possibility does not exist for Black after 6 B-Q3 as the KB also then protects the KP.

8 ...   QxP +
9 K-R1   N-B3

Obviously such a move must be playable. However, even better may be 9 ... QN-Q2 to eventually position the Knight on QB4 for applying pressure on the KP.

10 N-Q2   ...

An "elegant" maneuver, but what better things does the Knight do on QN3 than at KB3? Well, none; and it takes at least one pure tempo loss to get there. More logical were 10 Q-K1 or even 10 B-Q3.

10 ...   P-QR4

Preparing to bother the Knight as soon as it gets to QN3.

11 N-N3   ...

If 11 N-B4 (threatening with 12 B-K3 Q-N5; 13 P-QR3 to trap the Queen), 11 ... B-N5! gets Black out of all possible difficulties.

11 ...   Q-N3
12 P-QR4   ...

What else?

12 ...   N-QN5

Starting off very definitely as the Pirc, the opening has turned into a type of position which formerly often arose from the Sicilian Dragon with White having castled on the Kingside. This position is fully satisfactory for Black and the game could continue: 13 B-B3, B-K3 (threatening 14 ... NxBP!); 14 N-Q4, B-B5 etc. Instead ...

13 P-N4??   ...

THE LOSING MOMENT

In his eagerness to attack, Bobby carelessly runs into an opening trap well known in the old Sicilian Dragon. This is the only instance of Fischer falling into a known trap.

13	...	BxP!
14	BxB	NxB
15	QxN	NxP

The point. With the double attack on the Knight and Rook, Black wins back the sacrificed material.

| 16 | N-N5 | ... |

This decentralizing move is forced as the Knight at N3 must stay put to protect the Rook, can't be protected directly and the indirect attempt at protection via 16 Q-Q1 fails after 16 ... QxN; 17 R-R3, Q-B5!; 18 QxN, QxR mate!

| 16 | ... | NxR |
| 17 | NxN | Q-B3 |

White is about even in material, having two minor pieces for a Rook and two Pawns. Yet positionally he is quite lost: his minor pieces are awkwardly placed (to put it mildly!), Pawns are weak and King position is loose.

| 18 | P-B5?! | ... |

Realizing that he is completely busted, Fischer tries a desperate "go for broke" attack. For purposes of prolonging the game, moves

such as 18 Q-N2, 18 Q-B3, or 18 Q-K2 were in order.

18	...	Q-B5!
19	Q-B3	QxRP
20	N-B7	QxN!

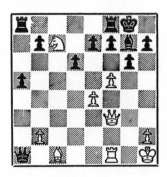

| 21 | N-Q5 | ... |

A move neither to be criticized nor praised. Bobby saw that after 21 NxR, RxN he is positionally lost and will wind up, depending on the variation, from one to three Pawns down, so he tries to "complicate things." Chances for success here are, of course, close to zero.

21	...	QR-K1
22	B-N5	QxP
23	BxP	...

Or 23 NxP+, RxN!; 24 BxR, B-K4! with play similar to the game: e.g., 25 R-B2, Q-B8+; 26 K-N2, R-K1!; 27 PxP, RxB etc.

| 23 | ... | B-K4! |

Demonstrating the weakness in White's King position.

24	R-B2	Q-B8+
25	R-B1	Q-R3
26	P-R3	PxP!

Korchnoi concludes very forcefully. As "compensation" for his lost position, White has a material inferiority of three Pawns.

27	BxR	RxB
28	N-K7+	K-R1
29	NxP	Q-K3
30	R-KN1	P-R5!
31	R-N4	Q-N6
32	Q-B1	P-R6
33	R-N3	...

This position is a joke. Of course, now 33 ... BxR wins instantly (34 N-Q4, Q-K6 etc.). Instead, Korchnoi decides to have a bit of fun.

33	...	QxR

WHITE RESIGNS

After 34 NxQ, P-R7 and 35 ... P-R8(Q) Black gets his Queen back, but White's Rook is gone forever.

GAME 36

White: R. Fischer
Black: E. Geller (USSR)

Played at Curaçao (Netherlands Antilles) Candidates Tournament, May 16, 1962, Round 9

With the help of an opening novelty, Geller equalizes. When the partners could agree on a draw, Fischer, instead, makes a rash winning attempt and soon thereafter lands in an inferior endgame. He continues making things worse for himself and, understandably enough, soon commits the losing mistake. An endgame which has made the textbooks.

Sicilian Defense (Sozin Variation)

1	P-K4	P-QB4
2	N-KB3	P-Q3
3	P-Q4	PxP
4	NxP	N-KB3
5	N-QB3	N-B3
6	B-QB4	...

Fischer has made this move his trademark from the very beginning of his career through the 4th match game against Spassky in 1972. Only after Spassky had demonstrated a clear equalizing method there did Bobby turn to 6 B-KN5 later in the match. There is no question that 6 B-QB4 is "Fischer's move" both

from the standpoint of his many contributions to its theory and lifelong play. It is true, however, that the Russian master Sozin was the first one to pay serious attention to it, so my objection to naming it the "Sozin Variation" is relatively mild and I have followed the conventional usage here.

6	...	P-K3
7	B-N3	...

The Bishop retreats voluntarily, before there is an actual threat. A flexible, modern approach yet not always infallible. The move does cost a tempo immediately and there are instances where the Bishop can advantageously retreat to Q3 (e.g., after Black's ... N-QR4). For 7 B-K3 see Game 54.

7	...	B-K2
8	P-B4	...

A very sharp approach, pressing in the center while delaying castling. Fischer had scored a full point with it at Stockholm 1962 against Olafsson and was eager to repeat. But Geller, who of course had been there also, is ready. For 8 O-O see Game 38.

8	...	O-O
9	B-K3	NxN!

With this and the following move Black takes advantage of the fact that White's development is not completed.

10	BxN	P-QN4!
11	P-K5	...

White has nothing better as 11 P-QR3, B-N2 is obviously in Black's interest. The disadvantage of the KB as an onlooker on QN3 is apparant.

11	...	PxP
12	PxP	N-Q2
13	O-O	...

If 13 NxP, Q-R4+; 14 N-B3, NxP and Black's is position better.

13	...	B-B4!

Geller's improvement on 13 ... P-N5?; 14 N-K4, B-N2; 15 N-Q6 with advantage to White in Fischer–Olafsson, Stockholm 1962. Black immediately strikes at the weakness in White's position—the KP.

14	BxB	...

There is nothing better, as 14 NxP, Q-N3 is good for Black.

14	...	NxB
15	QxQ	RxQ
16	NxP	...

Otherwise White is left with a weak KP with no compensation for it.

16	...	B-R3!
17	B-B4	...

This clumsy maneuver is required since 17 N-B7, BxR 18 NxR, B-N4 (also good is 18 ... BxP) puts

White's Knight in great danger of being lost.

17	...	QR-N1

In a later game—against Perez, Havana 1965— Geller took off the Knight immediately with 17 ... BxN, which is to be looked on as an improvement, at least from the standpoint of giving Black greater practical winning chances.

18	P-QR4	NxP!

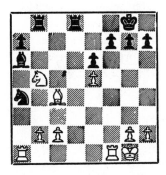

Black has defended perfectly and both sides could now agree on a just draw, in view of 19 RxN, BxN; 20 BxB, RxB; 21 RxRP, RxNP; 22 R7xP, RxP, etc. Instead, Fischer makes an incomprehensible winning attempt.

19	N-Q6?	BxB

Did Bobby truly expect 19 ... RxN?; 20 PxR, BxB; 21 RxN!, BxR; 22 KxB, RxP; 23 RxP and White wins?

20	NxB	NxP
21	N-Q6	...

Endgames with a Pawn down rarely offer *winning* chances and this is fully true here, too. For drawing purposes, a simpler way was 21 NxN to enter a double Rook endgame, as given in the notes after Black's 18th move, but with the significant difference that White now is one move behind.

| 21 | ... | R-Q2 |
| 22 | KR-N1 | R-B2 |

Too dangerous was 22 ... R-N3 as, after 23 P-B4, N-R5 White has 24 P-B5!! with mate threats on the back rank preventing both 24 ... NxP (25 RxR!) and 24 ... RxR+ 25 RxR, NxP.

23 P-R3? ...

What does this have to do with the game? White surely was in no danger of being mated! It was obvious to Bobby by now that White has no winning chances, but his attitude from here on is just as unhealthy: "No matter what I do, the game is a dead draw!" As Fischer himself has proved so many times from the opposite side of the board, this is just not so! The logical move was 23 P-B4! after which Black must find the only move—23 ... R-N5!—to retain any winning prospects.

| 23 | ... | R-N3! |
| 24 | P-B4 | P-KR3! |

With a well-calculated maneuver Geller ensures that he'll be a safe Pawn ahead in the following Rook endgame. What will then happen—well, the future can only tell, but it's nice to have such a position against Fischer!

25	N-N5	R-B4
26	RxN	P-R3
27	R-KB2	...

No matter what White plays, he'll be a Pawn down, e.g., 27 R1-N1, PxN; 28 RxP, R3-B3! etc.

27	...	PxN
28	R-R7	RxKP
29	R/2xP	R-N4

30 R/B7-N7 ...

One of the principles of play states that the materially stronger side should try to exchange pieces only, whereas the side with material down should exchange Pawns only. Since Bobby is a Pawn down, his offer to exchange Rooks is not too logical. True, it is difficult to win single

Rook endgames with a Pawn plus
if all the Pawns are on one side
(as will be soon here), but it is even
more difficult to win double Rook
endgames under such conditions!
Therefore the better play was 30
PxP, R3xQNP; 31 R-B2! and it is up
to Black to show he can make
progress.

30	. . .	RxR
31	RxR	PxP
32	R-QB7	. . .

White wins one Pawn back—big
deal!

| 32 | . . . | R-KB4 |
| 33 | RxBP | . . . |

Endgames with Rook and three
Pawns against Rook and two Pawns,
with all Pawns on the same side,
are usually dead draws. This position
should also be a draw, but it is
far from a "dead draw," because the
extra Pawn is a passed Pawn. Since
Bobby has so often won positions
of this type where he is the stronger
side, we could expect that he'll be
able to draw for the weaker side
with ease. But no such luck! Fischer
here is in a completely different
role and unfortunately "acts that
role."

| 33 | . . . | K-B2 |
| 34 | P-N4 | . . . |

White's King will now be cut off
from the third row. More accurate
was 34 P-N3.

34	. . .	R-B6
35	K-N2	R-Q6
36	R-B7 +	K-B3
37	P-R4	R-QR6
38	R-N7	R-QB6
39	P-N5 +	. . .

An extremely significant and potentially dangerous decision to make,
two moves before time control and
possible adjournment, as it is
obvious that White's KNP will
remain chronically weak. It is still
good enough for a draw, yet in
reality prepares the decisive error.
As an example of strategy to use in
going for the World Championship,
it is beyond logical comprehension.
From a practical standpoint, White
simply should shuttle back and
forth with his Rook on the seventh
rank.

39	. . .	PxP
40	PxP +	K-N3
41	R-K7	R-K6
42	K-B2?	. . .

THE LOSING MOMENT

After a long string of second-rate moves, finally comes the decisive blunder. And it was played unnecessarily on the board before adjournment. The proper tournament strategy was for White to seal his obvious 41st move and then in home analysis discover the proper drawing technique. While Geller now pondered his sealed move, Fischer said something like "It's a hopeless draw." This must be considered a psychological ploy to "pressure" Geller into a gentlemanly offer of a draw. Even if the position after the text move was a theoretical draw (which it no longer is), you can be sure that if Bobby was Black here, not in a million years would he have offered a draw to Geller or anyone else. No, he would have continued to squeeze his opponent for another 50 or so moves. The only King move which would still keep the draw was 42 K-R2! so that if 42 . . . R-K4 43 K-R3! and unlike the game, Black can't get his Rook off the King file with *check*. White's Rook continues to attack the KNP and KP and there is no way Black can win White's KNP without losing one of his own, in a position where White's King is properly placed for the draw.

42 . . .   R-K4

The obvious sealed move which wins by force the KNP and thus eventually the game. There is no way for White to prevent the following check. Fischer had finally subjected the position to a required amount of analysis, but for nought now—the damage already has been done.

43   K-B3   R-KB4 +
44   K-K3   . . .

Fischer's analysis had shown that 44 K-K4 was no better. If then 44 . . . P-K4??, Black loses both Pawns after 45 RxNP+, KxR; 46 KxR and 47 KxP even though the King and Pawn endgame is still drawn. Instead, Black wins with 44 . . . R-B2!; 45 RxP+, KxP and with White's King cut off from the KN file, the position is won for Black. This is similar to what happens later in the game.

44   . . .   P-K4
45   K-K4   RxP
46   R-K8   . . .

Of course 46 RxKP?, RxR+; 47 KxR, K-N4! leads to an easily won King and Pawn endgame. According to endgame theory, Rook and KP and KNP vs Rook endgames are won and this is no exception, even though for a few moments White's pieces appear to be favorably placed. The general technique consists of sacrificing, at the proper moment, one of the Pawns to obtain a theoretically won R + P vs R endgame.

46	...	R-N8!

Black starts his regrouping. Again the KP is indirectly protected.

47	K-B3	R-KB8+
48	K-N3	R-B4
49	R-QN8	K-N4
50	R-K8	K-B3
51	R-KB8+	K-K3
52	R-K8+	K-B3

With the next time control at move 56, Black repeats moves to save time without fundamentally changing the position so that he can then later get a "good think" about the position with a new full hour at his disposal. Compare this approach with Fischer's *before* the adjournment. On such "non-chessic" factors do chess results often depend.

53	R-KB8+	K-K3
54	R-K8+	K-Q4
55	R-QR8	R-B2
56	K-N4	R-K2

For maximum efficiency in Rook endgames, Rooks belong behind passed Pawns (such as here behind the KP) or as a second choice to the side of them (for the KNP here).

57	R-R5+	K-K3
58	R-R6+	K-B2
59	K-B3	R-K3

Compared to the position after move 45, Black has made slow yet very steady progress. Black's pieces are placed very harmoniously and the end is near for White.

60	R-R8	P-K5+
61	K-K3	P-N4
62	R-R1	K-N3
63	R-QN1	R-K4
64	K-Q4	K-B3
65	R-K1	

65 R-KB1+ would have prolonged resistance. After the text move, Geller finishes off very instructively.

65	...	R-R4!
66	RxP	K-B4!

(Position after 66 RxP)

With White's King on the Queen's file, Black's KNP is enough to win. But not here 66 ... R-R5+??; 67 K-K3 with a draw as the King and Pawn endgame is also drawn.

67	R-K8	K-N5!
68	K-K3	K-N6!

WHITE RESIGNS

For master chess the win is elementary. One demonstration: 69 K-K2, P-N5; 70 R-KN8, R-KB4!; 71 R-N7, K-R6; 72 R-N8, P-N6; 73 R-N7, K-R7; 74 R-KR7+, K-N8; 75 R-KN7, P-N7; 76 R-QR7, R-KR4!; 77 K-B3, K-R8! and the KNP queens.

GAME 37

White: R. Fischer
Black: T. Petrosian (USSR)

Played at Curaçao (Netherlands Antilles) Candidates Tournament, May 23, 1962, Round 13

Surprised in the opening, Bobby reacts with a third-rate "innovation." Petrosian establishes a pull and with direct, simple-looking moves carries the position to a convincing win. His moves *look* so simple that the first impression is that White must have missed thousands of obvious draws. Only a careful search for viable alternatives for White leads to the conclusion that each of the "simple" moves has a lethal punch. A game where Petrosian and classical chess are shown at their best.

French Defense
(MacCutcheon Variation)

1	P-K4	P-K3
2	P-Q4	P-Q4
3	N-QB3	N-KB3

The older and quieter of the two fighting alternatives here. Rather passive, though theoretically playable, is the Rubinstein or Exchange Variation: 3 . . . PxP.

4	B-KN5	B-N5

This is the MacCutcheon Variation, the sharpest move here, yet theoretically not quite sound. It is not part of Petrosian's normal opening repertoire and thus unquestionably came as a great surprise to Fischer. Petrosian has never liked the classical line, 4 . . . B-K2, here, but quite frequently plays the Burn variation: 4 . . . PxP. With the latter he obtained a winning position in the third match game against Fischer in Buenos Aires 1971, even though Bobby escaped with a draw.

5	P-K5	P-KR3
6	B-Q2	. . .

Long accepted as the best move. It has been known for over 70 years that 6 PxN, PxB; 7 PxP, R-N1 only looks good for White, but in reality Black doesn't have any problems.

6	. . .	BxB

That this capture is forced is the main disadvantage of the Mac-Cutcheon. 6 . . . N-K5?? loses a piece after 7 NxN, and after 6 . . . KN-Q2; 7 Q-N4, White has a very favorable version of the Winawer Variation (3 . . . B-N5).

7	BxB?!	. . .

Surprised by Petrosian's choice, Fischer decides to take his opponent "out of the book." Unfortunately, the move is clearly inferior to 7 PxB, N-K5 8 Q-N4 and it is up to Black to demonstrate how he can equalize.

7	...	N-K5
8	B-R5?	...

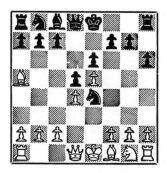

An extreme example of Fischer's "I can play anything!" attitude. How did he decide on such a silly, stupid move? Well, he didn't like leaving it on QB3 (though 8 Q-N4, K-B1; 9 B-Q3 is still best and retains equality for White—but no more as he will have difficulties defending the Pawn at QB3 after 9 ... NxB; 10 PxN, P-QB4), 8 B-N4 is unattractive after 8 ... P-QB4; 9 BxP (9 PxP?, NxKBP!; 10 KxN, Q-R5+ is worse for White) 9 ... NxB; 10 PxN, N-Q2, so what else is left except moving the Bishop one square further? Hardly a scientific approach to the game!

8	...	O-O!

Petrosian now gets an advantage and retains it all the way through. Only one question remains: where in the following course could White improve to escape with one black eye—a laborious draw?

9	B-Q3	N-QB3
10	B-B3	...

A rather total admission of the error of 8 B-R5, yet even less attractive was 10 BxN, PxB!; 11 B-B3, Q-N4 followed by ... P-QN3.

10	...	NxB
11	PxN	P-B3!

Immediately striking at White's center.

12	P-KB4	PxP!
13	BPxP	N-K2!

The Knight is very well placed here as it guards Black's weak KN3 and KB4 squares.

14	N-B3	P-B4
15	O-O	Q-R4

Black has a clear advantage as White has no compensation for his Queenside Pawn weaknesses.

16	Q-K1	B-Q2
17	P-B4	...

Uncharacteristically, Fischer voluntarily allows an inferior endgame. Apparently, he underestimated the resulting difficulties. A reasonable middle game move was 17 R-N1, since 17 ... QxRP allows White a draw with a perpetual attack on Black's Queen: 18 R-R1, Q-N7; 19 R-N1, Q-R6; 20 R-R1 etc.

17	...	QxQ
18	KRxQ	QPxP
19	B-K4	...

Also unattractive was 19 BxP P-QN4!

| 19 | ... | PxP |
| 20 | BxP | QR-N1 |

Black's advantage now derives from the fact that he is ahead some tempos in development—a direct result of White's time wasting QB maneuvers in the opening.

| 21 | B-R6? | ... |

THE LOSING MOMENT

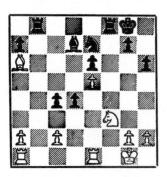

Surprisingly, this attacking move turns out to be the losing moment, as the Bishop remains out of the game long enough to make the difference. Correct was the centralizing 21 B-K4!—Black is better placed, but White can defend.

| 21 | ... | R-N5 |
| 22 | QR-Q1 | ... |

Or 22 NxP, P-B6!; 23 N-K2, N-Q4. From now on White only has a choice of evils.

22	...	P-Q6!
23	PxP	PxP
24	RxP	...

The same move would follow after 24 BxP.

24	...	B-B3
25	R-Q4	RxR
26	NxR	B-Q4
27	P-QR4	...

In spite of the meager material remaining, White can not prevent the loss of a Pawn. Thus if 27 R-K2, R-B5; 28 R-Q2, N-N3.

27	...	R-B5
28	R-Q1	N-N3
29	B-B8	K-B2
30	P-R5	NxP
31	P-R6	R-N5!
32	R-Q2	N-B5
33	R-KB2+	K-K2
34	N-N5	N-Q3
35	NxN	...

For drawing purposes it was probably beneficial to exchange the QRPs after 35 NxP, R-QB5 36 B-N7. The resulting endgame Pawn formation then is almost like in the previous game, but here the extra minor piece on the board increases Black's winning chances.

| 35 | ... | KxN |
| 36 | B-N7? | ... |

An error which makes Black's task very easy. Required was 36 R-N2 and White can prolong resistance.

| 36 | ... | BxB |
| 37 | PxB | K-B2! |

Fischer had overlooked this possibility and was hoping for 37 ...

R-N5; 38 R-B7, P-QR4; 39 RxP, P-R5?!; 40 R-N4! with a draw.

38	P-R3	R-N4
39	R-N2	K-N1
40	K-B2	R-Q4!

Black now picks off the QNP for nothing and remains then two clear Pawns up.

41	K-K3	R-Q2
42	K-K4	RxP
43	R-KB2	...

WHITE RESIGNS

The game was adjourned here and Fischer resigned without continuing it. Black's QRP is of decisive importance.

GAME 38

White: R. Fischer
Black: V. Korchnoi (USSR)

Played at Curaçao (Netherlands Antilles) Candidates Tournament, June 8, 1962, Round 19

By virtue of his superior theoretical knowledge, Fischer obtains an advantageous endgame. But his overeagerness quickly dissipates pretty much all of his advantage and from a level position a series of unbelievably careless moves leads to a most unexpected loss.

Sicilian Defense (Sozin Variation)

1	P-K4	P-QB4
2	N-KB3	N-QB3
3	P-Q4	PxP
4	NxP	N-KB3
5	N-QB3	P-Q3
6	B-QB4	P-K3
7	B-N3	B-K2
8	O-O	O-O
9	B-K3	N-QR4

Through the passage of time many approaches have been tried by Black to secure equality. With the help of hindsight, it is not surprising that the decentralizing text move is not fully satisfactory. It remained, however, for Spassky (or more likely one of his trainers or seconds) to discover and demonstrate in his 4th

Match Game against Fischer in 1972 the correct continuation: 9 ... P-QR3; 10 P-B4, NxN!; 11 BxN, P-QN4!; 12 P-QR3, B-N2; 13 Q-Q3, P-QR4! with full equality.

10	P-B4	P-QN3

The point of Black's setup: he prepares for quick fianchetto of the QB and is ready at his convenience to exchange off White's KB. The debit side of the strategy is that influence in the center is temporarily lessened.

11	P-K5!	...

White must strike quickly to take advantage of the latter factor. After 11 Q-B3?!, B-N2; 12 P-N4?, R-B1; 13 P-N5, RxN! Black already was better in Padevsky–Botvinnik, 1956 Moscow Olympiad.

11	...	N-K1

Other moves are significantly worse: 11 ... PxP; 12 PxP, N-Q2; and now 13 RxP!! wins material. And after 11 ... N-Q2; 12 PxP, BxP; 13 NxP White wins prosaically.

12	P-B5!	...

Not bad is 12 Q-B3, B-N2; 13 Q-N3, but the text move is stronger.

12	...	QPxP

12 ... NxB?; 13 N-B6, Q-B2; 14 NxB+, QxN; 15 P-B6! wins quite simply.

13 PxP!   NxB

The only reasonable move. If 13 ... P-B3?; 14 N-B5, NxB; 15 N-Q5!! and White wins.

14 N-B6   Q-Q3

14 ... QxQ? allows the *Zwischenzug* 15 NxB+ and 14 ... Q-B2? is refuted by 15 N-Q5!, QxN; 16 NxB+ and 17 NxQ.

15 QxQ!   . . .

This transition into a favorable endgame is the right way to proceed. It is not a Fischer innovation, as a fairly extensive analysis of the move had already been published by Polish master Kostro in the Polish chess magazine *Szachy* in January 1958. Characteristically, Fischer was fully familiar with it, while many of his contemporaries were not. Only visually attractive is 15 N-Q5?, as Black can advantageously play 15 ... B-R5! After 16 PxP+? (better 16 RPxN, BxP; 17 N5-N4, P-QR4!; but Black is still significantly better) 16 ... RxP; 17 RxR, NxR!; 18 Q-KB1, B-B3; 19 NxB+, NxN White resigned in Bilek–Petrosian, Oberhausen 1961.

15 ...   BxQ
16 RPxN!   BxP
17 NxRP   . . .

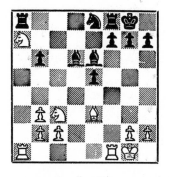

The basis of White's advantage is clear: Black's QNP is very weak while his Kright hinders back rank coordination. Also good was 17 RxRP or 17 N-N5.

17 ...   R-N1

The best try in an unpleasant situation. Everything else is hopeless, e.g., 17 ... B-QB4; 18 BxB, PxB; 19 N-B6! or 17 ... B-B2; 18 N3-N5, B-Q1; 19 N-B6, and in each case Black loses at least a Pawn.

18 R-R6?!   . . .

Fischer blindly follows Kostro's analysis, but the move is overeager. Correct was 18 N-K4! (threatening 19 NxB, NxN; 20 N-B6 winning a Pawn) and Black is in serious difficulties.

18 ...   N-B3!

A significant improvement over the 18 ... B-B2?; 19 N3-N5 considered by Kostro. Black by sacrificing a

Pawn is able to take advantage of the momentary misplacement of White's pieces.

19 RxP . . .

But not 19 BxP??, RxB; 20 RxR, B-QB4+ and Black wins. And 19 P-R3 is too slow, as Black defends everything with 19 . . . N-Q2.

19	. . .	RxR!
20	BxR	R-N1
21	B-B2	N-N5
22	N7-N5	. . .

White could try 22 N-B6, R-QB1; 23 N-R7, R-R1; 24 N7-N5, B-N5; 25 N-B7, but Black can repeat the position with 23 . . . R-N1! Bobby again is looking for more than a draw.

22	. . .	B-N5
23	B-R7	. . .

Fruitless is 23 P-R3, NxB; 24 KxN, B-Q2 and Black's two Bishops completely paralyze any hopes White may have on the Queenside.

23	. . .	R-N2
24	P-R3	BxN
25	PxB	RxN
26	PxN	BxKNP

A most interesting endgame has developed. White has three passed Pawns on the Queenside, while Black has a four to one majority on the Kingside. Despite his passed

Pawns being doubled, the fact that they are connected and already passed, gives White a slight advantage. With reasonable play on both sides the game should be readily drawn, however.

27	P-B4	R-N2
28	R-R1!	B-B4
29	P-B5?	. . .

While it is true that "passed Pawns must be pushed," some attention must be paid to material losses! Correct was 29 R-R2! with the point that 29 . . . BxP?? loses the Bishop because of the mate threat after 30 B-K3. However, after the correct 29 . . . R-Q2! aiming for the active Rook, Black should be able to get sufficient counterchances for the draw.

29	. . .	BxP
30	P-B6	RxP
31	P-N4??	. . .

THE LOSING MOMENT

Incredible. The "point" of the move is to prevent Black's Bishop from retreating to his KB4, yet Black simply can take off the Pawn for nothing! It was necessary to play 31 P-B7, B-B4 (not 31 ... R-QB6??; 32 B-Q4! and White wins); 32 B-B2, P-R4; 33 R-R8+, K-R2; 34 P-B8(Q), BxQ; 35 RxB, and the three Pawns are more valuable than the Bishop here, but the position is still a draw.

| 31 | ... | R-KN6+ |
| 32 | K-B2 | RxP |

Yum, yum, yum.

33	P-B7	B-B4
34	B-K3	P-R4
35	R-R8+	K-R2
36	P-B8(Q)	BxQ
37	RxB	P-R5

Four connected passed Pawns *always* win against a minor piece.

38	K-B3	P-B4
39	R-B8	K-N3
40	R-KR8	R-N6+
41	K-B2	P-B5
42	B-R7	P-R6
43	B-N8	K-B4
44	R-KB8+	K-K5
45	R-K8	R-N4

WHITE RESIGNS

The Pawns will inexorably move forward. The game was adjourned here and Fischer again resigned without continuing.

GAME 39

White: R. Fischer
Black: P. Keres (USSR)

*Played at Curaçao (Netherlands
Antilles) Candidates Tournament,
June 15, 1962, Round 21*

Keres "out-psychs" Fischer in the
opening and obtains the better
game. Eventually Bobby equalizes
and then even obtains the better
chances. Then it's even again.
Finally a very careless Knight's tour
leads to the loss of the Knight and
the game. This game, ending the
third cycle, was also the last one
Fischer lost. In the fourth cycle he
was actually the high scorer and with
two wins and four draws ended
that "mini-tournament" undefeated.
Unfortunately for Bobby, the
damage had already been done in
the initial three fourths of the
tournament.

Ruy Lopez (Closed)

1	P-K4	P-K4
2	N-KB3	N-QB3
3	B-N5	P-QR3
4	B-R4	N-B3
5	O-O	B-K2
6	R-K1	P-QN4
7	B-N3	P-Q3

It may be of interest to note that
Keres, one of the great attacking
players of our time, has never

showed much interest in the sharp,
attacking Marshall Gambit (7 . . .
O-O; 8 P-B3, P-Q4!?).

8	P-B3	O-O
9	P-KR3	. . .

The only point of this standard,
time-wasting move is to be able to
play P-Q4 without being bothered
by Black's . . . B-KN5.

9	. . .	N-QR4
10	B-B2	P-B4
11	P-Q4	N-Q2

This unusual move has an interesting
idea behind it: to "give up" the
center by exchanging the Pawns and
then to apply pressure there by
pieces. Tactically Black has some
good possibilities, but strategically
the concept is somewhat suspect
and White should be able to achieve
the better game. The variation was
introduced into tournament praxis
by Keres at this tournament and
justly carries the name "Keres
Variation." Yet note, Keres introduces a variation and *it is* called
"Keres Variation"; Fischer introduces
a variation and it is called *everything but* "the Fischer Variation."
We have already met the regular
move, 11 . . . Q-B2, in Game 5
and will see it again in Game 46.

12	P-Q5?	. . .

A surprising move for many reasons.
In the first place, Fischer has a
natural aversion to blocked centers

so that he will not enjoy such a position. Here it occurs at a most inopportune moment, since Black's KN has already unblocked the KBP and Black is able to achieve counter-play much faster than is usually the case. In the debut of this variation, in the Round 7 game Fischer–Keres, Bobby had played 12 PxBP and won in fine style. Apparently Fischer had looked no more at the variation, being quite sure that Keres wouldn't dare to play it again against him. Now that Keres has played it again, what does it mean and what to do about it? Very uncharacteristically, Bobby "chickens out" from challenging Keres again. For an example with 12 PxBP see Game 44. Also good is 12 QN-Q2 even though Tal lost with it in Round 16 against Keres.

| 12 | ... | N-N3 |
| 13 | P-KN4? | ... |

Consistent, to prevent Black's ... P-KB4 after, e.g., 13 QN-Q2, P-B4; 14 PxP, BxP; 15 BxB, RxB; 16 N-K4, Q-Q2 and Black stands well. After the Kingside weakening text move, Black, however, stands even better than in the note variation.

| 13 | ... | P-R4! |
| 14 | N-R2 | ... |

What else?

| 14 | ... | PxP |
| 15 | PxP | B-N4! |

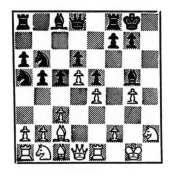

Black gladly offers to trade the dark square Bishops, as then White's Kingside will have additional holes. In addition, Black will remain with the "better" Bishop. White can not prevent this for any length of time.

| 16 | N-Q2 | P-N3 |
| 17 | QN-B3 | ... |

Otherwise the Queenside cannot be developed.

17	...	BxB
18	QxB	K-N2
19	Q-N5!	...

A move Fischer must have hated to play. Yet a lifeless endgame is unquestionably superior to being mated in the middle game.

19	...	N-N2
20	QxQ	RxQ
21	P-R4	...

With the Queens off, White enjoys a brief respite on the Kingside and Fischer uses this time for some counteraction on the Queenside. This is the best practical approach.

21 ... **PxP**

Otherwise White plays 22 P-R5 and 23 P-N4 and binds down Black's Queenside. White now is able to get rid of his "bad" Bishop, but at the cost of leaving the white squares very weak.

22	BxP	NxB
23	RxN	B-Q2
24	R-R2	...

Not so much to protect the QNP as to be ready for doubling Rooks on the QR file against Black's QRP.

24 ... **P-B5**

A major positional decision. To gain the lovely QB4 square for his Knight, Black accepts a permanently weak QBP and cuts down on the usefulness of his Bishop which now cannot infiltrate via White's Queenside and additionally must spend time protecting the QRP and QBP. For winning purposes the more promising move appears to be 24 ... R-R1 immediately and if required, protect the QRP by simply pushing it to R4 and possibly R5.

25	N-Q2	B-N4
26	N/R2-B1	R-R1
27	N-K3	R-R5
28	K-N2	QR-R1

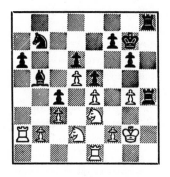

Black's Rooks look very menacing, but lack sufficient help to bring down White's King. Bobby defends very well and all Black's efforts get nowhere.

29	N-B3	R-R6
30	N-B1	N-B4
31	N-N3	B-Q2
32	P-N5	P-B3
33	PxP+	KxP
34	R-K3	K-K2
35	N-Q2	R-R7+
36	K-N1	B-N4

Required to protect the QBP. In certain positions the Bishop functions as only a glorified Pawn. Thus it is not surprising that Black's clear space advantage is insufficient for a win.

| 37 | R-R1 | R7-R5 |
| 38 | K-N2 | R-KB1 |

With the threat 39 ... N-Q6.

| 39 | R-B3 | R-QN1 |
| 40 | K-N1 | ... |

Both sides "kill time" and await adjournment.

40	...	R-QR1
41	R-R5	R-QB1
42	R-R3	...

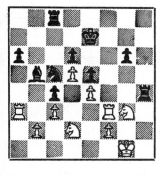

The game was adjourned here and White sealed this move. Black's position is optically better and he needs a win to stay in the race to be the Challenger. It is thus quite logical for Keres to continue playing for a win. Yet the position really does not offer many winning possibilities and by trying too hard, not surprisingly, soon Keres errs and suddenly it is White who has the better prospects.

42	...	R-QR1
43	R-R5	R-QR2
44	K-N2	N-N2
45	R-R1	P-R4

Black continues to play for a win, but a more sensible approach was a draw offer. The QRP advance now is ineffective since the positional liability— the QBP—still remains.

46	N3-B1	N-B4
47	N-K3!	P-R5

For a variety of tactical reasons 47 ... NxP 48 N3xP! is completely satisfactory for White, e.g.: 48 ... N-B3; 49 NxQP; 48 ... N-N4 49 NxRP!; 48 ... BxN 49 NxB, N-B4 and again 50 NxRP with the threat 51 N-B6+.

48	R-KR3	RxR
49	KxR	N-Q6
50	R-R2!	NxBP+
51	K-N3	N-Q6
52	N3xP	R-R1
53	N-N6	R-R3
54	N6-B4	N-B4

No draw!

55	K-B3	R-R1?!

One move before the time control, Black overlooks the following shot. In a way it turns out to be a blessing in disguise as the position then becomes more complicated, even though White has a slight advantage.

56 P-N4! . . .

Based on the fact that Black's Rook is unprotected. White now also gets a passed NP, though on the other side of the board! Black's QRP is no problem as the Knights are ideally located for blockading purposes.

56 ... **N-N6**
57 N-R3 ...

Not 57 NxN??, BxN.

57 ... **B-Q2**
58 K-N2 ...

To prevent a check on KR6 after, e.g., 58 R-N2, R-R1; 59 NxN, R-R6+; 60 K-N2, RxP!

58	...	**B-N5**
59	N3-B4	R-QB1
60	N-K3	B-Q2
61	P-B4	R-QN1!
62	P-N5	N-B4
63	N-Q1	K-Q1
64	N-QB3	R-R1

Keres has defended well and White could agree to a draw here. If he wanted to continue "playing" then 65 N2-N1! was the correct move, which would help blockade the QRP and free the Rook for action. Instead, Bobby starts his Knight on a suicidal mission.

65	N-B3?!	K-B2
66	N-N5?	K-N3
67	N-B7??	...

Fischer is bent on losing the Knight. White has lost lots of time already, but there was just sufficient time left for the return 67 N-B3 and if 67 ... K-R4; 68 R-N2, P-R6; 69 R-N1!.

67 ... **R-KB1!**
68 R-KB2? ...

White can't play 68 NxQP, K-B2! trapping the Knight. The Rook defense allows a deadly pin. The best practical move was again the return via 68 N-N5.

68 ... **P-R6!**

So the passed QRP is decisive after all.

69 R-B3?! ...

69 N-N5 was still better; 69 NxQP again loses the Knight after 69 ... RxR+; 70 KxR, K-B2 as 71 N-B7 allows 71 ... NxP+!; 72 NxN, P-R7.

69	...	B-N5
70	R-B2	P-R7!
71	NxRP	NxP
72	R-B1	B-B4!

The end. 73 ... RxN is threatened
and 73 N-R6 allows 73 ... B-R6ch
winning the exchange and the game.

Bobby gives one desperation check
before resigning.

73	P-B5ch	PxP

73 ... NxP would allow 74 N-N5
even though White is then hopelessly lost anyway.
WHITE RESIGNS

GAME 40

White: V. Ciocaltea (Rumania)
Black: R. Fischer

*Played at Varna (Bulgaria) Olympiad,
October 1, 1962, Finals, Round 5*

One more proof of Fischer's fantastic success with the Sicilian is that only once—here—has he lost to the Closed Variation. His handling of the opening is very lackadaisical, something of a cross between thoughtlessness and carelessness. This was an unfortunate character-istic of Bobby's play at that time. By the time he wakes up, the position is already too bad. Twice he almost gets sufficient counter-play, but "almost" turns out to be not good enough.

Sicilian Defense (Closed)

1	P-K4	P-QB4
2	N-KB3	P-Q3
3	P-Q3	...

A somewhat unusual sub-variation of the Closed Sicilian which is usually entered by 2 N-QB3. The text variation has the advantage that the QBP can be used for central purposes, but the disadvantage that the early development of the KN blocks the KBP and makes White's attacking chances on the Kingside

difficult to realize. The disadvantage is somewhat more important than than the advantage, thus the game continuation rarely occurs from the pure Sicilian Defense and is much more apt to result from a KB-fianchetto opening such as 1 P-KN3 or 1 N-KB3.

3	...	N-QB3
4	P-KN3	P-KN3
5	B-N2	B-N2
6	O-O	P-K4!

Effectively counters White's plan of P-QB3, P-Q4 etc.

7	P-B3	KN-K2
8	N-R4	...

See comment to move 3. Without the KBP White has no attacking chances.

8	...	O-O
9	P-KB4	PxP!
10	PxP	...

This position with an extra tempo for White (QN already on Q2) occurred via a completely different order of moves ten years later in DeFotis–Reshevsky, 1972 U.S. Championship, where Black first played 11 ... K-R1 and after 12 QN-B3, P-Q4 obtained an excellent game. An immediate 11 ... P-Q4 was even better.

| 10 | ... | P-B4?! |

One of the rules of thumb says that an attack on the flank is best countered by action in the center. So also here where 10 ... P-Q4! would give Black an excellent position since 11 P-B5 is tactically faulty: 11 ... QPxP!; 12 P-B6, BxP!; 13 RxB, N-Q4 with advantage for Black. Fischer's move, though playable, is second-rate because it weakens the Kingside and partially locks in the QB, all for no good reason.

11	N-Q2	K-R1

Not required. An immediate 11 ... P-Q4 was playable.

12	N2-B3	PxP??

THE LOSING MOMENT

Horrible and thoughtless! Black voluntarily gives White a strong center and lengthens White's KB diagonal—absolutely for no reason. Either 12 ... P-Q4 or 12 ... N-KN1 still would have sufficed for an approximately even game.

13	PxP	P-Q4

Apparently the "idea" behind 12 ... PxP??. It works out badly, but here there is already nothing good to recommend.

14	PxP	QxP

14 ... NxP; 15 N-N5 is also very unpleasant for Black.

15	QxQ	NxQ
16	N-N5!	...

White has a winning advantage: his KB has a fantastic diagonal, meaning that Black's QNP and the advanced QBP are quite weak. Also White's P-QB3 takes away any play Black may have hoped for in the center or on the Queenside.

16	...	N-N3

Removing the Knight from its nice central location can't be too good, yet 16 ... N3-K2; 17 B-Q2, followed by 18 QR-K1 also gives White a lovely position.

17	B-K3	N-R5
18	QR-K1!	B-Q2
19	B-B1	B-B3
20	N4-B3!	B-B4
21	N-K5	N-K2
22	N-K4	B-R5
23	R-Q1	QR-B1

There was no way to prevent material loss, e.g., 23 ... QR-N1; 24 N-Q6, P-N3; 25 N-B6! NxN; 26 BxN.

24	N-Q6	R-QB2
25	N-N5	R2-B1
26	NxRP	R-R1
27	N-N5	R-R4

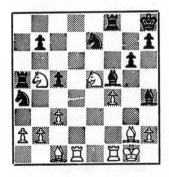

As so often happens, Black after losing a Pawn gets some play on the "missing Pawn" file. Objectively, though he is quite lost—a Pawn for nothing is a winning advantage.

28 P-B4 ...

In the approaching time pressure White plays inexactly, which makes the win more difficult. Decisive would have been 28 N-Q6!, P-QN4; 29 NxB!, NxN; 30 R-Q7, and White has a won position apart from being a Pawn ahead!

28	...	N-N3
29	N-QB3	N-R5
30	N-N5	N-N3

In this position even Bobby would be happy to draw with Black!

31	N-R3	B-B3
32	R/B-K1	N-R5
33	N-N5	...

33 N-Q7! was much stronger.

33	...	N-N3
34	N-QB3	N-B3!

Bobby does a good job here in trying to mix it up as much as possible.

35	BxN	PxB
36	P-N3	N-Q2
37	N-R4	...

Faster winning was 37 NxN, QBxN; 38 N-K4!, B-Q5+; 39 B-K3, but it is understandable that in time pressure White wanted to avoid the "complications" after 39 ... RxBP, though in fact White wins easily after 40 NxP!, R-N5+; 41 K-R1, BxB; 42 RxKB, RxN; 43 RxB.

37	...	NxN
38	PxN	B-R5
39	R-B1	K-N2
40	R-Q6	R4-QR1
41	B-K3	...

The time control is over and White can take a deeper look into the position. At the cost of a further weakening of his Queenside Pawns, Black has obtained the two Bishops and a considerable weakening of White's King position. He comes close to having sufficient counter-play for a draw, but not close enough.

| 41 | ... | B-R6 |

As good as any. The attack is simply not strong enough to compensate for the missing Pawn and the loose Queenside Pawns.

42	RxR	RxR
43	R-Q1	R-B4
44	NxP	R-B6
45	B-Q4	R-B5
46	P-K6+	K-B1
47	B-K5	B-B7+

An immediate 47 ... R-N5+ also gets the saving reply 48 B-N3.

| 48 | K-R1 | R-N5 |
| 49 | N-Q7+ | ... |

49 B-N3??; BxN

49	...	K-K2
50	B-N3	KxP
51	R-Q6+	...

To chase the King back; an immediate 51 R-Q2 is also playable, but not 51 BxB?, B-N7+; 52 K-N1, B-B6+; and the Rook is *en prise*.

51	...	K-K2
52	R-Q2	BxB
53	PxB	RxNP

Black has the Pawn back only for the moment; the weakness of the remaining Queenside Pawn turns out to be decisive.

54	N-K5!	P-B4
55	K-R2	R-K6
56	N-Q3	B-B4
57	NxP	...

The Pawn race turns out to be quite unequal. In the first place, three Pawns are more powerful than two; and secondly, White's King is able to provide some defensive help.

57	...	P-R4
58	P-R4	P-R5
59	P-R5	P-N4
60	P-R6	K-B3
61	P-R7	R-K1
62	R-R2	R-QR1
63	P-N4	P-N5
64	P-N5	P-N6+
65	K-N2	K-N4
66	P-N6	K-N5
67	P-N7	P-R6+

68 K-B1! . . .

After 68 K-N1?? R-Q1! *Black* would be the surprising winner, e.g., 69 R-R1, P-R7+; 70 K-N2, R-Q7+; 71 K-R1, K-R6 or 69 K-B1, P-R7!.

In chess utmost care is required to the very end!

68 . . . **P-N7+**
69 RxP+ . . .

Good enough also was the prosaic 69 K-B2.

BLACK RESIGNS

A fight both contestants can be proud of.

GAME 41

White: R. Fischer
Black: J. H. Donner (Holland)

*Played at Varna (Bulgaria) Olympiad,
October 3, 1962, Finals, Round 6*

After a promising but, for Fischer,
uncharacteristic piece sacrifice, he
continues carelessly and simply
remains a piece down. Donner in
time pressure makes it hard for
himself, yet a piece is still a piece
and Bobby resigns after adjourna-
ment. Except for the 1959 Candidates
tournament, this is Fischer's only
other loss against the Caro-Kann.

Caro-Kann Defense

1	P-K4	P-QB3
2	P-Q4	P-Q4
3	N-QB3	PxP
4	NxP	B-B4

The introduction to the so called
"B-B4 Variation." Black achieves
sound piece development, but has
to content himself with a fundamentally somewhat passive position.
A reasonable approach when playing
for a draw, something which would
satisfy Donner completely.

5	N-N3	B-N3
6	P-KR4	P-KR3
7	N-B3	N-Q2
8	B-Q3	...

It is in White's interest to precede
this with P-R5, thus fixing Black's
Kingside Pawns.

8	...	BxB
9	QxB	P-K3
10	B-B4	Q-R4+
11	B-Q2	Q-B2
12	P-B4	...

At the time of this game Spassky's
fine maneuver was not yet known:
12 O-O-O, KN-B3; 13 Q-K2!,
O-O-O; 14 N-K5 (threatening 15
NxKBP), and White has a powerful
grip on the important K5 square.
(White's KRP is usually on R5 in this
variation.)

12	...	KN-B3
13	B-B3	...

Castling Queenside is more
promising.

13	...	P-QR4!
14	O-O	B-Q3

The logical follow-up to his previous move was 14 ... B-N5 with complete equality. If anyone's King-side then is weak it is White's.

15	N-K4	NxN
16	QxN	O-O
17	P-Q5	...

White's Bishop now has a fine diagonal.

17	...	KR-K1
18	PxBP	PxP
19	QR-Q1	B-B1
20	N-Q4	R-R3

Donner is not interested in defending a somewhat inferior endgame after 20 ... QR-B1, 21 QxBP, QxQ; 22 NxQ, RxN; 23 RxN, RxP; 24 P-KN3. But the Rook on QR3 is very awkwardly placed.

21	N-B5!?	...

21 P-QN3! would have stopped Black's counterplay.

21	...	N-B4
22	Q-K3	N-R5!
23	B-K5	Q-R2

Now 24 QxQ leads to nothing, and White must sacrifice a piece to retain winning chances. Objectively, the sacrifice is promising, but it is the intuitive "Tal type" of sacrifice rather than the strategically logical "Fischer type."

24	NxRP+!	PxN
25	R-Q4??	...

THE LOSING MOMENT

Bobby made this blunder without thinking or hesitating. Correct was 25 Q-KN3+, K-R2; 26 P-R5!, which prevents 26 ... P-KB4 because of 27 Q-N6 mate. White then has good practical chances on the Kingside, as three of Black's pieces are on the QR file shooting at nothing.

25	...	P-KB4!

Now Black's pieces can help out on the Kingside and White can't generate anything.

26	KR-Q1	N-B4
27	R-Q8	Q-KB2
28	RxR	QxR
29	B-Q4	N-K5
30	P-B3	P-K4!
31	PxN	...

Unfortunately, the Bishop has no moves, e.g., 31 B-N6, RxB.

31	...	PxB
32	Q-KN3+	B-N2
33	PxP	Q-K6+?!

Donner was in time pressure so his interest in exchanging Queens is understandable. However, White's Rook can now become very active and the game becomes close. Instead, 33 ... P-B4! getting the Rook into the game would win easily.

34	QxQ	PxQ
35	R-Q8+	K-B2
36	R-Q7+	K-B3
37	P-KN4	B-B1
38	K-N2	B-B4
39	R-KR7	K-K4!
40	K-B3	K-Q5!

Black's meaningful trump is the KP and it needs the help of the King for further advances.

41	RxP	R-N3
42	P-N3	P-R5
43	R-K6	PxP
44	PxP	K-Q6
45	P-N5	...

WHITE RESIGNS

The game was adjourned here, to be continued in the morning. A full night of analysis by Bobby and the American team showed that Black always comes first. One possible variation: 45 ... RxP; 46 P-N6, R-N8; 47 P-N7, R-KB8+; 48 K-N2, P-K7!; 49 P-B6, B-K6; 50 RxB+, KxR; 51 P-N8(Q), P-K8(Q); 52 Q-K6+, K-Q7! Bobby therefore asked me to reach Donner in the morning and tell him that Fischer resigns. I was scheduled to be up, anyway, to play off my adjourned game against Kramer (a won end-game). While searching for Donner I ran into Kramer and informed him also that Fischer had resigned. Kramer thought a while and then decided that he therefore should resign against me! Thus, Bobby's fine example of sportsmanship made my morning easier also.

GAME 42

White: R. Fischer
Black: S. Gligoric (Yugoslavia)

*Played at Varna (Bulgaria) Olympiad,
October 9, 1962, Finals, Round 11*

One of the very few times Fischer
has lost a won position and one
more proof of his unscientific play
at that time. The first part of the
game is unquestionably played by
Fischer, but then suddenly he turns
into a pumpkin and the name of
the player of the White pieces
during the second part is not known
to this writer.

*Sicilian Defense
(Scheveningen Variation)*

1	P-K4	P-QB4
2	N-KB3	P-Q3
3	P-Q4	PxP
4	NxP	N-KB3
5	N-QB3	P-QR3
6	P-KN3	P-K3

With this move Black sets up a
Scheveningen-type formation, which
is a perfectly reasonable approach.
Gligoric here writes that he played
this and the following moves
quickly, thus giving the impression
that Fischer's 6th move was no
surprise to him. Yet, considering
the fact that Bobby hadn't played

6 P-KN3 before (or since, for that
matter), whom did Gligoric think he
was fooling?
A perfectly safe and sound alternative for Black was the KB fianchetto
starting with 6 ... P-KN3. But why
play the Najdorf Variation of the
Sicilian if you want a safe and sound
position? The most consistent
continuation here is 6 ... P-K4
establishing the pure Najdorf. Bobby
has played this very successfully for
Black, showing that White's KB on
KN2 doesn't really have much to do.

7	B-N2	B-K2?!

The quick development of the Kingside leads to good attacking chances
for White and to nothing for Black.
The correct way of handling the
opening for Black is 7 ... B-Q2
followed by 8 ... N-B3.

8	O-O	O-O
9	P-B4	Q-B2
10	P-KN4!	N-B3
11	NxN!	. . .

11 P-N5? is faulty because of 11 ...
NxN 12 QxN, P-Q4! (13 PxN??,
B-B4) and the retreat 11 N-N3 is
time-wasting. The text move, theoretically speaking, does strengthen
Black's center, but because of his
passive position Black is not able to
do anything in the center. In the
meantime White has a free hand
on the Kingside.

11	...	PxN
12	P-N5	N-Q2
13	P-B5	R-K1
14	K-R1	...

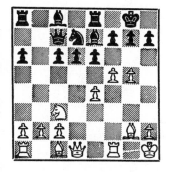

It is positionally somewhat surprising, but statistically unarguable, how helpful it is to prevent unwelcome checks on the KN1-QR7 diagonal.

14	...	B-B1
15	B-B4	N-K4
16	P-B6	P-N3

Extremely passive. A better practical approach may well have been 16 ... N-N3; 17 PxP, KxP; 18 B-N3, P-K4.

17	P-KR4	P-QR4
18	P-R5	B-QR3
19	R-K1	Q-N3
20	PxP	...

A more accurate order of moves is first 20 BxN, as now Black could get some counterplay chances with 20 ... NxP! If then 21 BxP?!, QR-Q1; 22 P-K5, NxP; 23 N-Q5!?, KPxN;

24 BxN, Q-B7, and who's position is better?

20	...	BPxP

After 20 ... RPxP? Black will go under because White will get two major pieces on the open KR file, but, as discussed above, a better try was 20 ... NxP.

21	BxN	PxB
22	Q-B3!	...

22 Q-Q7 only *looks* attractive; after 22 ... Q-B7 it is Black who has the attack.

22	...	R-R2
23	B-B1!	R-KB2
24	BxB	QxB

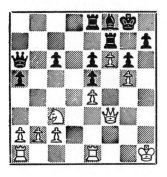

White has a significant set of advantages, e.g., the obviously superior Pawn formation, and the *potentially* much more valuable minor piece. Bobby had played quite quickly so far to establish this fine position, which simply testifies once

more to his great natural talent.
Here was the time to take stock of
the position and come up with the
right idea. Yet Bobby played the
next two moves in blitz tempo.

25 Q-N3?! ...

The fundamental turning point of
the game, as starting with this move
Fischer becomes unrecognizable.
The first objective for White should
be to get his Knight to a useful
square, e.g., one square forward to
QB4. For this purpose 25 N-Q1! was
in order. If then 25 ... B-B4; 26
P-N3! (26 N-K3, BxN; 27 RxB is
also in White's favor), Q-R2; 27
N-N2, P-R3; 28 N-B4. After 28 ...
PxP; 29 NxKP, B-Q5; 30 NxR, QxN;
31 QR-Q1, B-K4; 32 K-N2, R-KB1
Gligoric says "and the loss of the
exchange is still not the end of the
game." This is true enough in the
sense that there is no need yet for
Black to resign, but ahead an
exchange and with no particular
dangers, it is rather clear that
White has fantastic winning
chances after 33 R-KR1.

25 ... Q-N3
26 QxP? ...

It is rather stupid to exchange the
valuable QNP for a doubled KP.
Correct was still 26 N-Q1.

26 ... QxP
27 QR-Q1! ...

Here Bobby used a considerable
amount of time and thus came up
with the right move. During the
"blitzing" he hadn't noticed that
after 27 QR-N1, QxBP; 28 R-K2
Black's Queen escapes with her
bounty via 28 ... Q-Q6.

27 ... P-R3!

Black now achieves sufficient
counterplay and the chances are
about even. Of course, 27 ...
QxBP?? loses the Queen after 28
R-K2.

28 R-K3 B-N5!
29 PxP QxBP

With the threat 30 ... BxN 31 RxB,
QxR/Q8+.

30 R-KN1 K-R2
31 Q-N3? ...

The true dynamics of the position
is determined by the answer to
the question: Whose King is in
greater danger here? For this purpose the logical move was 31 R3-N3
or first 31 P-R3 and if 31 ... BxP
32 R3-N3! In these positions White's
Queen is well placed on the central
K5 square. Fischer's move, preparing
the superficially attractive protection
of the KBP by P-K5, is wrong,
because it goes against the true
spirit of the position. Gligoric doesn't
fall into the pretty trap 31 ... RxP?;
32 P-K5! and White wins (32 ...
R-B2; 33 N-K4). Instead ...

31	...	R-KN1!
32	P-K5	BxN!
33	RxB	Q-K5+!
34	R-N2	R-Q1
35	R-K3	Q-N8+
36	K-R2??	...

THE LOSING MOMENT

Almost unbelievable. White is dreaming of his attack, completely oblivious to the fact that it is Black who is doing the attacking! It should have been obvious that Black's Rook on Q1 is a more dangerous piece than White's R-K3, so 36 R-K1 was the right move. If then 36 ... R-Q8 37 RxR and with the exchange of a set of Rooks in a favorable position, White's defenses should be good enough for a draw.

36	...	R-Q8
37	Q-N4	R-R8+
38	K-N3	Q-QB8!
39	R-K4	...

A shade better was 39 Q-B3, though Black keeps the advantage with 39 ... R-R4!.

39	...	R-Q2
40	Q-K2	Q-N4+
41	Q-N4	...

This game was played in the last round of the Finals. Before the start of the round we had had an excellent chance for the silver or bronze medal, but by now things were rather bleak, since R. Byrne had already lost and Evans and Benko had drawn. To those who had watched Bobby play the last 15 or so moves it was painfully clear that he was like a punch-drunk fighter who was playing with his heart rather than with his head. This, then, was the moment to adjourn the game to see what could be saved. Yet, which team captain has the nerve to tell Fischer anything? Or would a Fischer listen?

41	...	R-Q6+
42	K-B2	R-Q7+

43	K-N3?	...

The final (inevitable) blunder. Correct was 43 K-B3! and there must be a win for Black, but it is not elementary. Thus if 43 ... R-B8+; 44 K-N3, RxR+; 45 KxR and compared to the game White is in much better shape, as Black's Rook stands much worse on KB8 than on KR8 because he takes away the KB8 and KN8 squares from Black's Queen.

43   ...   RxR+
WHITE RESIGNS

Here the game was finally adjourned and Black had sealed the above move. Bobby soon resigned when Gligoric showed him the simple wins after 44 KxR, Q-B8; e.g., 45 K-B3, Q-B8+; 46 K-K3, R-R6+; 47 K-Q4, Q-B7+; 48 K-B4, Q-B7+; 49 K-Q4, Q-B6 mate.

GAME 43

White: R. Fischer
Black: E. Mednis (United States)

Played in the U.S. Championship,
New York, December 16, 1962,
Round 1

Black obtains full equality after the opening, but some dilly-dallying later on leads to a slight plus for White at the first adjournment. The position is not to be won, however, and after a particularly impetuous "attacking" move by White, a position results which now gives Black excellent winning chances. Mednis makes progress very slowly, yet carefully and surely, and by the second adjournment it is clear that Fischer must be lost. In fact, he resigns without continuing the game. This was the first game Bobby lost in a U.S. Championship after winning the first four without a loss, and is one of only three games he has ever lost in U.S. Championship play.

French Defense (Winawer Variation)

1	P-K4	P-K3
2	P-Q4	P-Q4
3	N-QB3	B-N5
4	P-K5	P-QB4
5	P-QR3	BxN+
6	PxB	Q-B2

An old-fashioned move the primary purpose of which once was to prevent White's 7 Q-N4, as now after 7 ... P-B4 Black's KNP is protected. However, Uhlmann has long since shown that after 6 ... N-K2; 7 Q-N4, PxP! Black has no *objective* reason to fear the resulting complications.

7	N-B3	B-Q2

The modern approach is 7 ... P-QN3 to try to exchange the white-square Bishops after 8 ... B-R3.

8	P-QR4	N-K2
9	B-Q3	QN-B3
10	O-O	P-B5

The active KB must be chased away before Black can undertake anything. Immediately disastrous would be 10 ... O-O because of the well-known Bishop sacrifice: 11 BxP+!, KxB; 12 N-N5+, K-N1; 13 Q-R5, KR-B1; 14 QxP+, K-R1; 15 P-KB4! and Black has no defense to the threat 16 R-B3 and 17 R-R3+.

11	B-K2	P-B3

Black must look for counterplay opportunities against White's center.

12	B-R3	...

White puts the Bishop on a visually very attractive diagonal, yet there is no practical benefit from it. It was

over eight years later, in his first
match game against Larsen in 1971,
that Bobby came up with the
significant improvement 12 R-K1!.
The point is that if now 12 ... O-O
13 PxP! and Black is forced to
recapture with the Rook, because
the centrally indicated 13 ... PxP
is bad: 14 B-R6!, R-B2; 15 N-R4,
N-N3; 16 B-R5! and if 16 ... NxN;
17 Q-N4+.

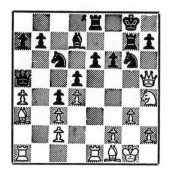

A very strong move, practically
forcing White's rather unattractive
reply. If, instead, 19 R-K3 then
simply 19 ... QxRP.

| 12 | ... | O-O |

It could be barely possible to accept
the Pawn sacrifice but I saw no
reason to tempt the fates or Fischer.
In fact, after 12 ... PxP; 13 PxP,
NxP; 14 R-K1 it could well happen
that by transposition the above-
mentioned Fischer–Larsen game
would be reached.

| 13 | R-K1 | R-B2! |
| 14 | PxP?! | ... |

Here this exchange is unmotivated
and leads to better chances for
Black. Correct was 14 B-KB1 with a
typical "French" struggle.

14	...	PxP
15	B-KB1	R-K1
16	N-R4	N-N3
17	Q-R5	R-N2
18	P-N3	Q-R4!

19	B-QN2	N-Q1
20	R-K3	N-B2
21	K-R1	N-Q3

Threatening 22 ... NxN followed
by 23 ... N-B4, so that White
decides to exchange Knights. However, this has the disadvantage of
strengthening Black's Kingside Pawn
formation and opening the KR file
for Black.

22	NxN	PxN
23	Q-K2	R-R2!
24	K-N1	K-B2
25	P-R4	P-B4
26	Q-B3	N-K5
27	Q-B4	...

Bobby has defended well and Black
was now faced with the problem
of what to play for next. Sharpest
was 27 ... R1-KR1 with the idea
... P-KN4. However, the following

text move is also okay. Black prevents a potential 28 BxP, PxB; 29 RxN and prepares for a slightly superior endgame.

27	...	R-QB1
28	B-N2	Q-B2
29	QxQ	RxQ
30	P-QR5	R-B3?!

Black now embarks on a whole series of inferior and time-wasting maneuvers, which are partly to be blamed on slight time pressure. Correct was 30 ... K-B3 followed by ... P-KN4 with a slight edge for Black.

31	B-QR3	R-QR3
32	B-N4	R-R1
33	R3-K1	B-B3
34	B-B3	N-Q7
35	B-K2	N-K5
36	K-N2	N-B3
37	R-R1	B-K1
38	K-B3	N-K5
39	K-K3	N-B3
40	P-B3	B-Q2
41	P-N4	B-K1
42	K-B4	B-N4

Here the game was adjourned and I had sealed this move. As a result of Black's dilly-dallying, White has unquestionably obtained the somewhat freer position. This game was started on a Sunday, which at that time meant that for most of the players the following week, Monday through Friday, was also a regular workweek at their normal jobs. Thus I had little time for analysis, but felt fairly sure that White has no winning breakthrough at his disposal.

| 43 | P-R5!? | ... |

Upon seeing my sealed move, Bobby gave me a brief funny look and then rather quickly played his move. He gave the impression that my sealed move was an error and that this was the way to take advantage of it. Even though fully playable, this offers no chance for anything more than a draw.

43	...	PxRP
44	QR-KN1	B-K1
45	K-K3	...

A good move. After a potential P-N5, White will have as a followup P-B4.

| 45 | ... | P-N3! |
| 46 | PxNP | RxP! |

For practical purposes Black is a Pawn ahead on the Queenside, so why not have the extra Pawn as a passed Pawn? Even if Black's QRP will be lost, White will have no advantage on the Queenside.

| 47 | R-R1 | R-N2 |
| 48 | B-Q6 | R-R2! |

With the Rook now protected, Black threatens 49 ... RPxP

| 49 | PxBP?? | ... |

THE LOSING MOMENT

From a deeper-thinking standpoint a rather incomprehensible move. The idea is to open up the position for "attacking purposes." Yet there is no realistic basis for expecting that White will be able to launch a successful attack against Black's King. What does matter now is that Black has a two (passed) Pawn advantage for which White has no compensation. A two-Pawn advantage is, of course, more than enough for a competent master. Considerable patience and care is

required, but there can be no doubt that Black must now win.
White's correct course was 49 P-N5, N-Q2; 50 P-B4 with a hard fight still to follow.

49	...	PxP
50	R-KR4	K-K3
51	B-R2	R-N7
52	K-Q2	R2-QN2
53	K-B1	R7-N3
54	B-B1	N-N1!

Black prepares to push his QRP and for this, additional protection of the KBP is required, as an immediate 54 ... P-R4 55 R-B4, P-QR5?! can be met by 56 B-R3.

| 55 | B-B4 | P-R4! |

The first tangible sign of progress by Black. Of course, the Pawn is taboo (56 RxQRP??, R-N8+ winning the Bishop).

56	R-KR2	P-QR5
57	B-R3	N-K2
58	B-N5	K-B2!

Indirectly protecting the KBP as now 59 BxN, RxB; 60 BxP?? loses a Rook after 60 ... R-K8+.

| 59 | R-K2 | ... |

Exchanges are in the interest of the materially superior side, yet there is simply no good "attacking" continuation for White.

59	. . .	R-K3
60	RxR	KxR
61	K-Q1	N-B1
62	K-Q2	B-Q2!

Again first safeguarding everything!

63	B-N2	R-R2
64	R-K1+	K-Q3
65	B-R6	P-R6
66	B-B8+	K-B3
67	B-B5	R-R1
68	R-QR1	P-R7
69	K-K3	N-Q3
70	K-B4	N-N4
71	B-N4	P-R5!

Passed Pawns must be pushed. The immobilization of White's pieces continues.

72	B-KR3	N-B2!

Here the game was again adjourned and White sealed his next move. I was absolutely convinced that the position must be a win, and work or no work, I was determined to analyze this position to death. This one was not getting away! I considered all reasonable moves and, believe me, after pages of analysis, demonstrated wins against all of them. Included in this category were moves such as 73 B-B1, 73 K-K5 and 73 K-N5. Fischer had sealed another reasonable move.

73	B-K7	. . .

WHITE RESIGNS

White resigned without continuing the game. Black wins after 73 . . . R-K1!; 74 BxRP (otherwise . . . N-K3+ wins) 74 . . . R-KR1!; 75 BxP (or 75 K-N3, P-B5+), 75 . . . R-KB1 and Black wins a piece and easily the game.

I have been asked innumerable times how it felt to receive Fischer's handshake. Well, it sure felt great to defeat Fischer, but I must admit that I didn't get Bobby's handshake nor, for that matter, any other direct communication from him. What happened was the following: Next time we were together was for Round 4, and before the games for that round started, Fischer went up to the referee, Hans Kmoch, and told him that he was resigning. Mr. Kmoch then came over to me and informed me, "Mr. Fischer has resigned."

PART THREE

Semi-Retirement

February 1963—February 1970

(Games 44 through 55)

The unhappiness with Curaçao was to affect Fischer's chess psyche for some time to come. All through 1963 he refused invitations to international tournaments. To everyone's surprise, he accepted invitations to play in two relatively minor open Swiss-type tournaments in the second half of the year and won both easily (Western Open and New York State Open). In the winter the U.S. Championship was annexed with the extraordinary score 11–0!

Rather than a good omen for the future, it had just the opposite effect. If Bobby's confidence in his greatness was reinforced, his skepticism toward the rest of the world deepened. The net result was that 1964 was chesswise a complete bust. Fischer refused to participate in the 1964 Interzonal Tournament, despite the fact that the U.S. Chess Federation had obtained at the FIDE Congress a complete restructuring of the system for determining the Challenger. The new system consisted of a series of individual matches to replace the Candidates Tournament, the very thing Bobby had insisted on! Now that he had got his way at FIDE, he simply said "No," he won't play, anyway. He also refused to play on the U.S. Team at the Olympiad in Israel. Fischer's only public chess activity during the year was a cross-country simultaneous exhibition tour, not a particularly profitable undertaking in those days.

Only in the second half of 1965 was he again ready to play international chess, accepting an invitation to play in the great Capablanca Memorial at Havana. But now fate, in the form of the U.S. State Department, intervened and he was not given permission to go to Cuba. Where there is a will, there is often a way, and Bobby participated in the tournament from the Marshall Chess Club in New York via a telephone-teletype setup. His play was pretty good and he finished in a triple tie for second place with a 15–6 score, just a half point behind the winner, Smyslov, although defeating Smyslov in their individual game. But three games were lost, the first ones in almost three years! Ivkov and Cholmov, both on the Black side of the Ruy Lopez, outplayed him (Games 44 and 46). Geller did the same on the White side of a fine Samisch King's Indian (Game 45), a variation which was still giving Bobby trouble.

Heartened by his successful return to tournament chess, Bobby consented to play in the 1965-66 U.S. Championship. Despite two decisive defeats by R. Byrne and Reshevsky (Games 47 and 48), he won easily with 8½–2½ and copped his seventh straight U.S. title.

All was quiet on the chess front in the first half of 1966. The American chess public was eagerly waiting for midyear when the Piatigorsky Cup Tournament at Santa Monica was to be held. The top players of the world were to compete in a double round robin tournament. Of course, Fischer was invited, but would he play? The answer finally was "Yes," but his start was lousy. After the first half (nine rounds) he was next to last with 3½ points and had already lost three games, while winning only one. Some incomprehensibly careless moves led to an unnecessary loss against Larsen (Game 49). Then both Najdorf and Spassky positionally outplayed the young American champion (Games 50 and 51). Bobby gave the impression of being complacent about his opponents and the chessboard. With the start of the second half, the tiger in him reawakened. His play and score (7½–1½) was grand and he placed a clear second, just a half point behind the victorious Spassky.

This time, success was a good omen, and soon thereafter Bobby led the U.S. team to a second-place finish at the 1966 Havana Olympiad. His play (this time in person!) was outstanding, with many fine wins against top grandmasters. He lost only one game—against the young Rumanian Gheorghiu (Game 52). Even here the result could have been a draw, had he accepted the draw offer which his opponent, out of respect, offered on move 15 although with a better position.

Fischer returned happy to New York and proceeded to sweep the 1966-67 U.S. Championship with a 9½–1½ score, undefeated and two points ahead of the field. This was his eighth and so far last title, as he has refused to play in subsequent championships.

The year 1967 also started on a good note. He won a small international tournament in Monaco, with only an unlucky last-round loss to Geller (Game 53) marring his performance. In the summer he was first in a mixed tournament at Skopje, Yugoslavia. This time the start was rocky: a draw in Round 1 against a weak master and then a short, sharp and undeserved loss against Geller (what, again?—see Game 54). Then came a series of wins and not even a deserved loss in the 12th round against Janosevic (Game 55) could stop the Fischer Express from a clear first.

The next step on Bobby's chess tour was the 1967 Interzonal Tournament at Sousse, Tunisia. The start was full of hope; the end a tragedy. Playing great chess, Bobby had scored 8½ points out of ten games actually played. Then disaster struck in the form of a series of disagreements regarding Fischer's refusal to play because of religious considerations. The United States Chess Federation had sent no one to look out for Bobby's interests; the organizers spoke no English and were not interested in learning, and many of the competitors in a grand display of selfishness did everything possible to egg Bobby on. The end result is well known to everyone: Fischer simply walked out of the tournament.

Despite this circumstance, Bobby was persuaded to return to international chess in 1968. He won two relatively minor tournaments—Netanya and Vinkovci—without the loss of a game. But then came another unfortunate event when Fischer simply walked out on the U.S. team at the 1968 Lugano Olympiad, complaining about poor lighting conditions.

The year 1969 brought even less cheer to Bobby's many admirers. He played only one serious game and even refused to participate in the 1969 U.S. Championship. He was impervious to the argument that since this championship was the Zonal Tournament for U.S. players his failure to compete would automatically rule out his chances for the World Championship. Fischer would not budge from his demands that the tournament contain at least 20 players or be a double round robin, so that "he wouldn't be unfairly affected if he lost an early-round game." From the rest of us, the argument made some sense, but coming from the man who had won the tournament each time he competed, it obviously did not hold water.

Thus the year ended on a gloomy note. What would now happen to the chess career of the only American with a realistic chance for the World Championship? Would he be a latter-day Paul Morphy and retire at the height of his ability?

GAME 44

White: R. Fischer
Black: B. Ivkov (Yugoslavia)

*Played at Capablanca Memorial
International Tournament, Havana
(Cuba)—with Fischer in New York
playing via telephone-teletype—
September 10, 1965, Round 10*

A game of changing fortunes. Ivkov
obtains some advantage in the early
middle game but then overlooks
a *Zwischenzug,* after which chances
are about equal. An attempt by
Black to continue playing for a win
allows White the better chances. But
Fischer comes up with a series of
weak moves and quickly lands in
a lost position. The first tournament
game Bobby had lost in almost three
years!

Ruy Lopez (Closed)

1	P-K4	P-K4
2	N-KB3	N-QB3
3	B-N5	P-QR3
4	B-R4	N-B3
5	O-O	B-K2
6	R-K1	P-QN4
7	B-N3	O-O
8	P-B3	P-Q3
9	P-KR3	N-QR4
10	B-B2	P-B4
11	P-Q4	N-Q2

So far the game is exactly like Game
39, where Fischer continued with
the inferior 12 P-Q5?. Here he
reverts to the idea which had given
him a fine win against Keres at
Curaçao 1962.

12	PxBP	PxP
13	QN-Q2	P-B3

A slight improvement over 13 ...
Q-B2 which landed Keres in trouble,
since White's QN, when it arrives
on Q5, then does it with a gain of
tempo.

14 N-R4!   ...

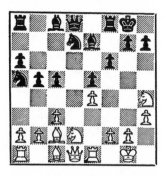

A powerful idea. Now that Black has
slightly weakened his Kingside,
White finds attacking objects there.

14 ...   N-N3

In Gilden–Karklins, 1973 U.S.
Championship, Black tried 14 ...
R-K1 without gaining equality: 15
N-B5, B-B1; 16 P-KR4!, P-N3; 17 N-K3,
N-N3; 18 P-R5, R-R2; 19 Q-B3 with

a clear plus for White, who went on to win in 34 moves. The problem with Black's position is that he has a weakened Kingside and no counterplay, whereas White has no weaknesses and fine attacking chances on the Kingside.

| 15 | N-B5 | R-B2 |
| 16 | NxB + ?! | ... |

Fischer spent 20 minutes on this move, but it simply cannot be fruitful to expend two tempos just to exchange off Black's inactive Bishop. He himself later pointed out that White keeps the advantage with 16 Q-N4, K-R1; 17 P-KR4! and if 17 ... P-N3; 18 N-R6!, R-N2; 19 Q-B3.

16	...	RxN
17	Q-B3	B-K3
18	N-B1	R-Q2!

Black has a considerable edge in development and stands very well. White's next order of business should be to complete his Queenside development. Thus a logical course was 19 P-QN3 with the idea 20 B-K3. As played, White runs into serious difficulties.

| 19 | N-K3?! | P-B5 |
| 20 | N-B5 | N-R5! |

A grandmasterly move. The Knight ties up White's Queenside and also at an opportune time threatens to move on to QB4 and Q6. Thus

White has nothing better than the following exchange, which, however, gives Black full command of his Q6 square and clear control of the Queen's file. These considerations far outweigh the Queenside Pawn weaknesses as White has no way of taking advantage of them.

21	BxN	PxB
22	B-K3	R-Q6
23	Q-N4	Q-Q2
24	B-B5	R-QB1
25	B-K7?!	...

Rather pointless. The normal moves 25 B-N4 or 25 B-R3 are preferable.

| 25 | ... | BxN! |
| 26 | QxB | ... |

Forced, as 26 PxB?? leaves the Bishop *en prise.*

| 26 | ... | N-B3 |
| 27 | B-B5 | ... |

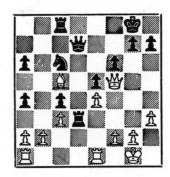

| 27 | ... | N-Q1? |

Ivkov was hoping to get the Knight to K3 with a gain of time, but is taken by surprise with a Fischer *Zwischenzug*. Correct play was 27 ... R-Q1 with a decided advantage for Black (28 B-N6?, R-N1).

| 28 | QxQ | RxQ |
| 29 | QR-Q1! | ... |

Thanks to the unfortunate Knight placement, White is able to neutralize the Queen's file. The chances are even.

| 29 | ... | R-Q6!? |

A risky attempt at winning. Safe equality results after 29 ... RxR; 30 RxR, N-K3; 31 B-R3, R-Q1! as after 32 RxR+; NxR there is no way White can take advantage of Black's weak Queenside Pawns.

30	B-R3!	N-B3
31	RxR	PxR
32	R-Q1	R-Q1
33	K-B1?	...

It is clear enough that the King should approach the QP, but this is a frightfully clumsy way. After the logical 33 P-B3! with the idea 34 K-B2, 35 K-K3 Black must play extremely accurately to hold the game. The only way seems 33 ... N-R4; 34 B-B5, N-B5; 35 P-QN3, PxP; 36 PxP, R-QB1!; 37 B-B2, N-R4!; 38 P-QN4, N-N6; 39 RxP, N-B8; 40 R-Q6 (or 40 R-K3, RxP! 41 RxR, N-K7+), 40 ... RxP; 41

RxRP, N-Q6! winning back the QNP thanks to the threat of 42 ... R-B8+; 43 K-R2, NxB. It can be said that Fischer's problems in this game occur because of his compulsion *not* to play P-KB3.

| 33 | ... | P-N3! |
| 34 | P-KN4? | ... |

A very serious and totally unnecessary weakening of the Kingside. 34 P-B3! leads to full equality.

| 34 | ... | P-B4! |
| 35 | NPxP? | ... |

THE LOSING MOMENT

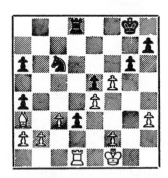

Too much is too much! White opens up the Kingside so Black can get in! The required move was 35 P-B3, with Black's position improved, but White should hold.

| 35 | ... | PxP |
| 36 | PxP?! | ... |

Bobby, please—36 P-B3!

36	...	P-K5
37	K-K1	...

This King move is no help, but the point of no return has already been passed. If 37 K-N2, R-Q4! wins.

37	...	N-K4
38	B-B5	N-B6+
39	K-B1	K-B2!
40	K-N2	...

Otherwise 40 ... R-KN1 will mate.

40	...	R-KN1+
41	K-R1	R-N8+

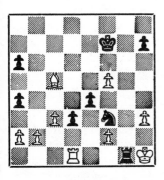

Ivkov spent over 30 minutes on this, the sealed move. It is not really certain what he was thinking about the whole time, as, chessically speaking, the move is a clear and simple way to win a piece for nothing. Maybe he was just enjoying the position!

42	RxR	...

Upon resumption of play, all the moves were played in virtual blitz tempo.

42	...	NxR
43	B-K3	N-B6
44	K-N2	P-Q7
45	BxP	NxB
46	K-N3	K-B3
47	K-B4	P-KR4
48	K-K3	N-B6
49	KxP	N-N4+
50	K-B4	NxP+
51	K-N3	N-N4
52	K-R4	KxP
53	KxP	N-K5

WHITE RESIGNS

A piece is a piece is a piece is a piece.

GAME 45

White: E. Geller (USSR)
Black: R. Fischer

Played at Capablanca Memorial International Tournament, Havana (Cuba)—with Fischer in New York playing via telephone-teletype—September 19, 1965, Round 17

Another positional masterpiece by Geller against Fischer. White obtains a slight advantage in the opening and steadily transforms it into a win. While it is true that with a super-perfect defense Fischer may have escaped with a draw, in actual practice such unpleasantly inferior positions invariably lead to a loss.

*King's Indian Defense
(Samisch Variation)*

1	P-QB4	P-KN3
2	N-QB3	B-N2
3	P-Q4	N-KB3
4	P-K4	P-Q3
5	P-B3	...

The Samisch again—but for the last time in this book! The reason for the lack of further appearances is not that Fischer suddenly acquired fantastic expertise against the Samisch, but that he simply decided not to play the King's Indian if there was a realistic danger of having to meet the Samisch. He has been very successful in this new "prep-aration"—since this game he's had to cope with only two more Samisches!

5	...	P-B3

Two rounds earlier against Jimenez of Cuba, Bobby tried 5 ... O-O; 6 ... P-N3; 7 ... B-N2 but stood slightly worse all the way through before offering a draw on move 50. So here Fischer tries something new for him: the system called the Byrne Variation, named after American grandmaster Robert Byrne, who has over a ten-year period demonstrated its playability. Black's idea is to start counterplay as quickly as pos-sible on the Queenside with ... P-QR3 and ... P-QN4.

6	B-K3	P-QR3
7	B-Q3	...

The sharpest method for White is 7 Q-Q2 followed by 8 O-O-O and an attack on the Kingside with P-KR4, B-KR6, etc. Understandably, Geller has no interest in sharp tactics against Fischer at so early a stage. A healthy, sound position is his aim.

7	...	P-QN4?!

Modern master practice has shown that the required course is first 7 ... QN-Q2 to prevent White's P-K5.

8	PxP?!	...

The way to take advantage of Black's last move is 8 P-K5!, KN-Q2!; 9 P-B4 with a clear space superiority for White.

8	...	RPxP
9	KN-K2	O-O
10	P-QN4	QN-Q2
11	O-O	B-N2?!

Now Black will forever have a passive and cramped position. A much better way is 11 ... N-N3 as Black has no need to fear 12 P-QR4, PxP; 13 NxP, B-QR3!; 14 BxB, RxB; 15 Q-N3, Q-N1 with equality, as in Pachman–Geller, Moscow 1967.

12	Q-Q2	P-K4
13	KR-Q1!	PxP
14	NxQP	N-K4
15	B-B1	N3–Q2
16	P-QR4!	N-N3
17	Q-QB2!	PxP
18	NxRP	NxN
19	RxN	RxR
20	QxR	...

The multiple exchanges have not lightened Black's task. He is stuck with a chronically weak QP; also. the QBP is weak and the QB has no scope. The net result is that Black's position is very uncomfortable, with Herculean efforts required for a draw and no chances for a win.

20	...	Q-K2
21	Q-N3	R-R1
22	N-B2	B-QB1
23	N-Q4	B-Q2?

Geller has started to feel the approaching time pressure, with about 17 minutes left for 17 moves. Thus to gain time he begins repeating moves. Fischer's last is both a psychological and practical error. In the first place, 23 ... B-N2 would have repeated the position and it is possible that against a Fischer, Geller may have felt that a draw in hand is worth more than a win in the bush. Secondly, the Bishop is poorly placed at Q2 as it takes away that square for a Knight retreat and also interferes with protection of the QP via a R-Q1.

24	P-R3!	R-N1
25	Q-R3	P-Q4

An unpleasant choice, as it allows White's QNP to become passed and saddles Black with an isolated QP, yet there was no other satisfactory way to counter White's threatened 26 P-B4.

26	PxP	PxP
27	N-B2	BxP?!

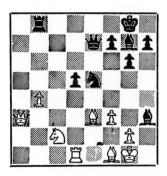

With Geller now in more acute time pressure, Fischer characteristically attempts active counterplay where tenacious defense is probably a better bet. The other way of going for complications, 27 ... N-B5, is also unsatisfactory: 28 Q-R7!, R-Q1; 29 RxP, NxB; 30 QxN! and Black is a Pawn down for nothing. One more example of the principle that going for complications from an inferior base position usually tends to boomerang. The patient 27 ... B-K3 or possibly 27 ... B-B4 was better.

28 B-B5!   ...

It is very difficult to prove (or disprove for that matter) whether Black gets enough for the piece after 28 PxB, NxP+ 29 K-B2!, Q-B3 30 K-N3!, yet it is clear that his practical chances are considerable.

28	...	Q-N4
29	P-B4	Q-R4
30	RxP	...

Geller again goes for "safety first," as after 30 R-Q2!? Black may retain sufficient counterchances with 30 ... B-B4!; 31 PxN, BxP (but not with 30 ... B-R3; 31 B-Q6!, BxBP; 32 BxR, BxR; 33 QxB).

30	...	B-B4
31	N-K3	N-N5
32	NxN	QxN
33	Q-R7!	R-K1
34	Q-B7	P-R4
35	R-Q8	RxR
36	QxR+	K-R2
37	B-K3!	...

Despite all Fischer's efforts, the net result is that White has a very strong passed QNP. The only glimmer of hope for Black is sufficient play against White's King.

37 ...   B-R3?

THE LOSING MOMENT

In his haste to "put Geller over," Bobby forgets that White can also have threats. Absolutely required was 37 ... P-R5! to try to exchange White's KNP and thus have White's King exposed enough to allow the possibility of a perpetual check. The draw is not guaranteed, but chances for it are reasonable.

| 38 | Q-B6! | ... |

The brutal threat of 39 B-Q4 forces Black's reply and White then is a clear Pawn ahead.

38	...	B-N2
39	QxBP	Q-Q8
40	Q-B4	P-R5?!

Now the Pawn is weak here without accomplishing anything positive. An immediate 40 ... Q-R8 was a shade better.

| 41 | Q-K2 | ... |

The sealed move.

| 41 | ... | Q-R8 |
| 42 | K-R2! | ... |

Unpinning the King. The win is not elementary, yet must be considered as a "matter of technique." After all, what is a grandmaster for, if not to win a game where he is a clear passed Pawn ahead?

| 42 | ... | B-Q5 |

Not fully satisfactory, but then again, nothing is.

| 43 | B-B2! | BxB |
| 44 | QxB | ... |

The weakness of Black's KRP is now readily apparent.

44	...	K-N2
45	P-N5	B-K5
46	P-N6	B-N2
47	Q-K2!	K-B3
48	Q-Q3	K-K2
49	Q-B4	K-B3
50	Q-Q3	...

Geller repeats moves to save time and thus to enable him to calculate the resulting King and Pawn end-game at his (relative) leisure.

| 50 | ... | K-K2 |
| 51 | Q-K3+ | K-Q3 |

The same reply would also follow on 51 ... K-B3.

52	B-K2!	Q-N7
53	B-B3	BxB
54	Q-K5+	QxQ
55	PxQ+	KxP

If Black tries to prevent the game continuation with 55 ... K-B3; 56 PxP, P-N4 White queens one of his Pawns after 57 P-K6.

| 56 | PxB | K-Q3 |
| 57 | P-B4! | ... |

BLACK RESIGNS

White wins by exactly one tempo after 57 ... K-B3; 58 K-R3, KxP; 59 KxP, K-B3; 60 K-N5, K-Q2; 61 KxP, K-K2; 62 P-B5, K-B1; 63 K-B6!, K-N1; 64 K-K7, etc.

White: R. Fischer
Black: R. Cholmov (USSR)

*Played at Capablanca Memorial
International Tournament, Havana
(Cuba)—with Fischer in New York
playing via telephone-teletype—
September 20, 1965, Round 18*

An outstanding strategic effort by
the Soviet grandmaster. Cholmov
comes up with a significant opening
innovation, follows it up with a
tactical shot, and then by positional
means transforms his superiority into
a win. A disappointing effort for
Bobby, as he is never in the game.

Ruy Lopez (Closed)

1	P-K4	P-K4
2	N-KB3	N-QB3
3	B-N5	P-QR3
4	B-R4	N-B3
5	O-O	B-K2
6	R-K1	P-QN4
7	B-N3	O-O
8	P-B3	P-Q3
9	P-KR3	N-QR4
10	B-B2	P-B4
11	P-Q4	Q-B2

The basic Tchigorin position which
we met in Game 5.

12	QN-Q2	N-B3

Over the years this has been thought
of as Black's most solid continuation: Black undertakes nothing and
tries to set up a healthy formation
against White's central play.

13 PxBP   . . .

The significant advances in chess
understanding during the last 10 to
15 years have *not* been the discovery
of new variations or even new
openings. After all, new discoveries
are simply the reflection of a living
science—including chess. What is
revolutionary is the large number
of ideas, formerly thought to be
worthless, which are now found to
be excellent, because the true concept behind the idea has been
discovered and understood.
For many years 13 P-Q5 had been
thought to be a duffer's move here,
yet Geller has shown that it is
actually White's best continuation!
After 13 . . . N-Q1 (if 13 . . . N-QR4;
14 P-QN3! and the QN looks
stranded, while White starts play on
the Kingside) 14 P-QR4!, R-N1 15
P-QN4! and White has a space
advantage everywhere while Black
can only sit back and suffer. The
text move, as has already been
pointed out several times, fits
Fischer's Ruy Lopez tastes and up
to the very recent years was thought
to be White's best. The point of
Black's system, of course, is that
because of the pressure against
White's QP White is prevented

from continuing with his normal development, e.g., 13 N-B1, BPxP; 14 PxP, NxQP!; 15 NxN, PxN and the unprotected status of the KB prevents White's 16 QxP and allows Black full equality.

13	...	PxP
14	N-B1	B-K3
15	N-K3	QR-Q1
16	Q-K2	P-B5!

This in combination with the next move is a significant innovation. After the formerly automatic 16 ... P-N3; 17 N-N5, B-B1; 18 P-QR4 White has a small yet noticeable advantage.

17	N-N5	...

After this logical move was shown to be fruitless, White's attention turned to 17 N-B5. It is a fully riskless continuation for White, but after some initial difficulties for Black, a satisfactory equalizing method was found: 17 ... KR-K1!; 18 B-N5, N-Q2; 19 BxB, NxB; 20 N-N5, N-B1!

17	...	P-R3!

A great idea! Black not only ignores White's threat of gaining the two Bishops while ruining Black's Kingside Pawn formation, but even forces White to execute it immediately! Normally Black cannot afford such weaknesses, but the position is just uniquely different here: all of White's pieces are passively placed and Black has a preponderance of key squares in his command after 18 NxB. There have been subsequent attempts to try to save the "unnecessary 17 ... P-R3" tempo for Black, but without positive results (e.g., 17 ... B-QB4; 18 N-Q5!). And an especially negative result came from the immediate piece sacrifice 17 ... N-Q5? After 18 PxN, PxP; 19 P-K5!, P-Q6; 20 NxB, PxN; 21 PxN!, PxQ; 22 PxB, QxP; 23 RxP, White's three minor pieces turned out to be stronger than Black's Queen and he won easily in Matulovic–Mecking, Sousse 1967.

18	NxB	PxN
19	P-QN4?	...

THE LOSING MOMENT

Bobby thought almost half an hour before this lemon, and there is no rational explanation for it except that he is having an off day. White not only ignores Black's tactical possibility, but even makes sure that it is extra powerful! Sufficient to keep the game in balance is 19 P-QR4, and 19 P-QN3 was also good enough in Suetin–Nei, Vilnyus 1967 for equality: 19 ... B-B4; 20 R-Q1, N-Q5!; 21 PxN, KPxP; 22 NxP, PxN; 23 PxP, P-Q6!; 24 RxP, N-N5!; 25 QxN, RxP; 26 B-K3, BxB; 27 RxB, RxB. A fine (or frightful!) example of the theoretical knowledge a modern master must have to survive in the chess jungle.

19	...	N-Q5!!
20	PxN	PxP
21	P-R3	...

It is obvious that Black must win back a piece anyway, so White protects the loose QNP. It is possible that Bobby had originally expected to play here 21 P-K5 (with the idea 21 ... QxP?; 22 N-B5!), but now noted that Black gets a won game after 21 ... P-Q6!; 22 PxN, BxBP!; e.g., 23 Q-N4, BxR; 24 QxKP+, Q-B2; 25 QxQ+, KxQ!; 26 B-Q1, P-Q7; 27 BxP, RxB; 28 B-R5+, P-N3; 29 RxB, PxB (as pointed out by Cholmov).

| 21 | ... | P-Q6! |

Good enough for equality was 21 ... PxN and 22 ... P-K4, but understandably Black goes for more.

| 22 | BxP | RxB |

Black now has a decided advantage: passed protected QBP, control of the Queen's file, White's weak KP. Silly would be 22 ... PxB?; 23 Q-R2!, K-R1! though Black is still okay.

| 23 | N-N4?! | ... |

The exchange of Knights turns out to be in Black's favor as he is then left with the superior Bishop. Therefore 23 N-B1 was worth a try.

| 23 | ... | K-R2! |
| 24 | P-K5?! | ... |

There is nothing good to suggest for White, yet the Pawn is a new fundamental weakness.

| 24 | ... | NxN |
| 25 | Q-K4+ | ... |

A waste of time.

25	...	P-N3
26	QxN	R-B4!
27	Q-K4	Q-Q2
28	B-K3	Q-Q4!
29	QxQ	...

29 ...   RxQ

The safe way to recapture, as Black
retains all of his previous advantages
while not allowing any counterplay.
However, 29 ... PxQ was equally
good, giving Black two connected
passed Pawns. In his recollections
of the game, Cholmov stated that
after considerable thought he
decided against it because of White's
strong counterplay after 30 B-B5. Yet
official time records show that Black
spent only one minute on the move!
What happened was that, understandably enough, Cholmov rather
automatically played the safe text
move against a Fischer. In fact, after
29 ... PxQ; 30 B-B5, R-B2!; 31
QR-Q1, RxR; 32 RxR, BxB; 33 PxB,
P-B6! Black wins rather easily.

30 P-B4   P-N4?!

But this second automatic "blitz"
tempo (two minutes' thought!) move
makes Black's job considerably
harder as White now is able to
protect his KP. Much stronger was
30 ... B-R5! and only after 31
R-KB1, P-N4!. Also unsatisfactory
for White was 31 KR-Q1, B-N6!; 32
RxR, PxR; 33 R-Q1, BxP; 34 BxB, RxB;
35 RxP, P-B6; 36 R-B5, R-B5, and
Black wins (Cholmov).

31	P-N3	PxP
32	PxP	R-B1!
33	K-N2	K-N3
34	R-KN1	R-Q6
35	K-B3+	K-B4!

At first glance somewhat dangerous,
yet help of the King is now required
for Black to make progress.

36	R-N7	B-Q1
37	R-N7	...

Required to prevent Black's 37 ...
B-N3. A pretty idea for White was
37 QR-KN1, so that if 37 ... B-N3??;
38 KR (or QR)-N5+!!, PxR; 39 RxP
mate!, but Black can cross White
up by 37 ... RxB+!; 38 KxR, B-N3+
followed by 39 ... BxR and a won
Rook and Pawn endgame.

37	...	R-N1
38	R-N8	...

Somewhat better was 38 R-KB7+,
K-N3; 39 R-QN7, K-R4!; 40 R-R2!,
B-R5; 41 K-K4, R-KN6; 42 B-B5,
though Black still must win after
42 ... R-Q8! (threat 43 ... R-K8+;
44 K-Q4, R-Q6 mate).

38	...	R-N2

Good enough to win, as the threat
of ... B-R5 and ... R-KN6+ is
renewed. Somewhat faster was 38
... P-KR4! with the same type of
idea ... P-R5 and and ... R-KN6+.

39	P-QR4	...

The position is lost and has been for
some time now. From the standpoint of further resistance 39 R-R2
was better, even though Black still
wins: 39 ... P-KR4; 40 R-Q2, RxR;

41 BxR, R-Q2; 42 B-K3, R-Q6!; 43
P-KR4, P-B6!; 44 K-K2, K-K5 etc.

39	...	P-KR4
40	PxP	PxP
41	RxP	...

Rather hopeless, yet 41 R1-R8, P-R5;
42 RxB, R-N6+; 43 K-B2, R/Q6xB
also leads to an easily won endgame
for Black. Now, however, all of
Black's pieces penetrate.

41	...	B-R5!
42	K-K2	R-N7+
43	K-B1	R-KR7
44	K-N1	...

If 44 B-N1, R-KB6+!

44	...	R-K7
45	B-N6	P-B6
46	K-B1	R-KR7

WHITE RESIGNS

What is White to do? If 47 K-N1,
R6xP; 48 R5-R5, P-B7; 49 P-N5,
R-R8+; 50 K-N2, R6-R7+; 51 K-B3,
P-B8(Q) and Black will be a Rook
ahead. One of the few games where
Fischer was behind his opponent in
time remaining all the way through!

GAME 47

White: R. Fischer
Black: R. Byrne (United States)

*Played in the U.S. Championship,
New York, December 1965,
Round 8*

Leading the field by two points
Fischer decides on an opening's
experiment. The experiment misfires
and is followed by a blunder which
quickly leads to a lost game
an exchange down. Only inertia
causes Bobby to play on as long as
he does.

French Defense (Tarrasch–Guimard)

1	P-K4	P-K3
2	P-Q4	P-Q4
3	N-Q2	...

The Tarrasch Variation is one of
many ideas of the German grandmaster and teacher Dr. Siegbert
Tarrasch (1862–1934) which have
stood the test of time. White
prevents the Winawer and enables
the QBP to support Q4 if so
required. As slight minuses (compared to 3 N-QB3) it must be said
that the Knight has less central
influence here and the QB is temporarily blocked. Overall, however,
the type of positions which result
allow White to retain a small yet
riskless initiative for many moves to
come. This is exactly the situation
that Bobby strives for as White,
thus the Tarrasch should suit him to
a T. Yet this is the only game where
he has played it! He has often stated
that the Winawer must be refutable
and he has continued to search
for the stone which can be turned
into gold. This is the only opening
where the mature Fischer still shows
signs of the "youthful stubbornness."

3	...	N-QB3

Argentinian grandmaster Guimard
introduced this into international
tournament practice in the middle
1940s. The idea is to put immediate
piece pressure on White's center.
The voluntary blocking of the QBP
makes the move a bit suspect positionally, though. The soundest way
to go for full equality is 3 ... P-QB4
but the resulting positions give
Black hardly any practical winning
chances. Of medium positional and
practical risk is 3 ... N-KB3.

4	P-QB3	...

This logical but too easygoing move
allows Black's surprising rejoinder.
Best for White is 4 KN-B3, N-B3;
5 P-K5, N-Q2; 6 N-N3, and Black
must work long and hard for the
potential equality.

4	...	P-K4!

Black now is able to undermine White's center and open lines for his own pieces, giving approximately even chances.

5	KPxP	QxP
6	KN-B3	PxP

The correct order of moves is very critical for Black. Wrong is 6 ... B-KN5?; 7 B-B4, BxN; 8 Q-N3!, Q-Q2; 9 NxB, with a huge advantage for White, as in Keres–Botvinnik, Moscow 1955.

7	B-B4	Q-KR4!
8	O-O	N-B3!

The preparation for Kingside castling is sounder than 8 ... B-K3 aiming for ... O-O-O.

9	Q-K1+?	...

At that moment in his career, R. Byrne was known to play the Guimard–French rather consistently, so that Fischer could prepare for it. The text move, planning to pin Black's KB, has a shallow point, which is completely overcome by Byrne's much deeper point. White has nothing better here than 9 PxP, B-K2; 10 P-QR3 (or 10 R-K1), 10 ... O-O; 11 P-QN4, B-Q3, with equality, as in Bouwmeester–Hort, Varna 1962.

9	...	B-K2
10	NxP	O-O!!

Black simply ignores White's threat. After the intended 11 NxN, 11 ... B-Q3! regains the piece with a strong attack: e.g., 12 N-K7+, K-R1; 13 N-B3 (13 P-KR3 BxP!), B-KN5, etc. Bobby's move, exchanging off a couple of minor pieces to reduce Black's attacking power is the right approach.

11	B-K2	B-KN5
12	NxN??	...

THE LOSING MOMENT

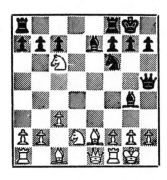

But what is this? In a moment of chess blindness White allows with greater force exactly what a move earlier he prevented! Required was 12 BxB. After 12 ... NxB; 13 N2-B3 (or 13 P-KR3, N5-K4), NxN; 14 PxN, B-Q3 Black already has the advantage but White should hold the draw.

12	...	B-Q3!

The mate threat wins an exchange.

13	P-KR3	. . .

Even worse is 13 P-KB4, BxB; 14
R-B2, N-N5!

13	. . .	BxB
14	N-Q4	BxR
15	QxB	. . .

So Black is a clear exchange up in
an obviously superior position and
it can be said very accurately that
"the rest is a matter of technique."
If in a dream, I or other masters
could choose our superior middle-
game position against Bobby, we
would choose Byrne's position here:
Black has a definite material advantage and White has absolutely
no counterchances anywhere.

15	. . .	KR-K1
16	N2-B3	P-QR3
17	B-N5	Q-N3
18	R-Q1	R-K5
19	B-K3	N-Q4!
20	B-B1	QR-K1

Black has command of the open
King's file.

21	N-Q2	R5-K2
22	N-B4	B-B5

Offering to chop wood.

23	N-B3	P-QB3
24	N-N6	BxB!
25	NxN	PxN

Black is not going to quibble over
an isolated Pawn here, as the Rook
penetration to the seventh rank
will be quickly decisive.

26	RxB	R-K7
27	R-N1	Q-B7!

Threatening 28 . . . RxP!; 29 QxR,
QxR+.

28	R-B1	. . .

Or 28 N-Q4, QxR!; 29 QxQ, R-K8+

28	. . .	QxNP
29	R-N1	QxBP
30	RxP	RxRP
31	K-R2	. . .

Why is Bobby playing on?

31	...	P-R3	34	QxQ	RxQ
32	Q-QN1	RxP	35	PxR	R-Q1
33	Q-B5	QxN	36	R-N6	P-Q5

WHITE RESIGNS

Or 33 ... RxN or 33 ... Q-KB3
or ...

Not too soon!

GAME 48

White: S. Reshevsky (United States)
Black: R. Fischer

*Played in the United States
Championship, New York,
December 1965, Round 9*

After uncharacteristically passive
play in the opening, Fischer lands in
a strategically inferior position.
Blending strategy and tactics perfectly, Reshevsky obtains a decisive
material advantage and wins convincingly. The length of the game is
somewhat deceptive: it is Sammy's
game all the way.

*Nimzo-Indian Defense
(Rubinstein Variation)*

1	**P-Q4**	**N-KB3**
2	**P-QB4**	**P-K3**
3	**N-QB3**	**B-N5**
4	**P-K3**	**P-QN3**

During the 1960s and through 1970
this variation was Bobby's method
against the Rubinstein. Of course,
he obtained fine results with it and
made many contributions to opening
theory. It was clear to him that the
Russians were prepared for it in
1972 and he crossed them up by not
utilizing the variation against
Spassky! What will he play in the

1975 World Championship Match?
Wait and see!
The most common method for Black
is 4 ... P-B4 and the noncommittal
4 ... O-O also has many adherents.
The dubious 4 ... P-Q4?! was seen
in Game 16. The point of 4 ...
P-QN3 is simple enough: Black
prepares to develop his QB on the
center diagonal (or after 5 KN-K2,
B-R3 against White's QBP) without
first committing his QBP or Queen's
Pawn. In the actual execution
Black must be most careful that
White does not achieve a sub-
stantial central superiority.

5	**B-Q3**	...

This normal developmental move is
one of two alternatives here, the
other being 5 KN-K2 with the idea
6 P-QR3, so that in case of 6 ...
BxN+ White can avoid doubled
Pawns by recapturing with the
Knight.

5	...	**B-N2**
6	**N-B3**	**O-O**

Black has truly a wide choice here.
He can start immediate central
action with either 6 ... P-B4 or
6 ... P-Q4. The most consistent
follow-up of the QB fianchetto is
6 ... N-K5. After 7 Q-B2, P-KB4!
Black has a grip on White's K4 and
equal chances. White's only real
try for an initiative is the Pawn
sacrifice 7 O-O! If Black takes the

Pawn, either way, White obtains more than enough compensation. Here too the best move is 7 . . . P-KB4, with reasonable chances for eventual equalization.

7   O-O   KBxN

Playable also is 7 . . . P-Q4 or 7 . . . P-B4.

8   PxB   B-K5

As Fischer has played this way for a second time—also against Reshevsky at Buenos Aires 1970, we can be pretty sure that Bobby is convinced of its fundamental soundness. Black tries to ensure possession of his K5 square, prior to starting to fix White's doubled QBPs with . . . P-QB4.

9   Q-B2!?   . . .

A most interesting strategic position has resulted after Black's 8th move. Reshevsky had already encountered it in his 1938 AVRO tournament game against Alekhine. There he had continued with 9 BxB, NxB; 10 Q-B2, but after 10 . . . P-KB4; 11 N-K5, Q-B1; 12 P-B3, N-KB3; 13 B-R3, P-Q3; 14 N-Q3, P-B4 Alekhine (Black) stood very well. Also known is the Bishop retreat 9 B-K2. Reshevsky used it in his 1970 Buenos Aires game against Fischer.

After 9 . . . P-B4; 10 N-Q2, B-N3; 11 B-B3, N-B3; 12 B-R3, R-B1; 13 PxP, Q-K2; 14 N-N3, N-K4 chances were about even and the very interesting game ended a draw on Move 41. The text move is a double-edged attempt at forcing an immediate decision from Black regarding what he is going to do about his BK5.

9   . . .   BxB?

As we know Bobby had lost in the previous round to R. Byrne. For this reason, in one of the very rare instances in his career, Bobby here decided to play safely for a draw. To achieve a draw, what is required is not safe moves, but *good* moves! Bobby, of course, knows this better than anybody else, for he has won countless games where his opponents were hoping for a draw. Yet here the master himself slips on the same pavement. In his *My 60 Memorable Games* Fischer recommends as playable 9 . . . BxN; 10 PxN, P-B4 with a fantastically unbalanced position. In the 1970 game, Reshevsky apparently had no interest in this position for White. A reasonable safe continuation is 9 . . . P-Q4 with only a slight plus for White.

10   QxB   P-Q3?

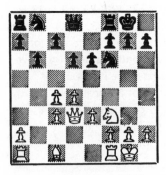

It seems rather harsh to call this early move the losing moment. Yet the strategic idea behind it is quite wrong, and against Reshevsky's thematic play Black just has no chance for a recovery. Correct was still 10 ... P-Q4; White has the advantage, but Black has reasonable chances for eventual equality.

| 11 | P-K4 | P-K4 |

This central Pawn formation would be quite satisfactory for Black *if* the white Bishops were still on the board. Then White's Bishop on Q3 would be locked in by his own Pawns and would be quite "bad," whereas Black's QB could be used effectively for both offensive and defensive purpose. But with the Bishops exchanged, White has no liabilities while Black has no strengths. Two individual superiorities: central influence and the QB being better than the counterpart Black Knight give White an overall decisive strategic superiority.

12	B-N5!	QN-Q2
13	N-R4!	P-KR3
14	B-Q2!	R-K1

This routine regrouping turns out to be fruitless. Maybe a better try was 14 ... K-R2 and 15 ... N-KN1.

15	QR-K1	N-B1
16	N-B5	N-N3
17	P-B4!	...

With all preparations complete, White starts a positional Kingside attack against which Black is defenseless. There are no improvements I can suggest in Black's play from now on; his position is surprisingly helpless.

| 17 | | PxQP |

There is only a choice of major evils. If 17 ... PxBP; 18 BxP, NxB; 19 RxN followed by doubling Rooks on the KB file would also give White a winning attack. From the standpoint of positional considerations this may have been worth a try, however, because if White misplays the attack, Black at least would be left with the superior Pawn formation.

18	PxP	P-B3
19	P-Q5!	PxP
20	BPxP	N-K2
21	N-N3	...

No need to lighten Black's burdens by exchanging off attackers.

21	...	R-QB1
22	B-B3	N-N3
23	B-Q4	K-R2
24	N-B5	R-B2

After 24 ... N-K2 the simplest win is 25 NxRP!

25	K-R1	R-N1
26	R-K3	N-R4
27	R3-B3	N-B3
28	R-R3	P-N4
29	P-N4!	...

Wins by force. The threat of 30 P-N5 can only be prevented by taking off the Pawn.

29	...	NxNP
30	Q-KN3	Q-K1

There is nothing else, as 30 ... N-B3 is met by 31 Q-N5! and there is no good way to prevent mayhem starting with 32 RxP+! (If 31 ... Q-KB1, first 32 BxN.)

31	NxQP	Q-K2
32	P-K5	N-B3
33	P-B5!	...

Wins at least a piece as both Knights are now under definitive attack.

33	...	NxQP

34	PxN+	...

There is no objective basis for criticizing this and the next move, as White's clear material superiority must be decisive in the long run. For those interested in the mathematically fastest wins it can be pointed out that 34 P-K6! with the brutal threat 35 PxP would have won sooner. After the only reasonable try, 34 ... N3-B5 White plays 35 NxBP! and the dual threat of 36 QxP+!!, RxQ; 37 RxP+, K-N1; 38 R-R8 mate, and 36 N-N5+, K-R1; 37 RxP mate cannot be prevented in a reasonable way. Of course, 35 ... NxR allows 36 Q-N6 mate.

34	...	PxP
35	N-B7	QxN

The threat was 36 N-N5+ followed by 37 P-K6 and 35 ... R-KB1 loses to, e.g., 36 P-K6, R-B5; 37 Q-K5,

N-B3; 38 RxN!, PxR; 39 Q-N5!! (39
... PxQ; 40 RxP+ and 41 R-R8
mate)—often in won positions many
beautiful combinations become
possible!

36	RxQ	RxR
37	P-K6	R-B8+
38	K-N2	R-B4
39	R-R4	R-K1
40	Q-Q6	R1-KB1
41	P-KR3	R-B1
42	R-K4	...

The sealed move. As Reshevsky
correctly points out, a faster win was
to be had with 42 Q-Q7, R-QB2;
43 R-K4! Then White threatens
decisively 44 BxNP! Of course after
the text move White must win also—
after all, he is a Queen ahead.

42	...	R-QB7+
43	K-N3	R-Q7

Or 43 ... N-B6; 44 R-K1, R-Q4;
45 Q-Q7! (Reshevsky).

44	P-K7	R-N4+
45	R-N4	NxP

Immediately losing was 45 ...
RxR+; 46 PxR!, NxP; 47 Q-K5, as
Black lacks ... N-B4+.

46	RxR	PxR
47	QxN	RxB
48	QxRP	...

In a way this endgame is similar to
that in Game 7: both were Queen
and Pawns vs Rook and Pawns, and
White had only one way of winning
and this thanks to *Zugzwang*. Yet,
one way is more than enough. So
also here.

48	...	R-KB5
49	Q-K7	R-B4
50	Q-K8!	R-B4

Black cannot prevent White's King
from reaching the Queenside as 50
... P-QN5 is no better after 51
K-N4, e.g., 51 ... R-R4; 52 Q-K6,
R-KB4; 53 Q-N3, R-N4; 54 Q-R4, etc.

51	K-B3	R-B7
52	Q-K6	R-B8
53	Q-N3	R-B4
54	K-K4	R-B4
55	K-Q4	K-R1

55 ... K-R3 56 Q-N8 loses as shown
later in the game.

56	K-B3!	K-R2

In the King and Pawn ending after 56 ... R-B6+; 57 K-N4, RxQ+; 58 PxR, White makes a new Queen ahead of Black and then wins the Queen vs three KNP endgame the usual way.

57	K-N4	R-K4
58	P-R3	K-R3

Black chooses the fastest way out of his agony. Otherwise White would again achieve a won King and Pawn endgame by an appropriately timed QxQNP Queen sacrifice.

59	Q-N8	P-N5
60	P-KR4	P-N4
61	P-R5!	....

BLACK RESIGNS

Black's only choice is whether he prefers to be mated by Q-KR7 or Q-KR8.

GAME 49

White: R. Fischer
Black: B. Larsen (Denmark)

*Played at the Second Piatigorsky
Cup International Tournament,
Santa Monica (California),
July 25, 1966, Round 6*

A tough fight between two great
fighters which Larsen deemed worth
including in his book of best games.
Somewhat untypically, Fischer goes
for mate from the very beginning,
only to make an inconsistent
defensive move at a critical junction.
The game is still in balance when
Bobby in *Larsen's* time pressure has
a hallucination. A most shockingly
sudden end.

Ruy Lopez (Open)

1	P-K4	P-K4
2	N-KB3	N-QB3
3	B-N5	P-QR3
4	B-R4	N-B3
5	O-O	NxP

Rather appropriately, this variation
is named "Open Variation" since
the resulting positions definitely
have an open, tactical nature. This
is especially true when comparison
is made to the Closed Variation—
5 . . . B-K2. Which is better for
Black, the Open or Closed Variation? Well, the Closed Variation is

played much more often in master
tournaments so it must be better,
right? No, not really. True enough,
White obtains some pull in the
Open Variation, but as master
practice over the last ten years has
shown, the Closed Variation is no
bed of roses either for Black. The
reason for the lack of popularity
of the Open Variation is based
on the selection of the opening
as part of the general game
plan. If Black wants an unbalanced
open fight he usually selects the
Sicilian or Alekhine or Pirc defenses.
As a reply to 1 P-K4, 1 . . . P-K4 is
usually chosen with a view to a
positional, strategic, maneuvering
type of game; the Closed Variation
fullfils this objective admirably while
the Open does not.

Shortly before the beginning of this
tournament, Larsen had completed
writing a monograph on the Open
Variation where he recommended its
adoption for the "club player."
Thus he was fairly familiar with
its ideas and ready to try them out.
Since the publication of the booklet,
Larsen, however, has rarely played
the variation which he officially
championed. Paradoxical? In a way,
yes, but there is a practical side to
it too: his opponents had the opportunity to prepare for it, especially
by looking for possible holes in
Larsen's analysis.

6	P-Q4	. . .

White should try to open the position against Black's King as quickly as possible. The reasonable looking 6 R-K1 yields no advantage after 6 ... N-B4!

6 ... P-QN4

The Riga Variation (6 ... PxP; 7 R-K1, P-Q4) does not lead to a forced loss for Black—"only" an inferior position.

7 B-N3 P-Q4

Here too, 7 ... PxP; 8 R-K1, P-Q4; 9 N-B3! leads to a clear advantage for White.

8 PxP ...

Apparently not quite satisfied with the opening results in this game and in Round 14 against Unzicker, Fischer employed the quieter 8 NxP against Addison in the 1966-67 U.S. Championship. After White missed an opportunity for some advantage, the game quickly petered out into a draw.

8 ... B-K3
9 P-B3 ...

The older and more positional of two good continuations. With the aggressive 9 Q-K2 Bobby scored a convincing victory against Ree at Netanya 1968. As far as Fischer is concerned, that is his "last word" in the Open Variation.

9 ... B-QB4

An aggressive Bishop placement against White's KB2. The move does also have negative aspects: the Kingside is less protected and the QB4 square is taken away from Black's Knight or possibly the QBP. The safer continuation is 9 ... B-K2, as played by Unzicker in Round 14. Inferior to the Bishop moves is 9 ... N-B4.

10 QN-Q2 O-O
11 B-B2 ...

Black must now decide what to do about his attacked Knight: should he exchange it with 11 ... NxN, protect it by 11 ... P-B4, or sacrifice it after 11 ... NxKBP. Objectively, all these possibilities are of equivalent value; however, the nature of the resulting positions is much different. In each case, with super-perfect play Black can eventually hope to equalize.

11 ... B-B4

A relatively new idea at the time of this game: an alternative, though unusual because of the time loss, way of protecting the Knight. It's about as good as the other moves mentioned above.

12 N-N3 B-KN5

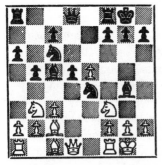

White already had the material threat of 13 NxB, winning a piece and the positional threat of 13 KN-Q4. A subsequent innovation, 12 ... B-KN3, was shown to be clearly inferior in Karpov–Savon, Moscow 1971 after 13 KN-Q4!

13 NxB ...

The immediate unpinning 13 Q-K1! is worthy of note. After 13 ... BxN 14 PxB, N-N4 15 Q-K2, White has good attacking chances along the open KN file, and if instead 14 ... NxKP then 15 K-N2! wins material.

13 ... **NxN**
14 R-K1 ...

As seen on the next move Fischer has a new idea. The most accurate execution, however, was an immediate 14 B-K3!. If then 14 ... N-K3, we get a forced transposition into the game continuation after 15 Q-Q3, P-N3, etc. And 14 ... N-Q2; 15 Q-Q3, P-N3; 16 QxQP, N/Q2xP, leads to an endgame where theo-

retically Black may be close to equality, but in practice the two-Bishops advantage in an open position would allow Bobby to grind on for the next 50 or so moves.

14 ... **R-K1**
15 B-K3 ...

Instead of the previously played defensive 15 B-B4, Fischer chases away the well-placed Knight.

15 ... **N-K3**
16 Q-Q3 P-N3?

Whether this is a decisive error or not depends on the correct evaluation of the position after Black's 27th move. In any case, we can safely say that it is foolish for Black to voluntarily weaken the black squares in front of his King. The sound alternative was 16 ... N-B1.

17 B-R6 N-K2

According to Larsen, the exchange of the white Bishops leads to a slight plus for White after 17 ... B-B4 18 Q-Q2, BxB 19 QxB, N-K2 20 N-Q4.

18 N-Q4 B-B4
19 NxB ...

With 19 Q-Q2 White could transpose into the above note; with the text move he goes for more.

19 ... **NxN**
20 B-Q2!? ...

Fischer's classical style usually makes him quite satisfied to exploit small positional advantages. In this game he finds himself under psychological pressure to go for a quick kill. This pressure is self-wrought, as the immediate tournament start was satisfactory with one win and four draws. Unnatural psychological pressure can be very disastrous, as the course of this game demonstrates. The strategic disadvantage of 20 B-Q2!? is that the QB, as a result of all attackable Black Pawns being on white squares and a majority of White Pawns on black squares, can quickly find himself being a bad Bishop. As a matter of fact, except for being utilized as a mating piece via, e.g., KB6, it *is* a bad Bishop.

The "normal" Fischer move here is 20 Q-R3! Whether Black exchanges Queens (with 21 ... Q-N4) or not after 20 ... NxB; 21 QxN/R6, in either case White has a clear advantage.

| 20 | ... | **Q-R5** |

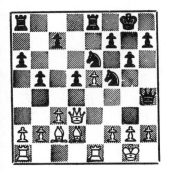

| 21 | **Q-B1!?** | ... |

A favorable endgame would result after 21 Q-B3!, N-N4; 22 Q-B4!, but Bobby wants "more" all the way through.

| 21 | ... | **N-B4** |
| 22 | **P-KN3** | ... |

22 BxN? would be only optically good. In actuality, White would have no chance of taking advantage of the doubled KBPs and Black's Knight would be much superior to White's bad Bishop.

| 22 | ... | **Q-QB5** |
| 23 | **Q-N2** | ... |

23 P-N3 is safe and good.

23	...	**N-Q6**
24	**BxN**	**QxB**
25	**B-N5**	**P-QB3!**
26	**P-KN4**	...

The awkward Queen location on KN2 shows itself in the unplayability of 26 QR-Q1? because of 26 ... RxP!

| 26 | ... | **N-N2** |
| 27 | **R-K3** | ... |

Again 27 QR-Q1? loses to 27 ... RxP!

| 27 | ... | **Q-Q7** |

If we look at this position two things are fairly clear: White has strong attacking chances against Black's weakened Kingside, and Black has effective counterchances against White Queenside. Thus White has two reasonable options here: either to proceed aggressively with the Kingside attack or to seek safety in an even endgame via 28 P-B3. As Larsen tells it, he had only 15 minutes left for the next 13 moves and was nervously worrying about how he could withstand the coming attack.

28   P-N3?   . . .

Most inconsistent as can be seen from the above discussion. Even though it does not have to lead to a loss, from practical considerations the question mark is warranted. Larsen in his book *Larsen's Selected Games* states that Black's position is satisfactory and considers only some variations starting with 28 B-B6. The best and logical way to continue the attack was 28 Q-R3!, with the special point that in certain positions the tactical possibility 29 QxRP+, KxQ; 30 R-R3+ and 31 BxQ becomes possible. After 28 Q-R3! Black must continue his counterplay with 28 . . . QxNP and after 29 QR-K1! the critical position occurs. Does Black have a satisfactory defense? The position is complicated enough to spend a week or so trying to exhaust all the possibilities. I have not seen a clear defense for Black yet and feel that until one is demonstrated, the position should

be considered "won" for White. Two possibilities for Black which illustrate the type of tactics involved are: a) 29 . . . QxRP; 30 Q-R6!, N-K3 (White threatened both 31 B-B6 and 31 R-R3); 31 B-B6, P-N4 (if 31 . . . Q-Q7; 32 P-N5! and there is no way to prevent White from 33 QxRP+!, KxQ; 34 R-R3+, K-N1; 35 R-R8 mate) 32 R-B3 and there is no good way to prevent White's major threat of R-KB5 followed by RxKNP+; b) 29 . . . P-Q5; 30 R-B3! N-K3; 31 B-B6 (again threatening 32 QxRP+, etc) 31 . . . P-N4; 32 Q-R6, Q-Q7; 33 K-B1, PxP; 34 R-B5, and the threat 35 RxNP+ is decisive.

28   . . .   P-N5!

If now 29 PxP??, P-Q5! and if the Rook moves White loses his Bishop. Required was 29 P-B3 with just a slight endgame advantage for Black. Instead . . .

29   Q-R3??   . . .

THE LOSING MOMENT

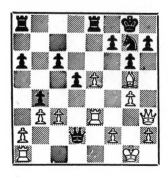

In *Larsen's* time pressure, *Fischer* has a hallucination! Lack of tactical sharpness bothered Bobby all through the first half of the tournament.

29	...	PxP
30	Q-R6	N-K3

WHITE RESIGNS!!!

Only now did Bobby notice that the intended 31 B-B6, P-Q5; 32 QxRP+??!, KxQ; 33 R-R3+ "with 34 R-R8 mate" allows the defensive resource 33 ... Q-R3. And otherwise the Black QBP turns into a new Queen!

GAME 50

White: M. Najdorf (Argentina)
Black: R. Fischer

*Played at the Second Piatigorsky Cup
International Tournament, Santa
Monica (California), July 27, 1966,
Round 7*

Despondent over the sudden
calamity against Larsen, Bobby puts
up very weak resistance in this, his
next, game. Najdorf plays magnifi-
cently, yet his opponent is not
really Fischer but a mere mortal
master.

*King's Indian Defense
(Averbach Variation)*

1	P-Q4	N-KB3
2	P-QB4	P-KN3
3	N-QB3	B-N2
4	P-K4	P-Q3
5	B-K2	O-O
6	B-N5	. . .

Introduced successfully into tournament practice in the early 1950s by
Russian grandmaster Yuri Averbach,
the variation soon started a ten-
year dormancy, only to reappear in
full force during the last five years
mainly as a result of significant
improvements by Uhlmann and
Polugajevsky. The move has no
immediate specific threats or points
(apart from the obvious prevention

of 6 . . . P-K4? because of 7 PxP,
PxP; 8 QxQ, RxQ; 9 N-Q5, etc.) yet
has lots of "bother value." At a
higher level of strategic thinking it
is something like the Ruy Lopez
move 3 B-QN5. The Bishop has no
immediate threat, but what, if anything, should Black do about it,
anyway?

6	. . .	P-B4

The immediate counter against
White's center is most logical and
fully in accordance with the ideas
behind the King's Indian. Over the
last two-three years some experi-
mentation has also been done with
the immediate kick 6 . . . P-KR3.
After 7 B-K3, P-B4; 8 PxP, Q-R4;
9 B-Q2!, QxBP; 10 N-B3, N-B3; 11
P-KR3, White has some advantage.

7	P-Q5	. . .

The full force of Black's plan appears
after 7 PxP?!, Q-R4; 8 PxP?, NxP.

7	. . .	P-K3

The old move is 7 . . . P-QR3 and
the supernew (1972–73 vintage) is
7 . . . P-KR3!.

8	N-B3	. . .

Now Black is okay. With Polugajevsky's 8 Q-Q2! White keeps a
slight but for Black unpleasant
advantage (thus the rationale for the
immediate 7 . . . P-KR3!).

8	...	P-KR3
9	B-R4	PxP
10	BPxP	...

10 NxP?, R-K1 is better for Black and with 10 KPxP White can hope for nothing more than static equality as the QB then is ineffective on KR4.

| 10 | ... | P-KN4! |
| 11 | B-N3 | P-N4?! |

At first glance a very attractive move and only the hindsight offered by this game allows us to stamp it inferior, almost the losing move—and so early! The position after White's 11th is fine for Black, and after some creative home analysis Bobby was prepared when Larsen in Round 15 repeated it: 11 ... N-R4!; 12 N-Q2, NxB; 13 RPxN, N-Q2; 14 N-B4, Q-K2! Black here stands at least equal: the KB has a fantastic diagonal and Black's Queenside can be effectively mobilized, while White can't get anything started on the Kingside. The strength of this new Fischer discovery has made White's opening approach in this game obsolete.

| 12 | N-Q2! | ... |

Black would stand well after 12 BxNP, NxKP! 13 NxN, Q-R4+. Najdorf's Knight maneuver is the positional refutation of Black's plan. Black remains with a chronically weak Kingside, weak and attackable

QP and vulnerable Queenside—and no compensation for these ills.

| 12 | ... | P-R3 |
| 13 | O-O | R-K1 |

An alternative approach was to go for quick mobilization of the Queenside with 13 ... Q-K2 and 14 ... QN-Q2. In either case Black must defend most exactly.

| 14 | Q-B2 | Q-K2? |

THE LOSING MOMENT

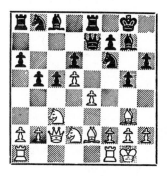

Black's position is so precarious, strategically speaking, that he cannot afford any more missteps, and the text move is exactly that. With the Queen as the lead, the pressure against White's KP is ineffective, giving White the opportunity to efficiently complete his development, after which Black's many weaknesses must tell. No better was 14 ... B-N5; 15 BxB, NxB (Reshevsky–Szabo, Tel Aviv 1958) and now 16 P-KR3, N-K4; 17 P-QR4, P-QN5; 18

N-Q1, with a big plus for White. For those who like muddy waters, the exchange sacrifice was worth a try: 14 ... P-QN5; 15 N-R4, NxQP!?; 16 N-B4 (maybe 16 B-B3!? offers more), N-B5; 17 BxN, PxB; 18 N/R4-N6 B-N2! The correct *positional* move was 14 ... R-R2 with the idea 15 ... R2-K2 when the attack on the KP makes it more difficult for White's Knights to swing into action. White is better off, of course, but Black has chances for survival. Now, however, Najdorf just walks all over Fischer.

15	QR-K1	QN-Q2
16	P-QR4!	P-QN5
17	N-Q1	N-K4

Or 17 ... NxKP; 18 B-Q3.

18	N-K3	...

White's grip over the key QB4 and KB5 squares is paralyzing. Even so, Black's next move is rather silly.

18	...	N-N3?!
19	N3-B4	...

Thank you!

19	...	N-B5

This blockade attempt misses by a mile, yet there is nothing good to suggest.

20	BxN	PxB
21	P-K5!	...

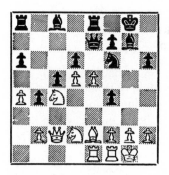

Gangway!

21	...	PxP

Or 21 ... NxP; 22 B-B3, etc.

22	B-B3	Q-B1

A better spot for the Queen must be 22 ... Q-R2.

23	NxP	B-N2
24	N2-B4	QR-Q1

The Queen would be lost after 24 ... BxP?; 25 BxB, NxB; 26 N-Q7.

25	N-B6!	RxR
26	RxR	R-K1
27	R-Q1!	R-B1

No hope either here or in the future for 27 ... BxN as the passed QBP would win.

28	P-R3!	...

This *"luft"* (air) move for the King clearly indicates the helplessness in Black's position. Now 28 ... NxP? is punished by 29 N6-R5! and White wins a piece.

28	...	N-K1
29	N6-R5	R-N1
30	Q-B5	N-Q3?

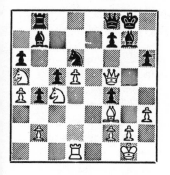

This tactical blunder shortens the agony. After the imminent 31 QxBP/4 Black would be on his last legs anyway.

31 NxN   . . .
BLACK RESIGNS

A piece is lost after 31 . . . QxN; 32 NxB, since 32 . . . RxN loses the Rook after 33 Q-B8+.

GAME 51

White: B. Spassky (USSR)
Black: R. Fischer

*Played at the Second Piatigorsky Cup
International Tournament, Santa
Monica (California), July 28, 1966,
Round 8*

With this loss, Bobby had three in a row—for the second and last time in his career. Even so, play in the succeeding rounds demonstrated the fighting qualities that set him apart from his fellow grandmasters. While Donner and Ivkov under similar psychological pressure floundered through the end of the tournament, Fischer started to play great chess and finished in second place just a half point behind Spassky.

With hindsight we can say then that this was the decisive game for determining the victor. In it Spassky shows all the qualities which best typify him: sound understanding of the principles behind his openings, strategic and tactical sharpness, consistency in the middle game and a fine evaluation and execution of technical endgames. Fischer does not play badly here; Spassky simply plays better.

*Gruenfeld Defense
(Exchange Variation)*

1	P-Q4	N-KB3
2	P-QB4	P-KN3
3	N-QB3	P-Q4

The Gruenfeld Defense, introduced into modern tournament practice by Austrian grandmaster Gruenfeld in the early 1920s, is the most extreme example of an opening where Black hands over immediate total central control to White, in the expectation of successful later challenge and neutralization. Fifty years of analysis and play have shown the objective soundness of the Gruenfeld. Yet it remains the most-delicate-to-handle opening for Black and one small inaccuracy is sufficient to transform White's attackable center into a sound, unstoppable, over powering, roaring lion. Ever since his 1956 "Game of the Century" against Donald Byrne, the Gruenfeld has remained one of Fischer's secondary weapons against the QP. He has not been particularly successful with it, however. Why not? The major reason, I believe, is that the Gruenfeld is too wild, unbalanced, almost "obscure" for Bobby's inherently clear strategic style. The reader may well ask: "How about the Najdorf Sicilian, which also is rather obscure? Doesn't Bobby have great results with that?" And the answer is, of course: "Yes." But here is the big difference. The

Najdorf is *his* defense to the KP, for
many years the sole defense. He has
studied it day after day, month
after month, year after year. His
feel for it and knowledge of it are
about as total as practically possible.
The Gruenfeld, as only one of his
secondary defenses, has got nowhere
as much attention. The defense is
not particularly suited to his style,
requires very delicate handling, and
he has not studied it as extensively
as some others—thus even Fischer
has had some reverses.

4   PxP   . . .

The Exchange Variation is the most
consistent way to start building a
strong center. Some of the deeper
strategists consider it a bit too naïve,
as the resulting positions allow
rather clear opposing plans. Spassky
has remained true to it since his
early tournament days. For 4 B-B4
see Game 59. Of course, 4 N-B3
is also good.

4	. . .	NxP
5	P-K4	NxN
6	PxN	B-N2
7	B-QB4	. . .

The attempt to take advantage of
Black's last move (in place of 6 . . .
P-QB4) by 7 B-R3 (to prevent . . .
P-QB4) is less than fruitless, as after
7 . . . N-Q2! Black gets in . . .
P-QB4, anyway, while White's QB
is permanently misplaced on QR3.

7	. . .	P-QB4
8	N-K2	N-B3
9	B-K3	O-O
10	O-O	. . .

Here we have the basic position in
the Exchange Variation. White has
considerably more central influence,
while Black has started to chip away
at it. Up to the time of this game,
the usual and normal continuation
for Black was 10 . . . PxP; 11 PxP,
B-N5; 12 P-B3, N-R4; 13 B-Q3, B-K3
with interesting play and eventual
equality for Black.

10	. . .	Q-B2

Originally played by Shamkovich and
later worked into a consistent system
by Smyslov, yet hardly noted by
anyone else. That is, until this game.
Despite his loss here, the chess
world reasoned that if Fischer plays
it, then it must be good! From then
on, this has become the "normal"
continuation in the Exchange
Variation.
There are various style leaders in
all walks of life. In chess it has long
been Fischer. Reference has already
been made to his followers' selection of the very demanding Najdorf
Variation. This game is another clear
trend-setter. Even his innocuous
remarks can take on enormous
meaning. As an example, in commenting on his game against Perez
(Black) at Havana 1965 (1 P-K4,
P-Q3; 2 P-Q4, N-KB3; 3 N-QB3,

P-KN3; 4 P-B4, B-N2; 5 N-B3, O-O;
6 B-Q3, N-B3; 7 P-K5, PxP; 8 BPxP)
Fischer criticized the move played
by Perez (8 ... N-Q4) and in print
stated something like "Spassky's
8 ... N-KN5 or *maybe even* [my
italics] 8 ... N-KR4 is better." And
suddenly 8 ... N-KR4 became the
main line of the variation!

But what of the move 10 ... Q-B2,
itself? Well, the Queen indirectly
threatens the Bishop (11 ... PxP;
12 PxP, NxP!), while the Q1 square
is made available for the Rook to
put additional pressure on the QP.

11   R-B1   ...

Some attempts have lately been
made with 11 Q-B1, but after 11
... PxP! 12 PxP, B-Q2 (Razuvajev)
with the idea 13 ... QR-B1, White's
Queen looks rather embarrassed.

11   ...   R-Q1

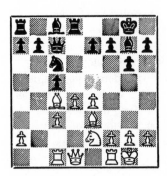

12   Q-K1   ...

As in any modern popular variation
many different approaches have
been tried here: 12 P-KR3, 12 K-R1,
12 P-B3, 12 P-B4, 12 Q-Q2, 12 Q-R4,
12 B-B4, etc. For 12 P-KR3 see Game
57. Most logical seems 12 P-B4. The
only disadvantage of Black's 11 ...
R-Q1 is that protection of the KBP
is lessened and thus it's in White's
interest to try to open the KB file
as quickly as possible. After Black's
best defense: 12 ... B-N5 play could
continue: 13 P-B5, NPxP; 14 P-KR3!,
BxN; 15 QxB, PxQP; 16 BPxP, Q-Q3!.
Black will eventually equalize, but
not without some difficulty.
The point of Spassky's 12 Q-K1 is
to remove the Queen from the
possible Rook threats as well as to
prevent the Knight pin after an
eventual P-KB4, B-KN5.

12   ...   P-K3?

The way to exploit the awkward location of White's Queen was with
12 ... Q-R4! After 13 R-Q1, PxP;
14 PxP, QxQ; 15 KRxQ, P-N3 the
endgame yields dynamically even
chances. After Black's passive text
move, White achieves a strong
attacking position.

13	P-B4	N-R4
14	B-Q3	P-B4
15	R-Q1!	P-N3
16	Q-B2	PxQP

White was threatening to win the QBP by simply taking it off. Rather ugly was 16 ... B-B1. Spassky states that he was planning 17 P-N4!? against it. Even stronger is 17 N-N3, B-QN2; 18 P-Q5!, PxKP; 19 NxP, PxP; 20 N-B6+, K-N2; 21 P-B5! (Zuckerman) with a winning attack. Bobby's move is the minor evil.

17	BxP!	BxB
18	PxB	B-N2
19	N-N3	Q-B2

White has a marked advantage, because Black's King position has been seriously weakened. Bobby's move is as good as any. Fischer has always been a great optimist as far as evaluating his position is concerned, and prior to achieving the highest level of chess maturity in 1970 he tended to be unobjective in some of his judgments. Whether he was White or Black, *his* position —almost any position—had to be "better." Thus after losing this game and seeing that 19 ... Q-B2 led to White's advantage, he seriously claimed that 19 ... Q-N2 "would have given Black the advantage." Well, KN2 is a pretty good square for the Bishop, but not the Queen, and it is not so difficult to see that with 20 B-B2!, PxP; 21 NxP, N-B3; 22 P-Q5! White gets a very strong attack after either 22 ... RxP; 23 B-N3! or 22 ... PxP; 23 N-N5; e.g., 23 ... Q-B3; 24 Q-R4, R-Q2; 25

RxP!, RxR; 26 QxP+, K-B1; 27 QxB and White must win.

| 20 | P-Q5!! | ... |

Spassky plays the attack very well and Fischer defends perfectly.

20	...	BPxP
21	PxP	QxKP
22	P-B5!	...

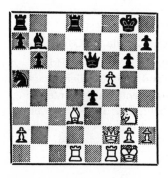

| 22 | ... | Q-B2 |

22 ... PxP? 23 NxBP would lead to quick annihilation: 23 ... Q-KB3 24 Q-K3 etc. as the Black King's open position is indefensible.

| 23 | BxP | RxR |
| 24 | RxR | R-KB1! |

24 ... BxB? 25 NxB allows the Knight to participate decisively in the attack.

| 25 | B-N1 | Q-B3 |
| 26 | Q-B2 | K-R1 |

And not 26 ... K-N2?; 27 PxP, PxP?;
28 N-R5+! (28 ... PxN; 29 Q-R7
mate!).

27	PxP	PxP
28	Q-Q2	K-N2
29	R-KB1	Q-K2
30	Q-Q4+	R-B3

This or 30 ... K-R3 seem equivalent:
Black is hanging on by the threads,
but he is hanging on.

31   N-K4   ...

There being no decisive continuation
of the attack, Spassky heads for a
superior endgame. Excellent practical tournament strategy! Interesting
was 31 BxP!?, KxB; 32 Q-KN4+ but
after 32 ... K-B2; 33 Q-R5+, K-B1
there only seems to be a draw in
the position.

31	...	BxN
32	BxB	Q-B4
33	QxQ	RxR+?

THE LOSING MOMENT

Bobby didn't like the endgame
resulting after 33 ... PxQ; 34 R-B1.
Yet in running from a poodle he
runs into a tiger! True enough that
after 34 ... P-B5; 35 R-B3 White
is still much better off, but as
Spassky has pointed out, Black has
reasonable drawing chances after
35 ... R-K3; 36 B-B3, K-B3; 37 K-B2,
P-N4. Or if 34 RxR, KxR and Black is a
significant tempo ahead of the game
continuation.

| 34 | KxR | PxQ |
| 35 | P-KR4! | ... |

Despite the paucity of material left,
the position is a win for White:
White's King will be much more
active than Black's since the latter is
stuck to protect the weak KNP and
the Bishop has much more scope
than the Knight. White will eventually infiltrate on the Queenside,
win Black's QRP and then queen
his own. Black's passed QBP is more
a weakness than strength here.

| 35 | ... | N-B5 |
| 36 | K-K2 | N-K4 |

No help either from 36 ... N-Q3;
37 K-Q3, N-B4 (37 ... NxB; 38 KxN
and White will win the King and
Pawn endgame because he makes
an outside passed Pawn on the
Kingside) as White has 38 P-R5.
Note that this would be impossible
with Black's King on KB3 (as after
33 ... PxQ!; 34 RxR, KxR).

37	K-K3	K-B3
38	K-B4	. . .

An obvious move three moves before time control, yet more effective was 38 B-B2! with the idea 39 K-K4.

38	. . .	N-B2
39	K-K3?!	. . .

Played to save "thinking time," but clearly a step in the wrong (ha ha!) direction. The correct way was 39 B-Q5, P-N4+; 40 PxP, NxP; 41 B-B4! and White's positional bind will be clearly sufficient for the win.

39	. . .	P-N4?

Forcing White to take a passed Pawn can't be the right idea. Either 39 . . . N-Q3 or 39 . . . N-R3 would require White to come up with the correct plan—yet there is really very little doubt that Spassky would!

40	P-R5	N-R3?!

Putting the Knight out of play is totally hopeless. After 40 . . . N-Q3 White would have to work much harder to infiltrate on the Queen-side, though eventually he must.

41	K-Q3	K-K4
42	B-R8!	K-Q3
43	K-B4	P-N5
44	P-R4!	. . .

Fischer has won this type of position for the stronger side many times. Here he must suffer, as Spassky does the same to him. There just is no way that Black's King can protect both the QBP and QRP. The QBP is not important by itself, but the problem is that after, e.g., 44 . . . K-B2; 45 KxP White's King has penetrated decisively into Black's side of the board and can't be stopped from a victorious trip to the Kingside.

44	. . .	N-N1
45	P-R5	N-R3
46	B-K4	P-N6
47	K-N5	N-N1
48	B-N1	. . .

Not required, but a "safety first" move.

48	. . .	N-R3
49	K-R6	K-B3
50	B-R2!	. . .

BLACK RESIGNS

Completely stifles Black, preparatory to 51 KxP. The immediate 50 KxP was also sufficient for the win: 50 . . . P-B5; 51 B-K4+! etc.

GAME 52

White: F. Gheorghiu (Rumania)
Black R. Fischer

Played at Havana (Cuba), Olympiad,
November 17, 1966, Finals,
Round 12

Fischer chooses a continuation
which is known to be strategically
inferior for Black. A thoughtless
draw refusal on move 15 leads to
the positionally logical result: White
wins.

Nimzo-Indian Defense
(Samisch Variation, by transportation)

1	P-Q4	N-KB3
2	P-QB4	P-K3
3	N-QB3	B-N5
4	P-B3	...

A rather brutal attempt to establish
full control of the K4 square by
hoping to play P-K4. It has the
obvious defect of neglecting Kingside development (where will the
KN go?).

4	...	P-Q4

Black must strike quickly in the
center, as otherwise he can easily
be smothered. The game often now
by transposition turns into the
Samisch Variation (4 P-QR3). Also
good is 4 ... P-B4; 5 P-Q5 N-R4.

5	P-QR3	BxN+

More complicated, but equally playable is 5 ... B-K2; 6 P-K4, PxKP;
7 PxP, P-K4!; 8 P-Q5, B-QB4.

6	PxB	O-O?!

With 6 ... P-B4 7 BPxP, NxP! a
well-known variation in the Samisch
would be reached, where Black has
fine chances for equality. Black's
better development allows him to
press sufficiently against White's
somewhat shaky center to keep the
game in balance. The "automatic"
castling is a little bit too easygoing.
The old rule of thumb "Castle only
when you have nothing better to
do" applies to Bobby also.

7	PxP	PxP?

In a strategic sense this is the losing
move. Much practical experience has
shown that White always gets in
P-K4, anyhow, and with that an
advantageous opening of the game
for the two Bishops. White also
keeps fine attacking chances on the
Kingside. Black's Pawn majority on
the Queenside is stilted and incapable of ready usefulness. In this
game White even gets play there.
Correct was 7 ... NxP with a fully
sound Pawn formation.

8	P-K3	N-R4
9	Q-B2	R-K1

If 9 ... Q-R5+; 10 Q-B2 and White
keeps his central advantage after the
exchange of Queens also.

10	P-KN4!	N-B5
11	P-KR4	...

At first glance such Pawn pushes look unsafe, but Black simply has no meaningful attacking objects, so that White can readily "expand" his space.

11	...	P-QB4
12	K-B2	N-N3
13	B-Q3	...

The theoreticians are fond of citing here the Gligoric–Averbach, Stockholm 1952 game where after 13 P-R5, N-B1 Black "obtained a good game." The developing text move is more logical, but the basics of the position would not be changed by the immediate 13 P-R5, either. Gligoric's problem in the game above simply came from inexact play later on.

13	...	N-B3
14	N-K2	B-K3
15	P-N5!	...

THE LOSING MOMENT

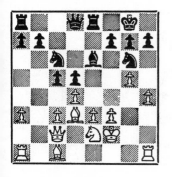

After this move, out of respect for Fischer and his great play at the Havana Olympiad, Gheorghiu offered a draw. Without any consideration of the position, Bobby automatically said "No, there is much play left." This is definitely true, but it is all on White's side! Black's game is strategically so inferior that his only hope is that White will overextend himself. This is a poor base for the future! Gheorghiu continues playing perfectly and there is nothing that Bobby can do to change the outcome.

15	...	R-QB1
16	P-R5	N-B1
17	P-N6!	KBPxP
18	RPxP	...

Step 1 completed: White has a clear advantage on the Kingside.

18	...	P-KR3
19	Q-N1!	N-R4
20	N-B4	P-B5

This removal of central tension makes White's task easier, but a satisfactory continuation is non-existent. If 20 ... PxP; 21 BPxP, and Black's QP will be very weak. The Pawn exchange led to unsatisfactory results in Game 32, so it is logical that Fischer tries the other approach here.

21	B-B2	R-B3
22	R-QR2!	N-Q2

After the exchange of Rooks 22 ... R-N3; 23 R-N2, RxR; 24 QxR, White would have a free hand in the center.

23	P-R4	N-B3
24	B-R3	Q-Q2
25	R-N2	P-N3
26	R-N5	...

Step 2 completed: White has the play on the Queenside.

| 26 | ... | N-N2 |
| 27 | P-K4! | ... |

With both flanks safe, White now proceeds onto step 3: breakthrough in the center.

| 27 | ... | PxP |
| 28 | BxP! | ... |

28 PxP would weaken White's King position. White's position is beautiful enough without needing another Pawn in the center.

| 28 | ... | R3-QB1 |

Probably better was 28 ... NxB+; 29 QxN, even though White still must win by piling up on the King's file.

| 29 | R-K5! | ... |

Threatens 30 P-Q5 or 30 BxN, and if 29 ... N-Q3 then 30 BxN, QxB; 31 RxB, RxR; 32 NxR, QxN; 33 B-B5.

| 29 | ... | B-N5 |

As good as any, but the Bishop doesn't threaten anything and didn't even take off a Pawn in getting here! Thus for a moment White can simply ignore him.

30	N-Q5!	RxR
31	NxN+	PxN
32	PxR	N-B4

After 32 ... Q-Q7+ 33 K-N3, both of Black's minor pieces are *en prise* and also hopeless is 32 ... B-K3; 33 BxN!, QxB; 34 PxP.

33	BxN	Q-Q7+
34	K-N3	BxP
35	BxB	RxB
36	Q-QB1!	...

After the exchange of Queens, Black's position is obviously resignable. As both sides continued to "blitz" (not that there was a reason!), going on with the game presented no inconvenience for anyone except commentators. This one will say no more.

36	...	QxQ
37	RxQ	RxP
38	K-B4	K-N2
39	B-K4	P-KR4
40	R-Q1	R-K2
41	R-Q5	K-R3
42	R-Q6	K-N2
43	R-B6	P-R5
44	RxQBP	P-R6
45	K-N3	K-R3
46	B-N1	R-K6+
47	K-R2	R-K8
48	B-Q3	R-K6
49	R-R4+	K-N4
50	P-N7	...

BLACK RESIGNS

For the whole game Gheorghiu needed less than one hour! Bobby was far behind in time, but with only one and a half hours used!

GAME 53

White: R. Fischer
Black: E. Geller (USSR)

Played at Monte Carlo (Monaco)
International Tournament,
April 4, 1967, Round 11

A very interesting psychological struggle takes place at the very outset: each contestant surprises the other with his moves, and Geller winds up playing Fischer's own variation against him! Thus Geller scores psychologically, but Bobby is very close to the actual full point until, in a crazy, wild, yet promising attacking position he misses the correct continuation. An undeserved loss.

Sicilian Defense
(Najdorf–Fischer's QNP)

1	P-K4	P-QB4
2	N-KB3	P-Q3
3	P-Q4	PxP
4	NxP	N-KB3
5	N-QB3	P-QR3

The first surprise! The Najdorf is not part of Geller's regular opening repertoire (in fact, after 6 B-K2 he has been a regular Najdorf nemesis), yet he is known for his careful theoretical preparation. Thus Fischer was quite sure that a special surprise awaited his 6 B-QB4. So . . .

6	B-KN5	. . .

The second surprise! The text move is the most usual, yet this is the only time Fischer has played it. This was the last round and Bobby was leading the field by a whole point. Second-place Smyslov was playing Gligoric (a likely draw) so Bobby felt pretty secure of his victory. Under these circumstances, why not try something new?

6	. . .	P-K3
7	P-B4	Q-N3

The third surprise! Geller plays Fischer's own variation against him! How did this come about? In the first place, Fischer's 6 B-KN5 had been such a surprise, that all of Geller's home preparation had gone out the window. Secondly, in the morning Geller had lost a difficult adjourned game against Larsen which had killed his chances for the very highest places, so he took a sort of devil-may-care attitude. Under the circumstances—Geller was Black and Bobby only needed a draw to clinch first place—Geller probably would also have been quite satisfied with a quick draw. But he knew that it is impossible to draw with Fischer except on the terms of the actual game position. The opening selection presages a sharp fight, and with his natural curiosity he decided to see what Bobby would do against his variation.

There is no knowledgeable chess person who does not give Fischer full credit for making 7 ... Q-N3 playable. After a few brief sorties in the middle 1950s, Black's debacle in Keres–Fuderer, Goteborg 1955, dissipated all confidence and interest in it. Until 1961, that is, when Fischer resurrected it against Parma at Bled. His never-ending stream of contributions and discoveries, analytical and practical, have clearly imparted his name to 7 ... Q-N3. Yet what is its name? Unaccountably, for over 15 years it had no name, just something like 7 ... Q-N3. This changed, for the worse at that, in the summer of 1972 when in the 7th match game against Spassky, Bobby played 7 ... Q-N3. Immediately after 8 ... QxP the phones rang at the Marshall Chess Club in New York: various radio, TV, and newspaper people wanted to know what to call the variation. A reply that it had no name obviously wasn't satisfactory. So someone (let him remain nameless) after some seconds of contemplation (media people are in a hurry) came up with "Poisoned Pawn Variation." And that's what it is called today. What a horrible appellation! It utterly slights the real discoverer, and is also inaccurate for there is no clear proof that the QNP is actually poison. It may be too late to do anything about it (the power of the media, etc.), yet I propose the following accurate, understandable short name: "Fischer's QNP."

What of the move itself? Well, it is the sharpest and most double-edged attempt to take advantage of the lack of White's QB on the Queen-side.

8   Q-Q2   ...

For the faint of heart (Fischer is not one of them) 8 N-N3 is a reasonable alternative.

8   ...   QxP
9   R-QN1   ...

Long the only and normal continuation. Yet who knows, by the time this book is published it may be called old-fashioned. By his selection of the Fischer's QNP Variation in the 7th and 11th match games against Spassky in 1972, Bobby clearly showed that he has confidence in Black's position after 9 R-QN1. For the new 9 N-N3, see Game 61.

9   ...   Q-R6
10   P-B5   ...

Of the three reasonable methods the only one still consistently used. The positional continuation 10 BxN, PxB; 11 B-K2 (seen in three Parma–Fischer encounters!) is thought to give White less than nothing after Parma–Fischer, Rovinj/Zagreb 1970: 11 ... B-N2; 12 O-O, P-B4; 13 KR-Q1,

O-O!; 14 PxP, PxP; 15 N-Q5, N-B3;
16 NxN, PxN; 17 N-K7+, K-R1; 18
NxB, KRxN. And the sharp 10 P-K5
PxP; 11 PxP, KN-Q2; 12 B-QB4 has
been stopped by Fischer's 12 ...
Q-R4! and Black is perfectly okay—
assuming one knows all the complicated variations 20 to 25 moves
deep!

10	...	N-B3
11	PxP	PxP
12	NxN	PxN
13	P-K5	...

The point of 10 P-B5 is to open
lines against Black's King as rapidly
as possible, and the text move is the
only consistent continuation. By this
time Smyslov and Gligoric had
played to a 10-move draw, so Bobby
was sure of first place. He could
freely play for "the beauty of chess"
(and more individual successes).

13	...	N-Q4?!

Chess theory has vacillated between
considering 13 ... N-Q4 or 13 ...
PxP as the best reply. Fischer un-

doubtedly subjected this game to a
most minute examination and in his
next (and so far last) attempt, as
Black of course!, he played 13 ...
PxP. So to me that means that
13 ... PxP must be the best move.
That game, Kavalek–Fischer, Sousse
1967, is very important for theory
also: 14 BxN, PxB; 15 N-K4, B-K2;
16 B-K2, P-KR4! (Bobby's improvement!) 17 P-B4, P-KB4; 18 R-N3,
Q-R5 and now the piece sacrifice
19 O-O led to an eventual draw.
Instead, 19 N-Q6+ is safer for White
but gives no more than even
chances.

14	NxN	BPxN
15	B-K2	...

Quick mobilization of the KB and
KR is in order. This also is a new
move by Fischer!

15	...	PxP
16	O-O	B-B4+

Possibly 16 ... R-R2 is better.

17	K-R1	R-B1
18	P-B4!	...

More open lines, please! At this
point Fischer was well ahead in time
as, understandably enough, Geller
was rather unfamiliar with the variation.

18	...	RxR+
19	RxR	B-N2

Worse is 19 ... R-R2?; 20 PxP, R-Q2; 21 Q-B2!, R-KB2; 22 B-R5, P-N3; 23 BxP! winning.

20 B-N4?   ...

THE LOSING MOMENT

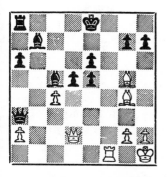

A look at the board after Black's 19th shows a crazy, wild, complicated, unbalanced position where Black has two extra Pawns and a reasonably strong center but with his King caught in the middle of the board. Yet there is no strategically clear way to proceed with the attack. What is required is an intuitive juggling of a number of tactical opportunities. This means that the position is not one where Fischer is at his best: yes, he's good in it but not great. It is truly a "Tal type" position and in fact Tal did defeat Bogdanovic at Budva 1967 soon thereafter, thus: 20 Q-B2!, P-K5; 21 B-N4, B-K2; (the point of 20 Q-B2! is that now 21 ... Q-Q6 allows 22 Q-R4+ and mate); 22 Q-B2!, O-O-O; 23 B-B4!, B-Q3; 24 BxP+,

K-N1; 25 Q-N6, BxB; 26 QxR+, K-R2; 27 R-QN1, Q-Q3; 28 BxP!, BxB; 29 QxQ, BxQ; 30 PxB, and Black resigns. Black would have been better off with 20 ... B-K2; 21 BxB, KxB; 22 QxP, R-QN1; 23 QxP+, K-Q3, but the fact that Fischer would not allow it against Kavalek must mean that it is also advantageous to White.

It is noteworthy that despite 20 minutes' consideration Bobby did not grasp the right concept. For those with academic inclinations it can be said that also better than 20 B-N4? was 20 B-Q1 (threatening 21 Q-Q3!!, QxQ; 22 B-QR4+, B-B3; 23 BxB mate) which leads to at least even chances for White.

20 ...   PxP!

Geller is a very brave man in this game!

21 BxP

Now too the better idea was 21 Q-QB2, though after 21 ... Q-Q6; 22 Q-R4+, Q-Q2; 23 QxBP, Q-Q4 White's compensation for the sacrificed Pawns is inadequate.

21 ...   Q-Q6!

After this powerful Queen centralization Black is the one with the attack.

22 Q-K1   B-K5!
23 B-N4?!

Such a middle-game position with two Pawns down is hopeless and joyless. An inferior ending, but with material equality, could be reached with 23 B-B5!, BxB 24 QxP+, K-Q2; 25 QxP+!, K-B3; 26 Q-B6+, B-Q3; 27 QxQB, QxQ; 28 RxQ. The advanced passed BP must win for Black, yet White has a few rays of hope.

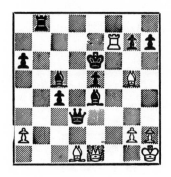

| 23 | ... | R-N1! |

The Rook joins the fight decisively.

| 24 | B-Q1 |

Or 24 B-B3, BxB; or 24 B-K2, R-N7!. Hope springs eternal now with the super-cheapo threat of 25 B-QR4+.

| 24 | ... | K-Q2! |
| 25 | R-B7+ | K-K3 |

WHITE RESIGNS

In this position 26 RxP, BxP+; 27 KxB, R-N7+ leads to mate. The sudden collapse in a promising attacking position is reminiscent of Game 49. And the next game offers another example!

GAME 54

White: R. Fischer
Black: E. Geller (USSR)

*Played at Skopje (Yugoslavia)
International Tournament,
August 7, 1967, Round 2*

Another short, complicated scrap with a sudden collapse by Fischer. It is agreed that White errs decisively on move 20. But what of the position immediately prior? Fischer in *My 60 Memorable Games* claims a forced win for White; I don't think so; Geller isn't talking, but keeps playing the variation for *Black*.

Sicilian Defense (Sozin Variation)

1	P-K4	P-QB4
2	N-KB3	P-Q3
3	P-Q4	PxP
4	NxP	N-KB3
5	N-QB3	N-B3

No more experiments with the Najdorf! Geller also does not like to allow the Richter–Rauser attack, 6 B-KN5, but is very confident that Fischer will stick to "his 6 B-QB4."

6	B-QB4	P-K3
7	B-K3	B-K2
8	B-N3	O-O
9	Q-K2	...

A sharp attacking idea, preparing for Queenside castling. Originated by the aggressive Yugoslavian grand-

master Velimirovic and used briefly by Fischer in the 1967-70 period.

9	...	Q-R4

Partly because of the atmosphere generated by this game and the Round 17 encounter Fischer–Sofrevsky, this variation has almost disappeared from tournament practice. The only high-level practitioner left is Geller and he has remained true to it through 1973. So he must remain convinced of its fundamental soundness. The latest approach for Black is 9 . . . P-QR3 and 10 . . . Q-B2. See Game 58.

10	O-O-O	NxN
11	BxN	B-Q2
12	K-N1	...

A useful precautionary move. 12 BxN?, BxB; 13 RxP, B-B3 threatening both 14 . . . BxN and 14 . . . Q-N4+ (followed by 15 . . . QxNP) is clearly in Black's favor. Also both 12 P-B4? and 12 P-N4? fail after 12 . . . P-K4!

12	...	B-B3

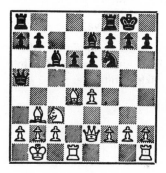

After the game, Geller and Fischer spent some time analyzing the illogical-looking 12 ... QR-Q1. To his sorrow, Sofrevsky in the last round decided to try it out in practice. Fischer was prepared, and after 13 Q-K3!, P-QN3? (the active Pawn sacrifice 13 ... P-QN4!? must be tried); 14 BxN, PxB? (giving up the Pawn with 14 ... BxB is a must) 15 N-Q5!!, KR-K1; 16 NxB+ (16 Q-R6 is even better), RxN; 17 RxP, R-QB1; 18 Q-Q4, B-K1; 19 QxBP and Black had had enough and resigned.

13 P-B4   QR-Q1

A routine playable move. Worth considering is the immediate 13 ... P-QN4!? After 14 BxN, BxB; 15 RxP, QR-B1; 16 P-K5, B-K2 Black's two Bishops give him good counter-chances on the Queenside.

14 KR-B1!   ...

White effectively prepares for either 15 P-K5 or 15 P-B5 (15 ... PxP; 16 RxP!). An immediate 14 P-B5 leads to nothing: 14 ... PxP!; 15 PxP, R-Q2!; 16 KR-B1, B-Q1.

14 ...   P-QN4!

Black must go for counterplay. After 14 ... P-Q4 or 14 ... P-K4 White keeps a riskless initiative.

15 P-B5   ...

Thinking that this is bad, Fischer and Geller in their post-mortem analyzed 15 P-K5 as the proper

continuation leading to advantage for White. While it is true that after 15 ... PxP; 16 PxP, N-Q2; 17 Q-N4, P-N5? White breaks through with 18 RxP!!, KxR; 19 QxKPch, K-K1; 20 QxQB, PxN; 21 P-K6 and White won in Jovcic–Radojcic, Yugoslavia 1969, after the correct 17 ... N-B4! Black is okay. The piece sacrifice 18 BxN, BxB; 19 BxP!?, P-N5!; 20 BxP+, RxB; 21 Q-K6, B-K1; 22 N-K4 is good enough for equal chances, but no more.

With his text move White prepares also a promising piece sacrifice. In either case, with correct play Black can equalize. This is as it should be for sound variations. It just can't be that after 1 P-K4 it's "White to play and win"!

15 ...   P-N5
16 PxP   ...

The Knight has no safe retreat square.

16 ...   PxN
17 KPxP+   K-R1
18 R-B5   Q-N5

The last moves have been rather straightforward. White has two Pawns for the piece and a dangerous attack. However, Black's pieces stand fairly well and he exerts immediate pressure on White's KP. How should White proceed?

19 Q-B1   ...

In regard to this move Bobby proudly states that it is not an easy one to find and that he spent 45 minutes on it. Considering that his next two follow-up moves are blunders, it is difficult to give much credit to Fischer here. Despite the immediate threat it contains, somehow such an awkward, passive, decentralizing move shouldn't be a winning one! In a fairly offhand article in the Russian magazine *USSR Today* Spassky here recommended 19 P-K5!?

19 ...   NxP!

Active and yet fairly obvious. Geller isn't about to fall for 19 ... BxP??; 20 RxN!, BxR?; 21 QxB!, PxQ; 22 BxP mate.

20 P-QR3?   ...

THE LOSING MOMENT

Chasing the Queen to a better square is the decisive error—no argument here. But what of the position after Black's 19th move?

Fischer in *My 60 Memorable Games* claims a win for White after 20 Q-KB4 and presents a number of beautiful variations as proof. However, after 20 ... PxP! 21 R-KR5, N-B3!! (not considered by Fischer), I see no winning opportunities for White (possibly a draw after 22 RxP+!?). A Yugoslavian chess source (probably International Master Maric) suggests that 20 R-KR5! would have led to a draw after 20 ... N-Q7+; 21 RxN, PxR; 22 RxP+, KxR; 23 Q-B5+, K-R3; 24 Q-R3+, K-N3; 25 Q-Q3+! with a perpetual; this would appear to be correct. Attempts by Black to improve on 20 ... N-Q7+ do in fact lead to a winning attack for White, as in effect White is a move ahead compared to the game continuation. What does Geller think of all of this? It would be interesting to know, but unfortunately he isn't talking. Yet in a way his actions speak louder than his words could: he keeps playing the variation for Black!

20 ...   Q-N2
21 Q-KB4?   ...

This serious loss of time (one move!) leads to an immediate collapse. The only chance for a draw was again 21 R-KR5!, threatening perpetual check after RxKRP+. Black's only winning method then is 21 ... N-N4!; 22 Q-B5, RxP!; 23 RxN, QxB!!; 24 BxP+ RxB; 25 PxQ, RxR; 26 Q-B7, R-N2; 27 Q-QB4, BxP

(Maric), though White keeps some practical chances with 28 QxP.

21 **...** **B-R5!!**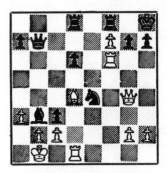

Black's attack now comes through exactly one move sooner than White's.

22 **Q-N4** **...**

Or 22 Q-R6, B-KB3; 23 RxB, BxB!— similar to the game.

22 **...** **B-KB3**
23 **RxB** **BxB!**

An example of one of White's threats is 23 ... PxR?; 24 QxN!! ...

WHITE RESIGNS

After the intended 24 R-B4 Black mates with 24 ... B-R7+!; 25 KxB, QxNP. And if 24 PxB, NxR Black is a Rook ahead, with no compensation for White.

GAME 55

White: D. Janosevic (Yugoslavia)
Black: R. Fischer

*Played at Skopje (Yugoslavia)
International Tournament, August
1967, Round 12*

A game where Fischer underrates
his opponent all the way. He selects
a dubious opening idea, plays the
middle game inexactly and misses a
draw (possibly intentionally, in hope
of a win) in the endgame. Janosevic
is not about to throw away all the
chances offered him and wins a
well-played endgame. And yet, the
loss of the game again demonstrated
Bobby's great fighting qualities: he
won the next five games in a row
to finish first, a half point ahead
of Geller who "only" scored 4½
out of 5.

Sicilian Defense (Najdorf Variation)

1	P-K4	P-QB4
2	N-KB3	P-Q3
3	P-Q4	PxP
4	NxP	N-KB3
5	N-QB3	P-QR3
6	P-B4	...

An active positional method of
meeting the Najdorf. White aims to
dislodge Black's KN by P-K5. Black
will have to prevent this by an
eventual . . . P-K4 leading to a
weakening of the KB3 square, which

then gives White good attacking via
a later Q-KR4, N-KN5, etc. It was
quite popular in the middle 1950s,
fell by the wayside when effective
defensive formations were discovered for Black, and has had a
resurgence of interest during the last
three-four years with the (inevitable)
unearthing of improvements for
White. Historically, Fischer hasn't
had any trouble against it.

6	...	N-B3?!

What had got into Bobby to get him
to try this unnatural-for-the-Najdorf
idea I don't know. Such an approach
for Black shows 5 . . . P-QR3 to
be a complete waste of time, something Black can ill afford in an open
position. Two rounds later, against
Nicevski, Fischer reverted to the
normal 6 . . . Q-B2; 7 N-B3, QN-Q2;
8 B-Q3, P-QN4; 9 P-QR3?!, P-KN3
and won in good style in 35 moves.

7	N-B3	B-N5

The questionable idea. Together with
the following KB fianchetto Black
hopes to exert pressure on White's
Q4 square. But the concept has no
sound strategic basis nor any
practical significance. White obtains
the two Bishops and a freer position
while Black has nothing.

8	P-KR3	BxN
9	QxB	P-KN3
10	B-K3	B-N2
11	B-B4!	...

Much better than the routine 11 B-Q3. The Bishop not only has some realistic possibilities against Black's KB2 but the QR will be well placed on the half-open Queen's file.

11	...	O-O
12	O-O	Q-B2
13	B-N3	P-QN4
14	P-N4?!	...

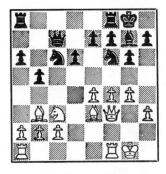

Grandmaster Janosevic is a very dangerous attacking player, though not always quite sound. The text move is a clear indication of his style, yet is premature. Indicated was first the completion of development by 14 QR-Q1! If then 14 ... P-N5; 15 N-Q5, NxN; 16 BxN, BxP; 17 P-B5, N-K4; 18 Q-N3, QR-B1; 19 B-R6 and White has a very strong attack (Janosevic).

| 14 | ... | P-N5 |
| 15 | N-R4 | ... |

The Knight is forced to the edge of the board to protect the QNP. Now 15 N-Q5 is insufficient: 15 ... NxN;

16 BxN, BxP with an attack on the QR. In effect White is then a move behind the above variation, as his 14 P-KN4 is of no practical benefit.

15	...	N-Q2
16	QR-Q1	N-R4
17	P-K5!	NxB

Not 17 ... PxP; 18 BxP+!

| 18 | PxP | PxP |
| 19 | BPxN | QR-K1 |

White still has the freer position, but with the Knight out of play and Queenside Pawns devalued, chances here are about even.

20	R-B1	Q-N1
21	KR-Q1	R-K3
22	B-B2	KR-K1
23	P-N5	...

Janosevic always moves forward!

| 23 | ... | P-R3 |
| 24 | P-R4 | R1-K2?! |

Surprisingly passive. Now White again gets a pull. More in the active Fischer tradition was 24 ... R-K5! If then 25 R-B4, P-B4! with complicated play and chances for both sides.

| 25 | Q-Q5! | Q-K1 |
| 26 | R-B2! | ... |

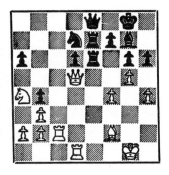

After 26 R-B6, R-K8+! Black gets a draw by perpetual check. So White protects his second rank. Fischer, too, now starts making some fine moves.

26	...	R-K5!
27	QxQP	B-B1!
28	QxRP	Q-N1!
29	Q-Q6	R-K8+!
30	K-N2	...

Not 30 BxR??, RxB+ and White's Queen is lost.

30	...	RxR
31	QxR/Q1	QxP
32	Q-B3!	PxP

Otherwise Black remains a Pawn down.

| 33 | QxQ | PxQ |

An interesting endgame position has arisen. Each has a three-to-one Pawn advantage on opposite sides, with a doubled Pawn somewhat devaluing each superiority. Overall, White has a slight plus because his

Rook is a bit more active and his King better and more securely placed.

34	R-B8	P-B3
35	N-N6	K-B2
36	N-Q5	R-K4?

Clearly the "automatic," active 36 ... R-K7 must be the right move. Fischer would be the first to know and realize it. He did not like that White could then force a draw with 37 R-B7, K-K1; 38 R-B8+; etc. Half a point is better than nothing, Bobby! With the text move, Black forces the Knight from its central position, but at the exorbitant cost of a Pawn.

| 37 | NxBP/4 | P-N4? |

THE LOSING MOMENT

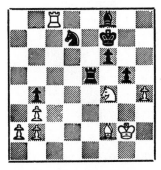

It is impossible to appreciate the fine points in a position if one plays without thinking. Here Black feels that the Kingside is completely "his," but overlooks White's possibilities. Correct was 37 ... R-KB4! with excellent drawing chances, as it will be very difficult for White to realize

his Queenside Pawn advantages,
e.g., 38 N-K2, R-QR4!

38 R-B7! K-K1

38 ... PxN; 39 RxN+ is also most
unattractive for Black.

39 N-N6 R-K7
40 NxB! ...

The first point. After 40 K-B1, RxP;
41 RxN, KxR; 42 NxB+, K-K1; 43
N-R7, PxP; 44 NxP+, K-B2; 45 BxP,
R-R7!; 46 B-N3, RxP there is insufficient material left for White to win.

40 ... NxN
41 P-R5! ...

The second point. Who would have
thought that, starting with a disadvantage of one to three Pawns
on the Kingside White would obtain
a passed Pawn there? As is well
known, the RP is the most difficult
Pawn for a Knight to stop.

41 ... RxP
42 K-N3 P-B4
43 B-B5 ...

The sealed move. Momentarily
material is even again, but the KRP
is a terror.

43 ... N-Q2
44 P-R6! P-B5 +

It is possible that a better practical
chance was 44 ... NxB. If then 45
P-R7, N-K5+, 46 K-B3, R-R7; 47

R-B8+, K-B2; 48 P-R8(Q), RxQ; 49
RxR, Black has drawing hopes after
49 ... N-B6. Thus the correct way
for White is 45 RxN! K-B2; 46 RxP+
K-N3; 47 RxP+!, KxP; 48 R-QR5!
(Janosevic) and White's King walks
over to pick up the QNP.

45 K-R3 RxP
46 B-Q4! ...

White avoids 46 P-R7, P-N5+; 47
KxP, R-R7!; 48 P-R8(Q)+, RxQ;
49 R-B8+, K-B2; 50 RxR, NxB; 51
R-R3, as there is no clear win after
51 ... K-K3!; 52 KxP, K-Q4!

46 ... P-N5 +

46 ... N-B1; 47 R-B8+, K-B2; 48
RxN+! wins.

47 KxP R-R7
48 B-N7 N-N3
49 R-N7 N-Q4
50 R-N5 N-K2
51 RxP ...

White now has two widely separated
Pawns. There is no way Black can
stop both. Meanwhile Black's BP
is not a viable threat to White.

51 ... N-N3
52 R-N6 R-KN7 +
53 K-B3 R-N6 +
54 K-K4 R-K6 +
55 K-Q4 ...

Black's Knight can't be protected
(55 ... R-N6; 56 RxN!, RxR; 57
P-R7) and if it moves to safety,
White's RP queens.

55 ...   K-B2

A last bluff.

56   R-KB6+   K-N1

57   P-N4   ...

And it worked! As Janosevic tells it,
Fischer appeared so confident here
that he was afraid that maybe the
position after 57 RxN, RxP is a
draw. However, since White's
Bishop is the right color (covers the
queening square) for his RP, White
wins rather easily. Even so there is
no reason to criticize the text move.
White simply pushes the QNP to

victory. Black is rather helpless about
it all. A fine psychological move
(the bluff) by Bobby, but unfortunately with no practical benefit.

57	**...**	**K-R2**
58	**P-N5**	**R-QN6**
59	**K-B4**	**R-N8**
60	**R-B7**	**K-N1**
61	**R-N7**	**R-QB8+**

If 61 ... P-B6 62 B-Q4! wins a piece.
Here the game was adjourned for
the second time.

62	**K-Q3**	**R-KR8**
63	**P-N6**	**P-B6**
64	**K-K3**	**N-R5**

A last attempt by a great battler.

65	**R-N8+**	**K-R2**
66	**P-N7**	**R-K8+**
67	**K-B2**	**R-K7+**
68	**K-N3**	**...**

Not 68 K-B1??, N-B4 and it is *Black*
who wins!

68	**...**	**P-B7**
69	**R-KB8**	**...**

BLACK RESIGNS

The QNP will cost Black the Rook.

PART FOUR

Artistry at the Highest Level

March 1970—September 1972

(Games 56 through 61)

Just as the night is darkest before dawn, so the gloom and doom of 1969 quickly transformed itself into the sunshine of 1970. When I talked of Fischer's semi-retirement, the reference was of course, to tournament play. Bobby never retired from chess and, most importantly, he never retired from his intensive study of chess. He studied everything: old opening variations and modern openings, old masters and recent ones, middle games and end-games. He works so hard in his studies, his concentration is so total, that for him this is equivalent to tournament play. Thus, as far as chess knowledge is concerned, Fischer was prepared as 1970 dawned.

It was also quickly apparent that he was ready to play chess again. His inner self had told him: "You know that you're the greatest, so how about going out and showing it to the world? It shouldn't be too difficult, should it?" Thus Bobby quickly accepted the invitation to play Board 1 on the World Team against USSR in the "Match of the Century" at Belgrade in March of 1970. When he arrived at Belgrade a potential roadblock emerged in Larsen's insistence that he, Larsen, be Board 1 because of his recent successes. A satisfactory resolution seemed impossible, but the new Fischer simply said, "Larsen has a point," and agreed to play Board 2. He had come to play and play he would! After brilliantly defeating Petrosian in the first two games, he held on tenaciously to draw the next two for a fine 3-1 win. He stayed in Yugoslavia to participate in "The Tournament of Peace" at Rovinj/Zagreb. A clear first place (13-4), two points ahead of the field, was his due. Only the young Yugoslav master Kovacevic was able to win a well-played game against him (Game 56).

After an absence of ten years Fischer returned to Buenos Aires, Argentina, in July 1970. Where ten years ago he had made the worst showing of his life, he now proceeded to score the most smashing tournament triumph of his (or probably anyone's) life. Playing strategically and tactically perfect chess, Bobby scored 13 wins, allowed only 4 draws, and finished 3½ points ahead of Tukmakov, who was second. Bobby decided that he now liked Argentina and stayed to spend some time there.

The next hoped-for start would be in September at Siegen, West Germany, for the 1970 Olympiad. Col E. B. (Ed) Edmondson, the Executive Director of the United States Chess Federation, was in constant contact by telephone with Bobby in Argentina and was quite pessimistic about the likelihood of his playing. Bobby had prepared his usual list of "25 demands" regarding playing conditions and these had been duly forwarded to the West German Chess Federation. But the Germans had said "no," and there did not seem much that could be done. Depending on Bobby's decision, I would be either the fifth or sixth man on the team. On the eve of departure for Germany, Edmondson had cabled Anthony Saidy, the first alternate, to come from Los Angeles and stand by in New York. Fischer was to arrive in Siegen directly from Argentina and he came right on time. The Germans had flatly refused 24 of his demands and partially agreed to the 25th. His table would be three feet (the others had no clearance) from the first row of spectators. Would he play? He had come to play; he would; and a happy Edmondson cabled Saidy to go back to Los Angeles.

Bobby's play in the Olympiad was good without being great. But the important thing was that he was playing at all! Personally disappointing to him, of course, was the loss to Spassky. Boris was visibly nervous before and during the game, chain-smoked all the way through, but kept his nerves and won when Bobby refused to realize that the position can't be won and can be lost (Game 57).

All through the Olympiad I could sense a new, realistic, practical Fischer. As an example, in the Finals he adjourned an endgame against Hort of Czechoslovakia. He was a Pawn ahead, but with a lousy Bishop against an excellent Knight. At adjournment, Hort offered a draw, saying, "I don't know who's better, but I offer you a draw, Bobby." And Fischer replied: "I don't know who's better, but I have a Pawn!" We analyzed the position at night, and what struck me as significant was Bobby's refusal to consider any variations which contained losing chances. He wanted very much to win, but only if the best moves led to this. There was to be no second-class effort at winning, if this could lead to losing. Again, it was the truth in chess that Fischer was interested in! (The game was resumed but ended in a draw, anyway.)

Within six weeks of the Olympiad, the eyes of the chess world would be on the Interzonal at Palma de Mallorca. But what of Bobby? Hadn't he forfeited his chance by not playing in the 1969 U.S. Championship? Here the U.S. Chess Federation made a masterful move at the FIDE Congress, asking for permission to use discretionary criteria in selecting its representatives to the Interzonal. Permission was granted, and after Benko and the rest of the U.S. Championship participants stepped aside, the way was cleared for Bobby.

There was one more major step that the USCF took for the Interzonal. This was the delegation of Executive Director Ed Edmondson to be Bobby's representative all through the tournament. The combination of Bobby's chess and Ed's everything else was unbeatable. A loss with White in a sharp Sicilian against Larsen (Game 58) was only a minor irritant. In Round 12 Fischer clearly showed that he has no psychological bugaboos. When Geller, his most dangerous opponent, playing White in a symmetrical English, offered a draw on move 7(!) Bobby growled a "no." Geller was so unnerved that he soon squandered away a Pawn and finally lost a tenable endgame. Bobby, of course, won the Interzonal decisively with a 3½ point edge.

Decisive also were his Candidates Match victories over Taimanov and Larsen. The combination of Fischer and Edmondson clicked like clockwork. With some luck, both Taimanov and Larsen could have been saved from 0-6 shutouts, but there was never a doubt of Bobby's sure triumphs.

Things were more difficult in Buenos Aires 1971 against Petrosian. Up to this moment, Fischer had won 18 straight tournament games and some letdown was a realistic danger. At the start Bobby was dangerously complacent. He was taking everything easy. No worries or complaints about anything, but few points also! Luckily, he was able to win the first game, because in the second (Game 59) Petrosian was a convincing victor. The following three games were drawn, with Fischer in some difficulty in two of them. But then Bobby got back his fighting spirit and in fine style swept the next four games and the match!

It is a cliché to say that the world awaited the match between Bobby and Boris, but how true it is! And it almost did not come off. In a fit of temper, Bobby had decided not to utilize further the invaluable help of Ed

Edmondson. This would seriously handicap him in both the final negotiations in New York and during the match in Iceland. Well, the match finally started, but what a lousy start! The very first game (Game 60) brought forth the worst one move blunder Bobby had made since Buenos Aires 1960. Statistically, a careless move every twelve years is not much, but when it occurs in a World Championship match, is it painful. Game 2, you will recall, was forfeited because Fischer failed to show up.

Everything was dark again, but again this was the darkness before the glorious day. Starting with Game 3 and continuing through Game 10, Bobby played the grandest chess ever seen in World Championship play.

Surprisingly broad opening preparation, deep strategic concepts in the middle game, tactical sharpness, and a fantastic will to fight were the tools that allowed Bobby to sweep the next eight games by 6½-1½ to establish a commanding lead. Everyone is entitled to one bad game in a match, and for Fischer this came in Game 11 (Game 61). Spassky won very easily. The second part of the match was contested more closely. Bobby's play showed many dangerous signs of complacency, overconfidence and carelessness, but Boris, with his poor form, was incapable of taking advantage of the offered chances. Thus the match ended 12½-8½ for Bobby and there was happiness in the land. . . .

GAME 56

White: R. Fischer
Black: V. Kovacevic (Yugoslavia)

Played at Rovinj/Zagreb (Yugoslavia)
International Tournament,
April 21, 1970, Round 8

A rare circumstance where Fischer is surprised in the opening by a better-prepared opponent. Being on unfamiliar ground, Bobby reacts inexactly and is simply swept off his feet. A grandmasterly effort of the highest quality by International Master Kovacevic. This is the last game Fischer has lost to someone who is not a front-line Grandmaster.

French Defense
(Winawer Variation)

1	P-K4	P-K3
2	P-Q4	P-Q4
3	N-QB3	B-N5
4	P-QR3	. . .

Suggested and played a few times in the 1930s by World Champion Alekhine, the move is unquestionably the most radical attempt to refute the Winawer. Yet modern opening knowledge has taught us that brute force at so early a stage is apt to be disappointing in outcome. Objectively the move is okay in that White retains even chances, but this is a rather modest goal for

White on move 4! Fischer has played the move periodically, with indifferent results. In this game, however, it can be considered the psychologically losing move. How come? Well, just two rounds earlier against Uhlmann, Bobby had employed it and won in good style. This meant that Kovacevic was forewarned and was able to prepare for it especially, which he did, and found or learned an important improvement, while Fischer rested on his laurels. Bobby was totally surprised and couldn't find the right concept in over-the-board play.

4	. . .	BxN +
5	PxB	PxP
6	Q-N4	. . .

Otherwise White remains a Pawn down.

6	. . .	N-KB3!
7	QxNP	R-N1
8	Q-R6	. . .

A most unusual and unbalanced position. White has the two Bishops (what is new about that in the Winawer?) and thus can theoretically look ahead to an advantageous opening of the position later on, and White also has possibilities of winning Black's isolated KRP. However, the other side of the coin is that White's center position is rather shaky, Black's advanced KP inhibits White's piece development and

White's Queen can find herself precariously placed. The chances are about even.

8 ...   QN-Q2

There is no logic in chasing the Queen away from her lonely position via 8 ... R-N3. After 9 Q-K3, N-B3; 10 B-N2, Q-Q3; 11 P-B3, PxP? (11 ... P-K4!?); 12 NxP, B-Q2; 13 O-O-O, O-O-O; 14 P-B4! White's position was better in Fischer–Uhlmann, Rovinj/Zagreb 1970 and 1-0 in 31.

9 N-K2   ...

Fischer had already played this against R. Byrne in the 1966-67 U.S. Championship, so that Kovacevic knew that he could expect it. However, the idea and move is rather slow and passive. Instead, Hort's 1971 suggestion 9 P-B3!? is worthy of note. Completely unsatisfactory is 9 B-N2?!, N-N3; 10 P-QB4, N-R5!; 11 O-O-O, B-Q2; 12 P-KB3, Q-K2! with Black favored in Foguelman–R. Byrne, Buenos Aires 1964.

9 ...   P-N3!

Black did all right with 9 ... P-B4; 10 N-N3, Q-B2; 11 Q-K3, Q-B3; 12 P-QR4, P-QR3; 13 PxP, QxBP; 14 QxQ, with equal play and a draw on move 31, as in the Fischer–R. Byrne game. It's possible that Bobby had prepared an improvement here. The text move seems sounder:

Black immediately develops his QB on the very useful center diagonal.

10 B-N5?   ...

THE LOSING MOMENT

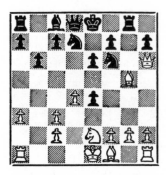

This is a most difficult game to analyze from the standpoint of fixing the blame for Fischer's defeat. White makes no obvious errors yet loses decisively in 30 moves! In retrospect, 10 B-N5? must be the losing move, since, in effect, White loses about two tempos with no recompense. The proof of it is far from obvious, yet Kovacevic is equal to the task. Simple development was required, such as 10 N-N3 and 11 B-K2. True enough that White has nothing—yet that is much better than pain and suffering.

10 ...   Q-K2!

Prevents 11 O-O-O and threatens to obtain a favorable endgame with 11 ... N-N5!.

11	Q-R4	B-N2
12	N-N3	...

After 12 N-B4, 12 ... P-KR3! is just as effective as in the game, e.g., 13 BxP, R-R1 or 13 QxP, O-O-O!.

12	...	P-KR3!
13	B-Q2	...

What is White to do? 13 QxRP? loses a piece after 13 ... N-N5; 14 BxQ, NxQ; 15 B-R4, R-N5. Also most unpleasant is 13 BxP, R-N5; 14 Q-R3, O-O-O; 15 B-K2, R5-N1; 16 Q-R4, R-R1. The suggestion 13 B-B1 is not to be taken seriously. The only basis for that is the hindsight that 13 B-Q2 turned out unsatisfactorily.

13	...	O-O-O
14	B-K2	N-B1!
15	O-O	N-N3!

Black is insistent on sacrificing the KRP for line opening. As 16 Q-R3, N-Q4! with the threat ... N3-B5 is also unsatisfactory, White decides to bite the bullet.

16	QxRP	R-R1
17	Q-N5	QR-N1
18	P-B3!?	...

Yes, this leads to a loss, but is by far the best practical try, since Black's play must be strategically deep and tactically perfect. The suggestion of 18 Q-N5 by some commentators is a joke, as obviously with White's Queen completely out of play, Black's Kingside attack must be successful. Somewhat better is 18 P-QB4, to take away the possibility of ... N-Q4 by Black, but after 18 ... N-R5; 19 Q-K3 (or 19 Q-B4, NxP! 20 KxN, P-K6+), 19 ... N-N5; 20 BxN, RxB Black has too many threats, including ... P-KB4, P-KB5.

18	...	P-K6!!

Only so—a fantastic rejoinder! It is obvious enough that 18 ... PxP; 19 BxP, is okay for White. Fischer's fine point shows if Black plays the apparently "winning" 18 ... N-R5?: 19 PxP!!, RxQ; 20 BxR, with at least even chances for White! The point of Kovacevic's move is to prevent the opening of the KB file and to gain some more attacking time—at the cost of another Pawn.

19	BxP	...

Black has it even easier after 19 QxP, N-Q4; 20 Q-B2 (or 20 Q-N5, P-KB3 21 Q-N4, R-R5), Q-R5.

19	...	N-B1
20	Q-N5	N-Q4
21	K-B2	...

There is no defense. After 21 B-Q2 Black comes through with 21 ... P-R3!; 22 Q-Q3, Q-R5.

| 21 | ... | P-R3! |

To eliminate a possible Q-K8+ by White, if Black plays ... Q-KR5.

| 22 | Q-Q3 | RxP |

The beginning of the harvest. White is both helpless and hopeless in warding off further damage. Kovacevic finishes off efficiently—but the difficult part was to get this far!

| 23 | R-R1 | Q-R5 |
| 24 | RxR | QxR |

Not 24 ... QxN+??; 25 K-N1.

25	N-B1	RxP+
26	K-K1	Q-R5+
27	K-Q2	N-N3!
28	R-K1	N3-B5
29	BxN	NxB
30	Q-K3	R-B7!

WHITE RESIGNS

There is no defense to the major threat: 31 ... NxB!; 32 RxN, RxN— not to mention the minor ones (31 ... BxP and 31 ... N-N7).

GAME 57

White: B. Spassky (USSR)
Black: R. Fischer

Played at Siegen (West Germany)
Olympiad, September 20, 1970,
Finals, Round 6

Unquestionably the high point of the 1970 Olympiad was the anticipated duel between World Champion Boris Spassky and Robert J. Fischer. As luck would have it, the USSR–United States match was scheduled for a Sunday so that people from far and near could attend. And come they did, in droves. All available space was sold out in the morning and the organizers had to improvise to provide demonstration boards and standing room for the late-comers. The USSR thought the match important enough to send their ambassador to West Germany, Mr. Tserapkin, as a personal observer. Of course, no such interest from our side!

As far as the game itself is con-cerned: Spassky played it very con-sistently, doing whatever the position required. This is always the very best practical approach and is a characteristic strength of Spassky's. Bobby's position was well enough out of the opening—sound equality —but his main concern was winning,

rather than good moves. The result was a most unwelcome loss.

Gruenfeld Defense
(Exchange Variation)

1	P-Q4	N-KB3
2	P-QB4	P-KN3
3	N-QB3	P-Q4

Spassky's order of moves allows White to achieve the Samisch against the King's Indian (3 . . . B-N2; 4 P-K4, P-Q3; 5 P-B3), Spassky's usual choice. Because Bobby doesn't allow the Samisch anymore when meeting its experts, he doesn't have much choice here—the Gruenfeld it must be.

4	PxP	NxP
5	P-K4	NxN
6	PxN	B-N2
7	B-QB4	P-QB4
8	N-K2	N-B3
9	B-K3	O-O
10	O-O	Q-B2
11	R-B1	R-Q1

Up to here as in Game 51, where Spassky continued with 12 Q-K1.

12	P-KR3	. . .

Again suspicious of a special prep-aration against the consistent 12 P-B4!, Spassky tries something else. The point of the move is to prevent a . . . B-KN5 and thus ensure White's P-KB4. However, the move costs a clear developmental tempo and this is sufficient for Black to equalize.

12	...	P-N3
13	P-B4	P-K3
14	Q-K1	N-R4

More cunning would be 14 ...
B-N2, and if 15 Q-B2, N-R4; 16 B-Q3,
P-B4! we would have Game 51 with
an extra tempo for Black. Here 17
P-K5? led to better chances for
Black in Gligoric–Smyslov, Yugo-
slavia–USSR Match, 1959.

| 15 | B-Q3 | P-B4 |
| 16 | P-N4!? | ... |

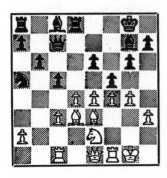

Spassky correctly realizes that with
the missing tempo there is no future
in 16 Q-B2, B-N2. One more
example: 17 N-N3, PxKP; 18 BxP,
N-B5! and White's QB has no retreat
squares available. With the text
move he goes for an immediate
attack against the KBP, even at the
cost of significantly weakening his
Kingside. It may well be that 16
R-Q1 is objectively sounder, but
Black clearly then has no problems
to solve. This is not so after the
aggressive text move.

| 16 | ... | PxKP |

Spassky obviously had no qualms in
pursuing this line, since he repeated
it a year later against Stein at
Moscow 1971. There Stein found,
for winning purposes, a more satisfactory continuation: 16 ... B-N2!;
17 N-N3, Q-Q2! After 18 NPxP,
PxQP!; 19 PxKP, QxP; 20 P-B5,
correct would have been 20 ...
Q-Q3! (with an attack on the
Knight) and probable advantage for
Black.

17	BxP	B-N2
18	N-N3	N-B5
19	BxB	...

Unsatisfactory is 19 B-KB2, BxB; 20
QxB (20 NxB, QxP), N-Q7; 21
QxKP+, K-R1; 22 KR-Q1, N-B6+
with advantage for Black.

19	...	QxB
20	B-B2	Q-B3
21	Q-K2	PxP

Or immediately 21 ... P-QN4.

| 22 | PxP | ... |

Not 22 BxP?, BxB; 23 PxB, RxP and
the Knight is protected.

| 22 | ... | P-QN4 |
| 23 | N-K4! | ... |

Spassky realizes that he must not
tarry with protection of the chronically weak QP and instead must get
the Knight into play.

23 ...   BxP!?

A look at the position after White's
23rd move shows that it is dynamically in balance—a tribute to Fischer's
strategically clear handling of the
opening. Objectively, Black should
be satisfied; after all, to achieve an
equal position with the Black pieces
against the World Champion is a
most satisfactory result. However,
Fischer is not interested in equality,
but in bringing down Spassky. This
is a much more formidable goal.
How to go about it? Well, unfortunately, this is very difficult to achieve,
as the position is already much
simplified. For winning purposes, the
misstep occurred on move 16.
Black's problem is that 23 ... R-K1
can be met effectively by 24 P-QR4,
P-QR3; 25 N-B5! and the simplifying
threat 26 NxRP, 27 PxP, and 28 QxN
keeps the position in balance. And
after 23 ... R-KB1 the same idea is
executed via 24 P-QR4, RxP; 25 PxP.
In chess usage the marks !? after a
move mean "an enterprising move"
or "a move deserving attention."
This is unquestionably true in regard
to 23 ... BxP!?. Bobby played it
because he felt that with the gain of
a Pawn he would have good winning
chances. Yet the choice turns out
most unlucky. It's an excellent move
for drawing purposes but a deceptively bad one for a win. We'll see
why.

24 N-N5   BxB+?

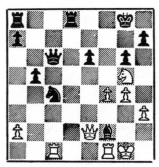

Unquestionably *psychologically* the
losing move, as Fischer is lulled into
continuing to look for wins when
instead he should be racking his
brains to find a satisfactory drawing
method. Practically speaking, it is
also the losing move. Black's Kingside is so weakened that White gets
a tremendous bind, even if no
Queens are on the board. Black's
special problem is his Knight:
apparently well positioned, but of
no use in guarding the King. However, the move may not lead to a
definitive loss—see the analysis after
move 30. Objectively correct was
only 24 ... B-N3! and an approximately even endgame after 25
QxP+, QxQ; 26 NxQ, R-Q7; 27
P-QR4!.

25 RxB   R-Q3

25 ... R-K1; 26 N-K4 does not look
reassuring either, while 25 ...
R-Q7?? drops the Rook after 26 QxR.

26 R-K1   Q-N3

There is little attraction in an inferior endgame via 26 ... R-Q7; 27 QxP+, especially when going for a win.

27 N-K4   R-Q5

No better or worse is 27 ... R-B3.

28 N-B6+   K-R1

Black's problem here is that after 28 ... K-N2 29 QxP, QxQ 30 RxQ the endgame is very unpleasant (30 ... R-Q3; 31 N-K8+, K-B2; 32 NxR, KxR; 33 NxP). So Bobby prefers to keep the Queens on. It is the right idea but for the wrong reason: Black plays it for winning purposes, whereas it actually offers better drawing chances.

29 QxP   R-Q3

Unfortunately for Black, the intended tactical 29 ... R-Q8 fails after 30 Q-B7!!, e.g., 30 ... RxR+; 31 K-N2, Q-B3+ (or 31 ... N-K6+ 32 K-N3, R-KN8+; 33 K-R4); 32 K-N3, R-K6+; 33 K-R4, RxP+; 34 KxR, Q-R8+; 35 R-R2.

30 Q-K4   . . .

30 . . .   R-KB1?

After this utterly pointless move (White will play 31 P-N5 anyway) it is definitely over. The obvious 30 ... QR-Q1 was correct, with chances for saving half a point after 31 P-N5, R-Q7; 32 R1-K2, RxR; 33 QxR by 33 ... Q-K6!, as after 34 QxQ Black has the *Zwischenzug* 34 ... R-Q8+!! (but not 34 ... NxQ?; 35 R-K2, N-B4; 36 R-QB2!, R-R1; 37 R-B7, N-N2; 38 R-N7, P-QR3; 39 K-B2, and with all of Black's Kingside forces immobile, White will win Black's Queenside Pawns thanks to *Zugzwang*): 35 K-N2 (35 K-R2, NxQ; 36 R-QN2, R-Q7+!; 37 RxR, N-B8+, and 38 ... NxR), 35 ... NxQ+; 36 K-B3, N-B4!, and White's Rook has difficulties in penetrating (36 R-K2? and 36 R-B2? are foiled by 36 ... N-Q5+). Thus Black has fair chances for the draw. Maybe it's possible to improve on White's play—it's so difficult to be 100 percent sure in these positions. In any case, having a possible problem draw in one out of a thousand variations is hardly a justification for playing 24 ... BxB+?

31 P-N5   R-Q7

Sacrificing the exchange with 31 ... R3xN can unquestionably prolong Black's resistance, but why shouldn't White win with his material advantage?

32 R1-KB1   . . .

Equally good is 32 R1-K2.

| 32 | ... | Q-B2 |

There is no defense, as 32 ... RxR;
33 RxR, Q-K6 loses to 34 QxQ and
35 R-K2 (see the endgame discussion
above) while 32 ... N-Q3 loses to
33 Q-K5!, Q-Q5; 34 Q-K7.

| 33 | **RxR!** | NxR |
| 34 | **Q-Q4** | R-Q1 |

Or 34 ... Q-N3; 35 QxQ, PxQ;
36 R-B1!, N-B5; 37 P-QR4! winning
easily—in all endgames Black is in
danger of being mated on his KR2!.

35	**N-Q5+**	K-N1
36	**R-B2**	N-B5
37	**R-K2**	R-Q3

If 37 ... Q-N3; 38 R-K8+ RxR;
39 NxQ.

| 38 | **R-K8+** | K-B2 |
| 39 | **R-KB8+!** | ... |

BLACK RESIGNS

The Queen is gone after 39 ... KxR;
40 Q-R8+. With the bounty that
Spassky collected for this game was
a big-brotherly kiss from Ambassador Tserapkin!..

GAME 58

White: R. Fischer
Black: B. Larsen (Denmark)

*Played at Palma de Mallorca (Spain)
Interzonal Tournament, November
20, 1970, Round 9*

A game which shows Larsen at his
shining best: a meaningful opening
innovation, a most exactly handled
combination of attack and defense
in the middle game, and a
matter of technique endgame.
Fischer doesn't feel comfortable
here in the ambiguous attacking
position reached immediately after
the basic force deployment, and
Larsen's perfect play doesn't allow
any recovery later on. This game
caused Bobby to give up on the
sharp variation used here.

*Sicilian Defense
(Sozin Variation)*

1	P-K4	P-QB4
2	N-KB3	P-Q3
3	P-Q4	PxP
4	NxP	N-KB3
5	N-QB3	N-B3

Larsen in his preparation could con-
fidently expect Fischer's reply, as up
to that point in his career Bobby
had played nothing but 6 B-QB4.

6	B-QB4	P-K3

The simplest and soundest reply.
Black shortens the diagonal of
White's KB, but otherwise proceeds
with good developmental moves
without paying too much attention
to 6 B-QB4. Black's underlying
assumption is that there is no reason
why the Sozin Variation "must win"
for White and that therefore no
unusual precaution is required in regard to White's KB. Also playable may
be the roguish 6 ... Q-N3!?; too passive is 6 ... B-Q2; for an outright
error look at 6 ... P-KN3?: 7 NxN,
PxN; 8 P-K5, PxP??; 9 BxP+ winning
the Queen.

7	B-N3	B-K2
8	B-K3	O-O

Possibly the first surprise for Bobby.
In an earlier successful game against
Norman Weinstein in the 1970 U.S.
Open, Larsen had started a Queen-
side attack with his King in the
center of the board.

9	Q-K2	. . .

As in Game 54, Fischer here also
plays the sharp Velimirovic Attack.
But for the last time! Bobby quite
correctly realized that the type of
rival ambiguous attacking positions
that result from this variation are not
really suited for his inherently clear
strategic style. It is not that Bobby
lacks greatness as an attacking player
—it is just that he excels in attacks
which have a clear underlying

strategic basis. With White, Fischer invariably is able to obtain a sound, healthy position with some initiative and at no risk, so he doesn't need to venture into muddy waters. His determination to avoid the Velimirovic was absolute: he avoided it twice against Larsen in the 1971 Candidates Match by castling Kingside and after Spassky in the 4th Match game in 1972 equalized against that, Bobby for the first time in his life switched to 6 B-KN5!.

9 ... P-QR3

The most modern approach. Black will put his Queen on QB2, preparatory to starting play on the Queenside via ... P-QN4.

10 O-O-O Q-B2
11 P-N4 ...

White's plan obviously calls for an attack against Black's Kingside, so the text move is a logical approach. To prevent Black's possible reply 11 ... NxN which forces 12 RxN (if 12 BxP?, P-K4! and White's KNP is loose), White also often chooses the preparatory 11 KR-N1, since the Rook is well placed on the KN file, anyway. Objectively speaking, though, 11 P-N4 and 11 KR-N1 are of equal value.

11 ... N-Q2!

After making this move, Larsen had only used up two minutes on his clock, thus there was no question

that he was playing a specially prepared variation. The move is a purposeful innovation: without waiting to be chased away, Black's KN is immediately redeployed to QB4. The Knight stands quite well there for both offensive and defensive purposes and Black can delay development of his QB and leave his QN on QB3 until the most effective posts for them become apparent. The major value of the move, however, is its psychological surprise factor, which forces the opponent, under the pressure of the ticking clock, to come up with the right concept and then the correct actual continuation.

Perfectly playable is also the older 11 ... NxN; 12 RxN, P-QN4; 13 P-N5, N-Q2 and now 14 R-N1!, R-N1; 15 Q-R5, P-N3!; 16 Q-R6, R-Q1; 17 P-K5, P-Q4 (Parma) with chances for both sides.

12 P-KR4? ...

Because he is in a relatively unfamiliar position, surprised by the innovation, and takes only ten minutes on the move, Fischer's response is understandably faulty. The KRP is not really a prime attacking vehicle so that the move is essentially loss of time at *this* stage. Here we have one of the rare instances where a Fischer idea has had no followers—and for a good reason! Instead, White has two logical ap-

proaches: 1) Pushing the KNP: 12
P-N5, N-B4; 13 K-N1 (or 13 P-B4,
P-N4; 14 K-N1, B-Q2; 15 P-B5, NxN;
16 BxN, P-N5; 17 P-N6—Gilden–
Sherwin, Goldwater–Marshall Tour-
nament, New York 1973—with a
double-edged position), 13 . . .
B-Q2; 14 KR-N1, NxB; 15 BPxN,
P-N4; 16 Q-R5!, P-N5; 17 N3-K2
with an unclear position in an even
way. 2) Pushing the KBP: 12 P-B4,
N-B4; 13 P-B5, B-Q2; 14 K-N1,
P-QN4; 15 PxP, PxP; 16 N-B5 and
maybe White is a shade better.

| 12 | . . . | N-B4 |
| 13 | P-N5 | . . . |

Why Fischer had spent 15 minutes
on this is unclear.

| 13 | . . . | P-N4 |
| 14 | P-B3? | . . . |

THE LOSING MOMENT

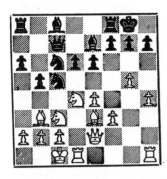

The position calls for a sharp attack
against Black's King and there is
no time to be lost for the laudable

purpose of protecting the KP. The
only practical chance was 14 P-R5!,
and if then 14 . . . P-N5; 15 N-R4,
NxP White unquestionably has a
strong attack after 16 P-N6. Note that
with White's King still on QB1 the
thematic combination 14 NxN, QxN
15 N-Q5 (with the idea 15 . . . PxN;
16 BxP and 17 BxR) fails after the
Zwischenzug 15 . . . NxB+!.

With the passive text move Fischer
loses another tempo for attacking
purposes and there just seems to be
no way of stopping Black's attack,
as perfectly executed by Larsen.

14	. . .	B-Q2!
15	Q-N2	P-N5
16	N3-K2	NxB+
17	RPxN	. . .

Unfeasible is 17 BPxN??, NxN+ and
17 NxN/3 just oils Black's Queenside machine better after 17 . . .
P-QR4 and 18 . . . P-R5.

| 17 | . . . | P-QR4 |
| 18 | P-N6 | . . . |

A standard line opening method.
It does not reach the desired mark,
yet is as good as any.

| 18 | . . . | BPxP |

This capture is possible because
Black's QB, thoughtfully developed
to Q2 (rather than QN2) protects
the KP.

19	P-R5	NxN
20	NxN	...

After 20 RxN Black also has 20 ...
P-N4!! 21 BxP, BxB+; 22 QxB, P-R5!;
23 R-B4 (23 Q-K7?, PxP), 23 ...
Q-N3; 24 R-N1, R-B2 with a winning
attack along the QR file in the
wings. And 20 BxN? allows 20 ...
P-N4 for free.

20	...	P-N4!!

Keeping as many Kingside lines
closed as possible. After 20 ...
PxP; 21 RxP White would have real
attacking chances along the open
KN and KR files.

21	BxP	...

Only marginally better was 21 P-R6,
as after 21 ... P-N3 and placing the
KR on KB2 Black's Kingside is safe
enough.

21	...	BxB+
22	QxB	P-R3!
23	Q-N4	...

Not 23 Q-K7?, R-B2; 24 NxP?, Q-B1!
and Black wins a piece.

23	...	R-B2!
24	KR-N1	...

Another opportunity for losing material was 24 NxP?, Q-B1; 25 RxP,
R-K2!

24	...	P-R5!

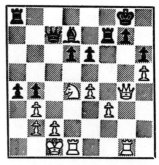

Larsen's play is a model of precision
in attack and defense. Wrong was
24 ... P-K4?; 25 N-K6!, Q-B1?; 26
RxP, and now 26 ... R-K2 (or 26
... R-R3 27 QxP+!, RxQ; 28 RxR+,
K-R1; 29 R7xB, RxR; 30 RxR, Q-N2;
31 R-Q8+, K-R2; 32 R-Q7+!, QxR;
33 N-B8+, and White wins (Due-
ball)) loses to 27 QxP+!, RxQ; 28
RxR+, K-R1; 29 R6xB. After the text
move this plan is no longer possible
as after 25 NxP, Q-B1; 26 RxP, Black
has 26 ... PxP with the mate threat
... QxP. And after White's forced
capture, 25 PxP, Black's QB5 square
has become available for his Queen.

25	PxP	P-K4!
26	N-K6?!	...

Playing an endgame with a piece
down must be absolutely hopeless
in the long run. Black obtains decisive attacks after either 26 N-N5,
Q-B4 or 26 N-B5, BxN; 27 PxB,
RxRP; even so there was more hope
in these. It is always possible to
misplay a winning attack, but almost
impossible not to win an endgame
with an extra piece.

| 26 | ... | Q-B5! |
| 27 | P-N3 | ... |

Equivalent to resignation. However, also after 27 RxP, Black wins easily enough: 27 ... P-N6; 28 P-B3, RxRP; 29 K-Q2, R-R3!.

27	...	QxN
28	QxQ	BxQ
29	RxQP	R-K1!
30	R-QN6	...

White does win the QNP and thus will have three protected passed Pawns on the Queenside. Yet they are rather immobile, and Black of course has an extra piece to help contain them. Meanwhile White's KBP and KRP are goners and Black then will have also protected passed Pawns: KNP and KRP. Just a bit of care is required on Black's part and Larsen shows the conclusion to be a relatively simple matter of technique.

30	...	RxP
31	RxQNP	R-QB1
32	K-N2	...

32 P-B4, R-B7 keeps the White King contained on the first rank.

32	...	R-B7
33	R-QB1	B-B2
34	P-R5	R-R1!
35	R-N5	...

Even after the better 35 R-QR1, 35 ... R-B3 puts a stop to everything.

35	...	BxRP
36	RxP	B-K7!
37	R-QB5	P-R4!
38	P-K5	B-B6
39	K-B3	P-R5
40	K-Q3	R-K7
41	R-B1	R-Q1+
42	K-B3	B-K5
43	K-N4	R-N1+
44	K-R3	P-R6

A new Queen coming up!

| 45 | P-K6 | BxP |

Nothing wrong with 45 ... P-R7, of course.

| 46 | P-N4 | R-K6+ |

The sealed move.

47 K-N2 . . .

Why did Bobby resume playing this hopelessly lost position? Was he hoping that Larsen would oversleep?

47	. . .	B-Q6
48	R-QR1	B-R3
49	R-B6	RxNP+
50	K-B2	B-N2
51	R-B3	R-K7+
52	K-Q1	R-KN7

WHITE RESIGNS

It was high time to pull down the curtain.

GAME 59

White: T. Petrosian (USSR)
Black: R. Fischer

*Played in Candidates Match Finals,
Buenos Aires (Argentina), October
5, 1971 Game 2*

At the time of this game Fischer had
won in a row 19 actual tournament
games and some kind of letdown
was long overdue. Nevertheless,
Bobby shows himself to be well
prepared for the opening and is
about to come out of it with full
equality. Then, suddenly, his play
becomes careless and apathetic and
he doesn't put up any obstacles at
all in his opponent's way. A game
which Petrosian plays in the best
"Fischer style": strategically clear,
positionally active and aggressive,
tactically decisive and perfect.

Gruenfeld Defense (4 B-B4)

1	P-Q4	N-KB3
2	P-QB4	P-KN3
3	N-QB3	P-Q4

Petrosian is a virtuoso in handling
the White side of the Samisch
against the King's Indian and Bobby
will have none of that. At Belgrade
1970, under similar opening circumstances, Fischer decided on the
Gruenfeld. Petrosian then continued
with 4 N-B3, B-N2; 5 PxP, NxP; 6

B-Q2, P-QB4; 7 R-B1, NxN; 8 BxN,
PxP; 9 NxP, O-O; 10 P-K3, Q-Q4;
11 N-N5, QxQ+; 12 RxQ with a
slight endgame edge for White.
Bobby finally equalized and drew
on move 52. (Game 4 of mini-
match).

4	B-B4	. . .

Tigran varies first. The Bishop move
forms the Classical Variation, where
White tries quickly to get his QR
to QB1 to apply pressure against
Black's Queenside and particularly
the QBP. In addition, also the
Bishop aims at the Queenside.

4	. . .	B-N2
5	P-K3	. . .

Also good and even a bit sharper is
5 N-B3.

5	. . .	P-B4

Instead 5 . . . P-B3 is somewhat
passive and 5 . . . O-O leads to a
theoretically much analyzed Pawn
sacrifice: 6 PxP, NxP; 7 NxN, QxN;
8 BxP. The immediate attack against
White's center with 5 . . . P-B4 is a
relatively new but promising approach.

6	QPxP	. . .

Rather childish is the attempt to win
a Pawn with 6 BxN, RxB; 7 Q-R4+,
B-Q2; 8 QxP. After 8 . . . BPxP; 9
QxQP, O-O!; 10 PxP, Q-R4!; 11 Q-Q2,

P-QN4; 12 B-Q3, P-N5; 13 QN-K2, QxQP Black's edge in development and two Bishops more than compensated the sacrificed Pawn and Black won decisively in Donner–Gheorghiu, Amsterdam 1969.

6	...	**Q-R4**
7	**R-B1**	...

A thematic defensive move (protecting the QN) and potentially attacking move (after Black's ... QxBP). White has nothing better: 7 Q-R4+ leads to an equal endgame; 7 Q-N3, PxP; 8 BxP, O-O; 9 N-B3, N-K5! to an equal middle game; while 7 PxP? opens up the gates for Black: 7 ... NxP!; 8 QxN, BxN+; 9 PxB QxBP/6+; 10 K-K2, QxR; 11 B-K5, Q-N8!; 12 BxR, B-K3 with a winning attack.

7	...	**N-K5!**

Black has reasonable chances for eventual equality with the older 7 ... PxP; 8 BxP, O-O. The text move, first played by Hort at the Palma 1970 Interzonal is considerably more effective. Bobby was there too, took a good note of the move, and added it to his repertoire.

8	**PxP**	...

The only logical approach. As compensation for his backward development White hopes to have an extra Pawn or at least a strong center. Ineffective was 8 N-B3?, NxN; 9 PxN, BxP+; 10 N-Q2, B-K3; 11 PxP, BxP; 12 P-K4!? BxRP; 13 R-R1!, P-K4! with Black's chances better in Reshevsky–Hort, Palma 1970.

8	...	**NxN**
9	**Q-Q2**	...

"With advantage for White" was the official theoretical evaluation prior to this game. But Fischer (and also unquestionably Hort) had bothered to look a couple of moves further and found that Black is perfectly okay.

9	...	**QxRP**
10	**PxN**	**Q-R4!**

True enough that after 10 ... QxQ+; 11 KxQ, N-Q2; 12 B-QN5 White keeps a sound Pawn advantage, but should theoreticians really overlook the obvious Queen retreat?

11	**B-B4**	...

The suggested 11 P-K4 makes sense after 11 ... QxBP/4?; 12 B-K3 and 13 B-Q4 but after the logical 11 ... N-Q2! and the imminent ... NxBP, White's unprotected KP will only be a liability.

11	...	**N-Q2**
12	**N-K2**	**N-K4**

An immediate 12 ... QxBP/4 is also good.

13	**B-R2**	**B-B4?**

A typical coffeehouse move, featuring automatic development and no thinking. Such an approach is only suitable for five-minute speed chess, where the emphasis is on completing the whole game in five minutes rather than making good moves. For tournament chess such an approach is suicidal.

After the good and obvious 13 ... QxBP/4 Black has full and sound equality. The passed QRP is a force to be reckoned with in a potential endgame.

14	BxN!	BxB
15	N-Q4	...

Fischer had completely overlooked White's last two moves and now has an unpleasant major positional decision to make: to allow doubled KBPs or to remain down the sacrificed QBP.

| 15 | ... | QxBP/4 |

Two moves too late! Objectively there was nothing better, yet more suitable for Bobby's active style was 15 ... B-Q2, though White keeps the advantage after 16 R-QN1!

16	NxB	PxN
17	O-O	...

White's positional advantage stems solely from the fact that because of the weakened Kingside Pawn formation, Black's King is unsafe both in the center or on the Kingside. In

addition, the advanced KBP is inherently weak and protecting it via ... P-K3 will lead to a further loosening of the King position.

| 17 | ... | Q-R4?? |

THE LOSING MOMENT

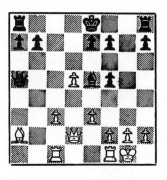

To voluntarily remove the Queen from a good central square to a meaningless spot on the edge of the board, while losing a tempo to do it, is altogether incomprehensible. As mentioned above, Black's immediate problems were the King's safety and the weak advanced KBP. A logical approach, then, was 17 ... P-B5!; and after 18 PxP, B-Q3 followed by Queenside castling. The opposite-color Bishops plus the fact that White's extra Pawn is a static doubled Pawn on the Kingside means that White's material advantage is of secondary importance. White stands better, of course, but the win is far out in the woods.

18 Q-B2!   P-B5
19 P-B4!   ...

White can ignore the KBP now and proceed effectively with his own attack.

19 ...   PxP
20 P-B5!   ...

In the first match game, Petrosian had obtained a promising attacking position but at the critical points simply refused to play attacking moves. He has obviously told himself that he will not make the same error again.

20 ...   Q-Q7

As good a chance as any. Without opportunities is 20 ... PxP+; 21 QxBP, O-O; 22 B-N1.

21 Q-R4+   K-B1

The King is quite unsafe here. Maybe 21 ... K-Q1 was better.

22 QR-Q1   ...

The sharpest. White is ready to sacrifice an exchange to keep his attack going. It could well be, however, that the positional 22 R-B2! was more effective.

22 ...   Q-K7

Fischer ignores the first way of winning the exchange: 22 ... P-K7; 23 RxQ, BxP+; 24 KxR, PxR(Q).

Indeed, Black's Queen is so badly placed that White breaks through after 25 P-Q6!.

23 P-Q6!?   ...

Petrosian continues with his newly found bravery. The move was much acclaimed in the chess world; yet Petrosian himself later recommended 23 P-N3! to first stop all possible counterplay.

23 ...   Q-R4?

This second way of winning the exchange is also hopeless. And if 23 ... PxQP; 24 Q-N3 wins similarly. Black, however, had a third way of winning the exchange and this would have given practically the best chances: 23 ... BxP+; 24 KxB, Q-R4+; 25 K-N1, P-K7. After 26 PxP+, K-N2!; 27 R-Q5! (not 27 R-Q3?, Q-R8+!! and Black wins), White has a strong attack but a forced win is difficult to prove.

24 P-B4!   ...

Decisive. Black takes the exchange as 24 ... B-B3; 25 R-Q5 is positionally hopeless.

24	...	P-K7
25	PxB	PxQR(Q)
26	RxQ	QxKP

What else?

| 27 | R-KB1! | P-B3 |

The "*Zwischen*-check" 27 ... QxBP+ is of no significance, but a bit further resistance was possible with the immediate 27 ... P-B4 though 28 Q-N3, P-K3; 29 QxNP, QxBP+; 30 K-R1, R-K1; 31 P-Q7, R-Q1; 32 BxP seems decisive.

| 28 | Q-N3! | K-N2 |

After 28 ... P-K3 29 QxNP is definitely curtains as Black's Queen is now tied to the defense of his KBP.

| 29 | Q-B7+ | K-R3 |
| 30 | PxP | ... |

| 30 | ... | P-B4 |

Clearly useless, but there is no hope; e.g., 30 ... KR-KN1; 31 B-N1, R-N3; 32 BxR, PxB; 33 Q-B8+ (R. Byrne), or 30 ... QR-KN1; 31 B-N1 threatening 32 RxP+, etc.

| 31 | RxP | Q-Q5+ |
| 32 | K-R1 | ... |

BLACK RESIGNS

The end is imminent.

GAME 60

White: B. Spassky (USSR)
Black R. Fischer

*Played in the World Championship
Match, Reykjavik (Iceland), July 11,
1972 Game 1*

Much has already been written about
the financial and personal problems
in getting The Match started. Also
chessically the start was most unpleasant for the American chess
public. In a static, dead-even endgame position, Fischer commits the
"blunder of the decade" and loses
his only remaining piece. Because
of the unique nature of the position,
there remain good practical drawing
chances. However, Bobby is too
dejected to hope for or look for any
good continuations and puts up no
fight at all.

So a most lucky start for Spassky,
yet with unfortunate and unforeseen
consequences. As already discussed
in this book (Games 23, 51, 57)
Spassky's prior successes against
Fischer came from tough, practical,
fighting chess. The gift half point
here apparently convinced Spassky
that he can do even better by playing safe "nothing" moves in the
expectation that Fischer will overreach. Yet points are scored by
making good moves rather than
safe moves, and by the time Spassky
woke up and realized this, the match
was almost out of reach.

*Nimzo-Indian Defense
(Rubinstein—Normal
Variation)*

1	P-Q4	N-KB3
2	P-QB4	P-K3
3	N-KB3	P-Q4

In Game 3 where a win was a must,
Fischer played the sharper 3 . . .
P-B4 and after 4 P-Q5 the Modern
Benoni was reached. One more
example of the transposition possi-
bilities in modern opening practice.

4	N-B3	B-N5

Bobby heads for the Ragosin again,
but why?

5	P-K3	. . .

Boris shows himself satisfied with a
quiet Nimzo-Indian.

5	. . .	O-O
6	B-Q3	P-B4
7	O-O	. . .

By transposition we have reached
the Normal Variation in the Nimzo-
Indian. Why the name? Well, over the
last twenty years when Black plays
the Nimzo-Indian this position occurs
much more frequently than any other.

7	. . .	N-B3

Perfectly good, sound, normal: the
Knight goes to a key central square.
The position is now completely
symmetrical except for the key difference of the KB locations. This

dissimilarity is sufficient to impart considerable life in the position. Also good and "normal" are 7 ... QN-Q2 and 7 ... QPxP.

8 P-QR3   B-R4

A modern retreat which keeps more tension in the position than 8 ... BxN; 9 PxB, QPxP; 10 BxBP, Q-B2.

9 N-K2   . . .

A rather tame continuation with which, however, Spassky had pleasant past experiences, so that his play here is quite understandable. More fighting chess results after 9 PxQP, KPxP; 10 PxP, BxN 11 PxB, B-N5.

9 . . .   QPxP
10 BxBP   B-N3

Before the game Bobby had decided to start the match off by a solid effort—and if the result is a draw, okay. More chances (for both sides) are offered by 10 ... PxP; 11 PxP where White has more freedom for his pieces, at the cost of the isolated QP.

11 PxP   QxQ!

After 11 ... BxP? 12 Q-B2! White's edge in development would be significant in the middle game. The position calls for the exchange of Queens, and Fischer quite correctly follows the call of the position.

12 RxQ   BxP
13 P-QN4   B-K2

As a result of the rather extensive maneuvers of Black's KB, White has some edge in development. In an endgame this is of less immediate value, and with the almost symmetrical Pawn formation Black is only a whisker away from equalization.

14 B-N2   B-Q2!

This innovation by Bobby makes the equality certain as Black will have 15 ... KR-Q1 as a follow-up. The tactical justification for the move is that 15 BxN?!, BxB; 16 RxB?? leaves the QR hanging. Instead of the text move, 14 ... P-QN3?! led to an advantage for White in Spassky–Krogius, 1958 USSR Championship: 15 N-B4, B-N2; 16 N-N5, N-Q1; 17 QR-B1, P-KR3; 18 N5xKP!.

15 QR-B1   . . .

Without further ado, Spassky accepts the indicated equality. True enough, 15 P-K4 is more "active," but after 15 ... KR-Q1; 16 P-K5, it is a moot point if the advanced KP signifies strength or weakness.

15	...	KR-Q1
16	N/2-Q4	NxN
17	NxN	...

Starting here and up to Black's 29th move, the game could be called a draw at any moment: the position is completely symmetrical with no strengths and weaknesses on either side. Why then isn't there a draw offer? Some commentators have suggested that Spassky and Fischer, by playing a short draw, didn't want to disappoint the spectators who had paid the equivalent of $5 admission. Poppycock! When going for the World Championship the last thing a competitor has on his mind is spectator happiness. You know what Bobby thinks of spectators, anyway! The true explanation is that both Spassky and Fischer are very proud men. Neither wanted to show the other that he is a bit more eager for the draw—which, in effect, is what a draw *offer* would have indicated. Thus they continued to play on in the full confidence that such a course would not harm their own position.

But what of the various expert commentators at this stage? It is almost superfluous to say that chess interest in the United States was at the highest pitch at the start of the match. As part of this interest, the Marshall Chess Club in New York City had a special program where all the games were demonstrated live to club members as well as a paying audience. I was senior commentator for this program as well as the "expert voice" during Public Broadcasting System's television coverage. The club rooms were chock full of TV and broadcasting people and equipment, and over and over, for the benefit of the media, I was saying that the position was so static that the game must end a draw. This was not my last error regarding the progress of the game!

17	...	B-R5!
18	B-N3	BxB

After 18 ... RxN?!; 19 BxB White would have a slight plus because of the two Bishops.

19	NxB	RxR +
20	RxR	R-QB1
21	K-B1	...

Or 21 BxN, BxB; 22 R-Q7, R-B6; 23 RxNP, P-N3 with equality.

21	...	K-B1
22	K-K2	N-K5
23	R-QB1	...

Anyone for a draw?

23	...	RxR

No one's talking—they're just moving!

24 BxR   P-B3

Rather useless. King centralization via 24 ... K-K1 was more logical. Of course, these comments are merely academic; practically, the position is a dead draw.

25	N-R5	N-Q3
26	K-Q3	B-Q1
27	N-B4	B-B2
28	NxN	BxN
29	P-N5!	...

After 29 P-R3, P-QN4! Black would have a slight advantage as White's Queenside Pawns would be fixed on the same color as Black's Bishop and thus theoretically could eventually be subject to attack. Actually, the position would still be drawn. Some spectators here had asked, "What if Black takes off the KRP?" I had just barely completed showing how that loses when over the teletype came ...

29   ...   BxKRP??

The shock left me dumfounded and flabbergasted. I couldn't see where I had erred in my analysis and also couldn't believe that Fischer was capable of such an error. How is such an error possible from a top master, or for that matter, from any master? Let us follow the train of thought that occurs in the master's mind in 99.9 percent (only a computer could do 100 percent) of the cases where a move like 29 ... BxKRP is legal: 1) Obviously the KRP can't be taken because after 30 P-N3 the Bishop is locked in and the White King returns to capture it. 2) I have lots of time left on my clock, so let me look just a bit deeper. Ah, after 30 P-N3, P-KR4; 31 K-K2, P-R5 White is "forced" to capture the RP since after 32 K-B3, P-R6!; 33 K-N4, B-N8; 34 KxP, BxP Black emerges with an extra Pawn. 3) That is almost too good to be true. Let me double check, just to be sure. Oops! After 35 B-Q2! the Black Bishop is still trapped and will be lost. What happened to Bobby was that in his eagerness he neglected to go through step 3 and impetuously made his final decision after step 2.

30	P-N3	P-KR4
31	K-K2	P-R5
32	K-B3	K-K2

Bobby now of course saw that 32 ... P-R6 is unsatisfactory, so rather quickly played the text move. More accurate would be to go for a Queenside Pawn clearing via 32 ... P-R3.

33 K-N2 ...

Perfectly logical. Much analysis has shown, however, that the sophisticated 33 B-Q2 may be most exact, as in certain positions it is in White's interest that his QRP is on the 3rd rather than 4th rank.

33	...	PxP
34	PxP	BxP
35	KxB	...

Under normal circumstances such positions are rather simple wins for White, since two Pawns are never sufficient compensation for the piece. In cases where the piece can't do any direct damage (as here), the win is accomplished thanks to *Zugzwang*: the defending King is pushed back while the stronger side's King penetrates. Here, however, two unique points regarding the Queenside Pawn formation make the win most problematical: 1) White's Bishop is of the wrong color for the QRP so that positions where White's only remaining Pawn is the QRP are drawn.

2) With the Kingside Pawns off the board (Black has good chances of achieving that) the following two types of positions are also drawn:
a) White: King any reasonable location, Bishop any reasonable location, P-QN6; Black: K-QB1, P-QN2, and b) White: King any, Bishop any,

P-QR5, QN6; Black: K-QB1, P-QR3, QN2.

In both these positions White can do nothing better than stalemate Black. For winning purposes in (2a) White's QNP must be on the fifth rank and in (2b) White's QRP must be on 4th or 3rd rank. Black then has a Pawn which can move; thanks to *Zugzwang* White will force the Pawn to move forward; White will then eventually win the advanced Pawn and in routine fashion the game.
All of the above means that if Black defends correctly the win is very difficult, if at all possible to achieve.

35	...	K-Q3
36	P-R4!	...

To be able to chase the King away from his QB4, e.g., 36 ... K-B4; 37 B-R3+.

36	...	K-Q4
37	B-R3	K-K5?

THE LOSING MOMENT

Bobby was thoroughly disgusted and dejected around this time and didn't bother to investigate whether there could be any hidden drawing possibilities. You can't find anything if you do no searching! Correct was the obvious 37 ... P-R3! with a view toward achieving one of the drawing Queenside Pawn formations shown above. For this purpose the King is well located on Q4 as he can readily get to the Queenside. After 37 ... P-R3! I have not been able to find a forced win. White comes close, but there is no victory. Instead, Fischer errs because he doesn't notice a tactical possibility. The result is that the text move costs a couple of tempos, enough to lose.

38 B-B5!   P-R3

After the intended 38 ... P-QN3? White breaks through with 39 BxP!, PxB; 40 P-R5! and either the QRP or the QNP queens.

39 P-N6   P-B4

"Prepares" a frightful idea. Even so there is no more salvation, e.g., 39 ... P-K4; 40 K-N4, P-N3; 41 K-N3! (a bit of *Zugzwang*), P-B4; 42 K-R4, P-B5; 43 PxP, KxP (43 ... PxP; 44 K-N5); 44 B-K7!, P-K5; 45 B-N5+, K-B6; 46 B-B1!, P-K6; 47 K-N5, P-K7; 48 B-Q2, K-B7; 49 KxP (Pachman) and White's King will win the QNP and the game.

40 K-R4!   . . .

At this moment another spectator at the Marshall Chess Club suggested pushing the KBP and had heard my reply (that this would be horrible as a Bishop can readily out-tempo two isolated Pawns) when Black's move came . . .

40 . . .   P-B5??

The remotest thought in my mind is that Mednis is better than Fischer and the only reason for recounting the actual events at the Marshall Chess Club during that horribly hot, humid, unhappy day is to show the reader how totally upset Bobby's machine-like chess mind had become as a result of the blundering 29 ... BxKRP??. After that move he just couldn't think straight anymore. Black must try to retain connected Pawns on the Kingside while trying to induce White to play the drawing P-QR5 on the Queenside. The only practical try was 40 ... K-Q4, though White still has a problem-like win after 41 B-N4!, K-B3; 42 B-R5!!, K-B4; 43 K-N5 K-B5; 44 K-N6, K-Q6; 45 KxP, KxP; 46 K-B6, etc.

41 PxP   . . .

The sealed move. An excellent tournament tactic, as it gives Spassky (and his grandmaster seconds) full opportunity to discover in home analysis White's best technique, starting with move 42.

41	. . .	KxP
42	K-R5!	. . .

Generally speaking, the winning technique will consist of drawing away Black's King from the Kingside Pawns, thanks to *Zugzwang*. Do note that this position would be a draw if White's QRP were on the 5th rank, as then Black's King need only reach his QB1 to establish a stalemate heaven. The particular advantage of having the White King on KR5 is that he can get to Black's QNP if Black goes after White's QRP: 42 . . . K-K5; 43 K-N6, K-Q4; 44 B-N1, K-B5; 45 K-B7! (time is money—the Bishop by itself can stop the KNP), 45 . . . K-N5; 46 KxP (this comes for nothing as it is on the way), 46 . . . KxP; 47 K-Q7, K-N4; 48 K-B7, etc. and White wins.

42	. . .	K-B4
43	B-K3!	. . .

This and the following maneuvers, though quite pretty and thematic, are still relatively simple for grandmaster play. It just goes to prove once more that a King and Bishop combination can tempo the hell out of King and two isolated Pawns.

43	. . .	K-K5
44	B-B2	K-B4
45	B-R4!	P-K4
46	B-N5	P-K5
47	B-K3	. . .

Thanks to *Zugzwang*, Black must now give ground.

47	. . .	K-B3
48	K-N4	K-K4
49	K-N5	. . .

Again Black must give ground someplace. Bobby could safely resign here—there is no practical saving chance left.

49	. . .	K-Q4
50	K-B5	P-R4
51	B-B2!	P-N4
52	KxP	K-B5
53	K-B5	K-N5
54	KxP!	. . .

No reason not to take it here.

54	. . .	KxP
55	K-Q5	K-N4
56	K-Q6	. . .

BLACK RESIGNS

After 56 . . . P-R5; 57 K-B7, K-R3; 58 B-Q4, Black's King will soon be forced (thanks to *Zugzwang* again!) to give up protection of the QNP.

GAME 61

White: B. Spassky (USSR)
Black: R. Fischer

*Played in the World Championship
Match, Reykjavik (Iceland),
August 6, 1972 Game 11*

The last game Fischer was to lose.
One of his worst efforts.

*Sicilian Defense
(Najdorf—Fischer's QNP)*

1	P-K4	P-QB4
2	N-KB3	P-Q3
3	P-Q4	PxP
4	NxP	N-KB3
5	N-QB3	P-QR3
6	B-KN5	...

Despite the lack of success with
this move in Match Game 7, Spassky,
being 3 points down, has to play
sharply.

6	...	P-K3
7	P-B4	Q-N3
8	Q-Q2	QxP
9	N-N3	...

This has the virtue of being less
analyzed generally, thus Spassky
felt that he has a better practical
chance with it than with the usual 9
R-QN1 (see Game 53). Objectively
though, 9 N-N3 does not look very
logical: the Knight is well placed

on Q4 and White's QR on QN1
also has a good location.

9	...	Q-R6

The threat was 10 P-QR3 and 11
R-R2, trapping the Queen.

| 10 | BxN | ... |

A quiet positional continuation.
White will simply play the game a
Pawn down in the hope of even-
tually taking advantage of Black's
somewhat loose position. In Match
Game 7, Spassky did poorly with
10 B-Q3, B-K2!; 11 O-O, P-KR3; 12
B-R4, NxP!; 13 NxN?!, BxB; 14 P-B5
PxP!

10	...	PxB
11	B-K2	P-KR4

"Automatically" preventing 12
B-R5. This seems a positional neces-
sity here.

12	O-O	N-B3
13	K-R1	B-Q2

Some commentators during and after
the match criticized Black's last two
moves. But why should such healthy
development moves be bad, especially since White is not undertaking
anything?

| 14 | N-N1!? | ... |

A move which was invariably given
two exclamation marks—14 N-N1!!
after the game. May I respectfully

suggest that if Spassky had proceeded to lose this game it would
have read 14 N-N1?? If we look at
the nature of the position, it should
be apparent that neither of these
extremes is warranted. White has
difficulties in how to continue, so
he decides to first kick Black's
Queen. However, this is an open
position and White's QN is placed
well on QB3. Retreating it to QN1
obviously cannot be a winning
maneuver. It is simply an interesting
concept, which works because
Fischer has an off game. Under the
circumstances 14 N-Q1!? would also
have probably won. As a historical
note, it may be stated that those
commentators who were loudest in
applauding 14 N-N1!? neither played
it themselves nor worried about it
when their turn came. One example
is Tal–R. Byrne, Leningrad Interzonal
1973 which continued instead 14
Q-K3, R-B1; 15 N-N1, Q-R5; 16
P-B4, N-R4; 17 Q-QB3, NxP; 18
QxBP, R-R3 and it turned out that
Black stood quite well.

14   ...   Q-N5

The dangerous looking 14 ... Q-N7
seems also playable, as does 14
... Q-R5; 15 P-QR3, N-K2!; 16
N-B3, Q-B3 and Black is safe enough.
True, White has compensation for
the Pawn, but what is so new about
that? He's had that since 8 ... QxP!

15   Q-K3   P-Q4??

THE LOSING MOMENT

Probably the worst move on the
board: Black gives up his valuable
QP for nothing and for no reason.
Almost any other move would be
better and sufficient for equality.
Interesting too is Paul Schmidt's
suggestion 15 ... P-KB4!? giving up
a *doubled KBP* for line opening.
One variation he gives: 16 PxP,
N-K2; 17 PxP, PxP; 18 P-B5, B-R3;
19 BxP+, K-Q1; 20 Q-Q4, QxQ;
21 NxQ, NxP; 22 NxN, PxN with a
fine endgame for Black. In variations like this the horrible location
of the QN on QN1 is very obvious.

16   PxP   N-K2
17   P-B4   ...

Bobby may have neglected to notice
that this move is possible. For his
sacrificed Pawn Black has a lost
position. No satisfactory defense
exists, but Bobby manages to lose
the fastest way.

17   ...   N-B4
18   Q-Q3   P-R5

Threatening 19 ... N-N6+; 20 PxN
PxP+; 21 K-N1, QxN!! and 22 ...
B-B4+. Spassky prevents it readily.

| 19 | B-N4! | N-Q3 |
| 20 | N1-Q2 | P-B4?! |

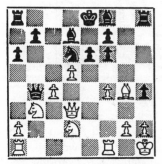

(Position after 20 N1-Q2)

Opening up the position for White!
Anything else would have been
better.

21 P-QR3,   Q-N3

If 21 ... Q-R5; 22 Q-QB3! and 23
N-B5.

| 22 | P-B5 | Q-N4 |
| 23 | Q-QB3 | PxB? |

Giving up the Queen is pointless.
23 ... R-KN1; 24 P-R4, B-N2 at
least would have kept it.

24 P-R4   P-R6?

After 24 ... Q-K7; 25 QR-K1, QxR
Black would get a Rook rather than
a Pawn for his Queen. That the game
would be hopeless, anyway, is
beside the point.

25 PxQ   ...

Starting now, the atmosphere at the
Marshall Chess Club became like
that of a morgue. But happily for
the last time in the match! Only
journalistic discipline makes me give
the rest of the game.

25	...	PxP+
26	KxP	R-R6
27	Q-B6	N-B4
28	P-B6	B-B1
29	QPxP	BPxP
30	KR-K1	B-K2
31	RxKP	...

BLACK RESIGNS

PART FIVE

1972–1997

Darkness Before Dawn

Just as Paul Morphy had done more than a hundred years earlier, so, too, Bobby Fischer returned from his European success to a tumultuous, triumphant reception in New York. A large public celebration was held outside City Hall, followed by a VIP reception inside in the Blue Room, both presided over by the mayor, John V. Lindsay. I had the pleasure of participating in a private five-minute chat with Fischer and Mayor Lindsay. Bobby was charming in every way and responded animatedly to my recollections of various examples of his past generosity. He was deservedly on top of the world.

As Fischer's star rose, the status of chess changed from a hobby to a respected profession. More people played, more chess books were sold, new sponsors appeared. Even the Soviet Union took the "capitalistic" step of significantly increasing tournament prizes. Yet the person who brought it all about quickly grew silent and invisible. The number of public appearances by GM Fischer over the next year barely reached the number of fingers on one hand. The brief list included an appearance on a Bob Hope TV special, meeting the players of the San Antonio International Tournament in November 1972, a TV interview with Dinah Shore, and playing an exhibition game against Ferdinand Marcos of the Philippines as part of the ceremonies for the 1973 Manila International Tournament. That was Fischer's last public appearance until his 1992 return match with Spassky. The reason that the commercial opportunities stopped was that Bobby turned all of them down. He had come to view every offer to him as an attempt to cheat him. The type of question that he raised in his mind was, "The only reason why XX Company is offering me $100,000 is because I'm worth more that this to them, isn't it so?" Thus every offer became unacceptable, including those where the initial offer had been increased substantially. Of course, the only negative impact of such behavior was on Fischer's own bank account. If Bobby did not want to exploit his status as world champion to become rich, that was his own business. It did not affect the chess world.

What did affect the chess world was Fischer's abstention from competitive chess. In the years before he became world champion, Bobby had become the loudest and most persistent critic of the relative lack of tournament activity by the then reigning champions, all of them from the Soviet Union. It would all be different if he ever had a fair chance to play for the title! (Fischer was certain that he would win any "fair" match). It was therefore both a shock and great disappointment to his fans and to the chess public that as soon as he became world champion, Bobby's interest in popularizing the game disappeared: no tournaments, no chess lectures, no chess writing (not even an analysis of the 1972 World Championship Match).

It soon became clear that nothing would be seen of Fischer's chess until the triannual World Championship match in 1975. Even here storm clouds were gathering. Because of Fischer's incessant complaints about the unfairness of the world champion having any advantage, FIDE changed its regulations. But as soon as he became champion, his attitude changed completely: he now vehemently insisted that "it's historical that the champion has advantages." When Col. Edmondson pointed out this inconsistency to Bobby, his response was simply, "Yes, I know. But the situation now is different."

A confident Fischer prepared his sets of "nonnegotiable demands" that FIDE would have to accept if it wanted him to defend his title in 1975. The initial reaction was cool, yet the brilliant work by Col. Edmondson, as well as the interest on the part of the chess public in seeing Fischer play again, led to the calling of an "Extraordinary General Assembly" in February 1975 at Bergen, Holland. Here all of Fischer's demands were met except the most extreme one: the challenger would need to win by at least a 10–8 (games won/lost) score to gain the title. Even this proposal lost by just a few votes—a tribute to Edmondson's work and the respect that Fischer commanded. Yet Bobby remained adamant: when he said "nonnegotiable" demands, that is exactly what he meant!

When the summer came and the deadline passed for agreeing to the FIDE-mandated match regulations, the inevitable happened. FIDE President Max Euwe crowned Anatoly Karpov as the new world champion. A title gained by default is real enough, yet obviously lacking respect and financial remuneration. It should be remembered that the prize fund guaranteed by the government of the Philippines for the proposed 1975 title match at Manila was $5 million.

Karpov realized that the right thing to do was to try to set up a match with Fischer under mutually agreeable conditions. He describes these negotiations at some length in his book *Karpov on Karpov*. These discussions started in person in Tokyo on July 25, 1976, and ended a year later in Washington, when Bobby refused to sign the final agreement.

Fischer's twenty years in the chess wilderness—from September 1972 through August 1992—were marked by initial promise and aborted hope. There were rumors of coming matches, perhaps against Miguel Quiteros of Argentina or Eugene Torre of the Philippines. There were reports of commercial chess agreements. Yet nothing came to pass. Bobby's only involvement with chess during this period was the playing of some private games against the Greenblatt computer chess program of the Massachusetts Institute of Technology in 1977. Of course, he easily won all games against the rather weak opponent.

As the years passed, it became increasingly doubtful that Bobby would return to chess. More and more "experts" published elaborate explanations on the theme "Why Fischer Will Never Play Again."

The question "Will Fischer play again?" was also asked of me many times. My answer was "I don't know." I explained that geniuses think differently from the rest of us. And I am hardly the only person who regards Fischer as a genius. In a September 1981 interview in *Playboy* magazine, James Michener, the best-selling author of *Tales of the South Pacific, Hawaii, Chesapeake, The Source,* and many, many other books was asked, "Of all the people you've met in your lifetime, who were the men of genius?" Mr. Michener responded, "I have met only two geniuses, a word that ought to be used with great care. . . . One was Bobby Fischer, the chess player, and the other was Tennessee Williams. . . . From the point of view of genius in action, Bobby Fischer is quite compelling."

Because Fischer is a genius and I am not, it was obvious to me that I had no basis for gauging his future actions. Nevertheless, the prospects seemed bleak. Not only had he turned down all opportunities, but he had also instituted a requirement that every proposal be accompanied by a nonreturnable check for $50,000. Apparently, one or two such checks were received. Not surprisingly, the proposals themselves were rejected.

Yet one small harbinger of hope appeared in the spring of 1990. Bobby Fischer traveled to Brussels to meet with Bessel Kok, president of SWIFT and Chairman of the Grandmasters Association. This meeting was widely reported to have concerned the new chess clock that Fischer had invented. Yet Kok, in an interview published in 1990 in *New in Chess Magazine,* had this to say about the meeting: "It [the plan] is very concrete and it has to do with chess. And it's not the clock only. . . ." What is significant here is that Bobby, apparently quite on his own initiative, had taken a step, however small, toward returning to the chess world.

Nevertheless, the expert opinion remained unanimous that Bobby Fischer's departure from chess was permanent. Arnold Denker, a lifelong friend and supporter of Fischer's, wrote "My own theory about why Bobby quit chess is based on the notion that chess—or rather his personal chess legend as an incomparable and undefeated genius—means everything to him. It is his raison d'etre—the single support for a very frail ego."

Fischer—Spassky 1992

On July 25, 1992, *The New York Times* carried an electrifying headline:
FISCHER AND SPASSKY SAID TO SIGN FOR CHESS REMATCH IN YUGOSLAVIA. The *Times*
reported that Jezdimir Vasiljevic, the owner of a Belgrade-based bank, had put
up a $5-million purse for the match, with the winner getting $3.35 million
and the loser $1.65 million. The first one to win ten games would win the
match. Other conditions required each game to be completed without
adjournment and that the Fischer-invented clock be used. The first part of the
match was to be held in the resort town of Sveti Stefan and the second part in
the capital, Belgrade.

Initial reaction from the chess public was a combination of excitement and
skepticism. The chess public wondered, What has caused Bobby to return?
The answers were of course varied: his need for money, the large prize fund,
the influence of his nineteen-year-old Hungarian girlfriend Zita Rajcsányi,
Fischer's realization that this might be his last chance for big money, and so
on. Again, I offer no expert opinions of my own. Only Bobby knows, and he
may not want to divulge the full answer.

As the date for the match, September 2, approached, the discussions turned to
chess. Was Fischer in good enough chess condition? Had he been keeping
up with chess theory during the previous twenty years? Reliable information
was again scant. Obviously Bobby was saying nothing. Only the supergrand-
masters who had visited Bobby in the wilderness era—Korchnoi or Spassky—
were willing to say something to reporters after their visits. The reports were
invariably general and positive, such as "He's still very strong," "He is current
in chess developments," "He has a low opinion of Karpov's and Kasparov's
chess." I must admit that I felt that Fischer had studied chess conscientiously
during his exile. How else would he have spent these twenty years? A close
study of the match games has forced me to change my mind. I think that
Bobby has spent very little time on chess studies (more about this later).

Perhaps the best way to describe the match course is "varied." Game 1 was
indeed a brilliant example of Bobby at his best. Unfortunately for his fans, the
euphoria was short-lived. Games 2 and 3 showed little; Games 4 and 5 were
disasters. In Game 4 Fischer forced his opponent to make a very promising

exchange sacrifice. Spassky got a good pawn and a strong bind for his small sacrifice. Black's position required very perceptive defending involving proper piece coordination. Yet Bobby never came up with a useful concept of what to do. His performance in Game 5 was even worse. Even though Spassky repeated the opening of Game 3 through Move 17, Fischer never rose to the requirements of the position. In the latter stages of the game he embarked on some obviously unsound sacrifices—something quite foreign to the "real" Fischer.

A great fighter, Bobby came back strongly. After a lucky draw in Game 6, he won nicely in Game 7, got a lucky win in Game 8, and then demolished GM Spassky right after the opening in Game 9. A hard-fought draw in Game 10 preceded an impressive strategic and tactical effort in Game 11. This ended the first part of the match with the score 5–2, and the scene moved to Belgrade.

The resumption was most inauspicious for Fischer. In Game 12 he handled the King's Indian Defense so passively that he was squashed in 54 moves. Not once was he able to come up for just a bit of air. The next three games were drawn, with Spassky having some advantage in Game 13 and Fischer in Game 15. Game 16 was all Fischer, with his opponent falling into an old opening trap on Move 9! This energized Bobby, and once he obtained a superior endgame in Game 17, he gave a virtuoso demonstration of how to win a Rook + Bishop vs. Rook + Knight endgame. Game 18 was a "GM draw," with little fighting effort on either side. Game 19 gave GM Fischer the opportunity to return a favor to Spassky, since he failed to win an elementary Queen endgame where he was two pawns up. The immediate result was a Closed Sicilian Defense that was very poorly played by Bobby. He did nothing right in the opening and the middle game and went down to defeat with barely a sign of life.

But again the problems were of short duration. Fischer squeezed out a nice endgame win in Game 21, drew comfortably on the black side of a Closed Sicilian in Game 22, and, even though he overplayed his hand in Game 23 still managed to escape with a draw. In game 24 Black achieved another good draw, followed by an impressive, successful attacking victory in Game 25.

The final phase of the match was just as mixed as the earlier ones had been. Fischer was again listless on the black side of a King's Indian in Game 26 and was ground down mercilessly in 58 moves. Games 27, 28, and 29 were normal draws. For Fischer fans, the match ended on truly a high note: in Game 30 Bobby came up with a creative opening and carried out his concept in active, thematic fashion. The final result: Fischer prevailed, 10 wins to 5, with 15 draws.

Was this the great Bobby Fischer or a pale facsimile? First, a few numbers. Using Fischer's 1972 rating of 2,780 and GM Spassky's prematch rating of 2,560, Fischer's performance rating works out to be "only" 2,618. The result is that the match cost him 59 rating points.

Bobby won the match simply because he was the better player: once great, always great. Yet during a large part of the match he was unrecognizable to me. It is important to remember that before his retreat from chess, he was acknowledged to be the most knowledgeable and creative opening expert of all time. In this match Fischer left the impression that during the preceding twenty years he had done no openings work at all. Consider that in 1972 he was recognized as the world's greatest expert on the King's Indian Defense. Yet in this match, in five of the seven games that he played the KID (Games 2, 8, 12, 26, 28) his performance was mediocre to poor. Only the last game, 30, showed the real Bobby Fischer.

What about the future? Will Bobby continue playing? As I write these lines, press reports are carrying news of a proposed match against Judit Polgar. But mere mortals like me are not qualified to forecast the future ways of geniuses like Bobby Fischer.

Epilogue
How to Beat Bobby Fisher

Can you defeat Bobby Fischer now? Can I beat him? Well, not really. Otherwise I would be out challenging him for million-dollar purses, rather than writing a book about it!

However, a close study of all his games, together with the detailed study of his lost games that we have just gone through, does give us some pretty effective do's and don'ts when playing Bobby.

First, some things not to do, if success is your aim.

1. Don't try to surprise Bobby with a doubtful opening variation. Either he already is familiar with it or will find the refutation over the board.

2. Don't weaken your position for some obscure compensation. He'll bore right in and through it.

3. Don't play any moves that you feel are not the best. If you see their weakness, why shouldn't he?

4. Don't voluntarily accept a slightly inferior game (middle game or ending) if the position is strategically straightforward, in the hope of holding on to a draw. Spassky and Petrosian couldn't do it and neither will you.

And now, for the ultimate advice in how to defeat Robert J. Fischer:

1. Play good sound openings, both for White and Black. He may overreach in storming a sound bastion.

2. When confronted with a clear positional threat and an obscure tactical one, *always* protect against the clear positional threat. Bobby does not like obscure tactics.

3. If the opportunity presents itself, go for a totally wild and unbalanced position. But be sure that it is truly uncontrolled with no clear strategic bench marks. Bobby is a fine tactician, but in crazy positions anyone can make errors and Fischer does not particularly enjoy such positions (see, e.g., Games 29, 53, 54, 58).

One further note on Bobby's opening selections is of interest. Fischer has played many variations once. The first time he plays something it is of no significance for the future. He may have prepared it just for a single surprise. When a variation has appeared the second time, however, this means that Bobby has become convinced of its fundamental soundness. Be prepared to meet it. And consider adding it to your own opening repertoire.

Okay, go out and beat the World Champ—even if it is in a simultaneous exhibition!

A CATALOG OF SELECTED
DOVER BOOKS
IN ALL FIELDS OF INTEREST

A CATALOG OF SELECTED DOVER
BOOKS IN ALL FIELDS OF INTEREST

CONCERNING THE SPIRITUAL IN ART, Wassily Kandinsky. Pioneering work by father of abstract art. Thoughts on color theory, nature of art. Analysis of earlier masters. 12 illustrations. 80pp. of text. 5⅜ x 8½. 23411-8 Pa. $3.95

ANIMALS: 1,419 Copyright-Free Illustrations of Mammals, Birds, Fish, Insects, etc., Jim Harter (ed.). Clear wood engravings present, in extremely lifelike poses, over 1,000 species of animals. One of the most extensive pictorial sourcebooks of its kind. Captions. Index. 284pp. 9 x 12. 23766-4 Pa. $12.95

CELTIC ART: The Methods of Construction, George Bain. Simple geometric techniques for making Celtic interlacements, spirals, Kells-type initials, animals, humans, etc. Over 500 illustrations. 160pp. 9 x 12. (USO) 22923-8 Pa. $9.95

AN ATLAS OF ANATOMY FOR ARTISTS, Fritz Schider. Most thorough reference work on art anatomy in the world. Hundreds of illustrations, including selections from works by Vesalius, Leonardo, Goya, Ingres, Michelangelo, others. 593 illustrations. 192pp. 7⅛ x 10¼. 20241-0 Pa. $9 95

CELTIC HAND STROKE-BY-STROKE (Irish Half-Uncial from "The Book of Kells"): An Arthur Baker Calligraphy Manual, Arthur Baker. Complete guide to creating each letter of the alphabet in distinctive Celtic manner. Covers hand position, strokes, pens, inks, paper, more. Illustrated. 48pp. 8¼ x 11. 24336-2 Pa. $3.95

EASY ORIGAMI, John Montroll. Charming collection of 32 projects (hat, cup, pelican, piano, swan, many more) specially designed for the novice origami hobbyist. Clearly illustrated easy-to-follow instructions insure that even beginning papercrafters will achieve successful results. 48pp. 8¼ x 11. 27298-2 Pa. $2.95

THE COMPLETE BOOK OF BIRDHOUSE CONSTRUCTION FOR WOODWORKERS, Scott D. Campbell. Detailed instructions, illustrations, tables. Also data on bird habitat and instinct patterns. Bibliography. 3 tables. 63 illustrations in 15 figures. 48pp. 5¼ x 8½. 24407-5 Pa. $2.50

BLOOMINGDALE'S ILLUSTRATED 1886 CATALOG: Fashions, Dry Goods and Housewares, Bloomingdale Brothers. Famed merchants' extremely rare catalog depicting about 1,700 products: clothing, housewares, firearms, dry goods, jewelry, more. Invaluable for dating, identifying vintage items. Also, copyright-free graphics for artists, designers. Co-published with Henry Ford Museum & Greenfield Village. 160pp. 8¼ x 11. 25780-0 Pa. $9.95

HISTORIC COSTUME IN PICTURES, Braun & Schneider. Over 1,450 costumed figures in clearly detailed engravings–from dawn of civilization to end of 19th century. Captions. Many folk costumes. 256pp. 8⅜ x 11¾. 23150-X Pa. $12.95

STICKLEY CRAFTSMAN FURNITURE CATALOGS, Gustav Stickley and L. & J. G. Stickley. Beautiful, functional furniture in two authentic catalogs from 1910. 594 illustrations, including 277 photos, show settles, rockers, armchairs, reclining chairs, bookcases, desks, tables. 183pp. 6½ x 9¼. 23838-5 Pa. $9.95

AMERICAN LOCOMOTIVES IN HISTORIC PHOTOGRAPHS: 1858 to 1949, Ron Ziel (ed.). A rare collection of 126 meticulously detailed official photographs, called "builder portraits," of American locomotives that majestically chronicle the rise of steam locomotive power in America. Introduction. Detailed captions. xi + 129pp. 9 x 12. 27393-8 Pa. $12.95

AMERICA'S LIGHTHOUSES: An Illustrated History, Francis Ross Holland, Jr. Delightfully written, profusely illustrated fact-filled survey of over 200 American lighthouses since 1716. History, anecdotes, technological advances, more. 240pp. 8 x 10¾. 25576-X Pa. $12.95

TOWARDS A NEW ARCHITECTURE, Le Corbusier. Pioneering manifesto by founder of "International School." Technical and aesthetic theories, views of industry, economics, relation of form to function, "mass-production split" and much more. Profusely illustrated. 320pp. 6⅛ x 9¼. (USO) 25023-7 Pa. $9.95

HOW THE OTHER HALF LIVES, Jacob Riis. Famous journalistic record, exposing poverty and degradation of New York slums around 1900, by major social reformer. 100 striking and influential photographs. 233pp. 10 x 7⅞. 22012-5 Pa. $10.95

FRUIT KEY AND TWIG KEY TO TREES AND SHRUBS, William M. Harlow. One of the handiest and most widely used identification aids. Fruit key covers 120 deciduous and evergreen species; twig key 160 deciduous species. Easily used. Over 300 photographs. 126pp. 5⅜ x 8½. 20511-8 Pa. $3.95

COMMON BIRD SONGS, Dr. Donald J. Borror. Songs of 60 most common U.S. birds: robins, sparrows, cardinals, bluejays, finches, more–arranged in order of increasing complexity. Up to 9 variations of songs of each species. Cassette and manual 99911-4 $8.95

ORCHIDS AS HOUSE PLANTS, Rebecca Tyson Northen. Grow cattleyas and many other kinds of orchids–in a window, in a case, or under artificial light. 63 illustrations. 148pp. 5⅜ x 8½. 23261-1 Pa. $4.95

MONSTER MAZES, Dave Phillips. Masterful mazes at four levels of difficulty. Avoid deadly perils and evil creatures to find magical treasures. Solutions for all 32 exciting illustrated puzzles. 48pp. 8¼ x 11. 26005-4 Pa. $2.95

MOZART'S DON GIOVANNI (DOVER OPERA LIBRETTO SERIES), Wolfgang Amadeus Mozart. Introduced and translated by Ellen H. Bleiler. Standard Italian libretto, with complete English translation. Convenient and thoroughly portable–an ideal companion for reading along with a recording or the performance itself. Introduction. List of characters. Plot summary. 121pp. 5¼ x 8½. 24944-1 Pa. $2.95

TECHNICAL MANUAL AND DICTIONARY OF CLASSICAL BALLET, Gail Grant. Defines, explains, comments on steps, movements, poses and concepts. 15-page pictorial section. Basic book for student, viewer. 127pp. 5⅜ x 8½. 21843-0 Pa. $4.95

BRASS INSTRUMENTS: Their History and Development, Anthony Baines. Authoritative, updated survey of the evolution of trumpets, trombones, bugles, cornets, French horns, tubas and other brass wind instruments. Over 140 illustrations and 48 music examples. Corrected and updated by author. New preface. Bibliography. 320pp. 5⅜ x 8½. 27574-4 Pa. $9.95

HOLLYWOOD GLAMOR PORTRAITS, John Kobal (ed.). 145 photos from 1926-49. Harlow, Gable, Bogart, Bacall; 94 stars in all. Full background on photographers, technical aspects. 160pp. 8⅜ x 11¼. 23352-9 Pa. $11.95

MAX AND MORITZ, Wilhelm Busch. Great humor classic in both German and English. Also 10 other works: "Cat and Mouse," "Plisch and Plumm," etc. 216pp. 5⅜ x 8½. 20181-3 Pa. $6.95

THE RAVEN AND OTHER FAVORITE POEMS, Edgar Allan Poe. Over 40 of the author's most memorable poems: "The Bells," "Ulalume," "Israfel," "To Helen," "The Conqueror Worm," "Eldorado," "Annabel Lee," many more. Alphabetic lists of titles and first lines. 64pp. 5³⁄₁₆ x 8¼. 26685-0 Pa. $1.00

PERSONAL MEMOIRS OF U. S. GRANT, Ulysses Simpson Grant. Intelligent, deeply moving firsthand account of Civil War campaigns, considered by many the finest military memoirs ever written. Includes letters, historic photographs, maps and more. 528pp. 6⅛ x 9¼. 28587-1 Pa. $11.95

AMULETS AND SUPERSTITIONS, E. A. Wallis Budge. Comprehensive discourse on origin, powers of amulets in many ancient cultures: Arab, Persian Babylonian, Assyrian, Egyptian, Gnostic, Hebrew, Phoenician, Syriac, etc. Covers cross, swastika, crucifix, seals, rings, stones, etc. 584pp. 5⅜ x 8½. 23573-4 Pa. $12.95

RUSSIAN STORIES/PYCCKNE PACCKA3bl: A Dual-Language Book, edited by Gleb Struve. Twelve tales by such masters as Chekhov, Tolstoy, Dostoevsky, Pushkin, others. Excellent word-for-word English translations on facing pages, plus teaching and study aids, Russian/English vocabulary, biographical/critical introductions, more. 416pp. 5⅜ x 8½. 26244-8 Pa. $8.95

PHILADELPHIA THEN AND NOW: 60 Sites Photographed in the Past and Present, Kenneth Finkel and Susan Oyama. Rare photographs of City Hall, Logan Square, Independence Hall, Betsy Ross House, other landmarks juxtaposed with contemporary views. Captures changing face of historic city. Introduction. Captions. 128pp. 8¼ x 11. 25790-8 Pa. $9.95

AIA ARCHITECTURAL GUIDE TO NASSAU AND SUFFOLK COUNTIES, LONG ISLAND, The American Institute of Architects, Long Island Chapter, and the Society for the Preservation of Long Island Antiquities. Comprehensive, well-researched and generously illustrated volume brings to life over three centuries of Long Island's great architectural heritage. More than 240 photographs with authoritative, extensively detailed captions. 176pp. 8¼ x 11. 26946-9 Pa. $14.95

NORTH AMERICAN INDIAN LIFE: Customs and Traditions of 23 Tribes, Elsie Clews Parsons (ed.). 27 fictionalized essays by noted anthropologists examine religion, customs, government, additional facets of life among the Winnebago, Crow, Zuni, Eskimo, other tribes. 480pp. 6⅛ x 9¼. 27377-6 Pa. $10.95

FRANK LLOYD WRIGHT'S HOLLYHOCK HOUSE, Donald Hoffmann. Lavishly illustrated, carefully documented study of one of Wright's most controversial residential designs. Over 120 photographs, floor plans, elevations, etc. Detailed perceptive text by noted Wright scholar. Index. 128pp. 9¼ x 10¾. 27133-1 Pa. $11.95

THE MALE AND FEMALE FIGURE IN MOTION: 60 Classic Photographic Sequences, Eadweard Muybridge. 60 true-action photographs of men and women walking, running, climbing, bending, turning, etc., reproduced from rare 19th-century masterpiece. vi + 121pp. 9 x 12. 24745-7 Pa. $10.95

1001 QUESTIONS ANSWERED ABOUT THE SEASHORE, N. J. Berrill and Jacquelyn Berrill. Queries answered about dolphins, sea snails, sponges, starfish, fishes, shore birds, many others. Covers appearance, breeding, growth, feeding, much more. 305pp. 5¼ x 8¼. 23366-9 Pa. $8.95

GUIDE TO OWL WATCHING IN NORTH AMERICA, Donald S. Heintzelman. Superb guide offers complete data and descriptions of 19 species: barn owl, screech owl, snowy owl, many more. Expert coverage of owl-watching equipment, conservation, migrations and invasions, etc. Guide to observing sites. 84 illustrations. xiii + 193pp. 5⅜ x 8½. 27344-X Pa. $8.95

MEDICINAL AND OTHER USES OF NORTH AMERICAN PLANTS: A Historical Survey with Special Reference to the Eastern Indian Tribes, Charlotte Erichsen-Brown. Chronological historical citations document 500 years of usage of plants, trees, shrubs native to eastern Canada, northeastern U.S. Also complete identifying information. 343 illustrations. 544pp. 6½ x 9¼. 25951-X Pa. $12.95

STORYBOOK MAZES, Dave Phillips. 23 stories and mazes on two-page spreads: Wizard of Oz, Treasure Island, Robin Hood, etc. Solutions. 64pp. 8¼ x 11. 23628-5 Pa. $2.95

NEGRO FOLK MUSIC, U.S.A., Harold Courlander. Noted folklorist's scholarly yet readable analysis of rich and varied musical tradition. Includes authentic versions of over 40 folk songs. Valuable bibliography and discography. xi + 324pp. 5⅜ x 8½. 27350-4 Pa. $7.95

MOVIE-STAR PORTRAITS OF THE FORTIES, John Kobal (ed.). 163 glamor, studio photos of 106 stars of the 1940s: Rita Hayworth, Ava Gardner, Marlon Brando, Clark Gable, many more. 176pp. 8⅜ x 11¼. 23546-7 Pa. $12.95

BENCHLEY LOST AND FOUND, Robert Benchley. Finest humor from early 30s, about pet peeves, child psychologists, post office and others. Mostly unavailable elsewhere. 73 illustrations by Peter Arno and others. 183pp. 5⅜ x 8½. 22410-4 Pa. $6.95

YEKL and THE IMPORTED BRIDEGROOM AND OTHER STORIES OF YIDDISH NEW YORK, Abraham Cahan. Film Hester Street based on Yekl (1896). Novel, other stories among first about Jewish immigrants on N.Y.'s East Side. 240pp. 5⅜ x 8½. 22427-9 Pa. $6.95

SELECTED POEMS, Walt Whitman. Generous sampling from *Leaves of Grass*. Twenty-four poems include "I Hear America Singing," "Song of the Open Road," "I Sing the Body Electric," "When Lilacs Last in the Dooryard Bloom'd," "O Captain! My Captain!"–all reprinted from an authoritative edition. Lists of titles and first lines. 128pp. 5³⁄₁₆ x 8¼. 26878-0 Pa. $1.00

THE BEST TALES OF HOFFMANN, E. T. A. Hoffmann. 10 of Hoffmann's most important stories: "Nutcracker and the King of Mice," "The Golden Flowerpot," etc. 458pp. 5⅜ x 8½. 21793-0 Pa. $9.95

FROM FETISH TO GOD IN ANCIENT EGYPT, E. A. Wallis Budge. Rich detailed survey of Egyptian conception of "God" and gods, magic, cult of animals, Osiris, more. Also, superb English translations of hymns and legends. 240 illustrations. 545pp. 5⅜ x 8½. 25803-3 Pa. $11.95

FRENCH STORIES/CONTES FRANÇAIS: A Dual-Language Book, Wallace Fowlie. Ten stories by French masters, Voltaire to Camus: "Micromegas" by Voltaire; "The Atheist's Mass" by Balzac; "Minuet" by de Maupassant; "The Guest" by Camus, six more. Excellent English translations on facing pages. Also French-English vocabulary list, exercises, more. 352pp. 5⅜ x 8½. 26443-2 Pa. $8.95

CHICAGO AT THE TURN OF THE CENTURY IN PHOTOGRAPHS: 122 Historic Views from the Collections of the Chicago Historical Society, Larry A. Viskochil. Rare large-format prints offer detailed views of City Hall, State Street, the Loop, Hull House, Union Station, many other landmarks, circa 1904-1913. Introduction. Captions. Maps. 144pp. 9⅜ x 12¼. 24656-6 Pa. $12.95

OLD BROOKLYN IN EARLY PHOTOGRAPHS, 1865-1929, William Lee Younger. Luna Park, Gravesend race track, construction of Grand Army Plaza, moving of Hotel Brighton, etc. 157 previously unpublished photographs. 165pp. 8⅞ x 11¾. 23587-4 Pa. $13.95

THE MYTHS OF THE NORTH AMERICAN INDIANS, Lewis Spence. Rich anthology of the myths and legends of the Algonquins, Iroquois, Pawnees and Sioux, prefaced by an extensive historical and ethnological commentary. 36 illustrations. 480pp. 5⅜ x 8½. 25967-6 Pa. $8.95

AN ENCYCLOPEDIA OF BATTLES: Accounts of Over 1,560 Battles from 1479 B.C. to the Present, David Eggenberger. Essential details of every major battle in recorded history from the first battle of Megiddo in 1479 B.C. to Grenada in 1984. List of Battle Maps. New Appendix covering the years 1967-1984. Index. 99 illustrations. 544pp. 6½ x 9¼. 24913-1 Pa. $14.95

SAILING ALONE AROUND THE WORLD, Captain Joshua Slocum. First man to sail around the world, alone, in small boat. One of great feats of seamanship told in delightful manner. 67 illustrations. 294pp. 5⅜ x 8½. 20326-3 Pa. $5.95

ANARCHISM AND OTHER ESSAYS, Emma Goldman. Powerful, penetrating, prophetic essays on direct action, role of minorities, prison reform, puritan hypocrisy, violence, etc. 271pp. 5⅜ x 8½. 22484-8 Pa. $6.95

MYTHS OF THE HINDUS AND BUDDHISTS, Ananda K. Coomaraswamy and Sister Nivedita. Great stories of the epics; deeds of Krishna, Shiva, taken from puranas, Vedas, folk tales; etc. 32 illustrations. 400pp. 5⅜ x 8½. 21759-0 Pa. $10.95

BEYOND PSYCHOLOGY, Otto Rank. Fear of death, desire of immortality, nature of sexuality, social organization, creativity, according to Rankian system. 291pp. 5⅜ x 8½. 20485-5 Pa. $8.95

A THEOLOGICO-POLITICAL TREATISE, Benedict Spinoza. Also contains unfinished Political Treatise. Great classic on religious liberty, theory of government on common consent. R. Elwes translation. Total of 421pp. 5⅜ x 8½. 20249-6 Pa. $9.95

MY BONDAGE AND MY FREEDOM, Frederick Douglass. Born a slave, Douglass became outspoken force in antislavery movement. The best of Douglass' autobiographies. Graphic description of slave life. 464pp. 5⅜ x 8½. 22457-0 Pa. $8.95

FOLLOWING THE EQUATOR: A Journey Around the World, Mark Twain. Fascinating humorous account of 1897 voyage to Hawaii, Australia, India, New Zealand, etc. Ironic, bemused reports on peoples, customs, climate, flora and fauna, politics, much more. 197 illustrations. 720pp. 5⅜ x 8½. 26113-1 Pa. $15.95

THE PEOPLE CALLED SHAKERS, Edward D. Andrews. Definitive study of Shakers: origins, beliefs, practices, dances, social organization, furniture and crafts, etc. 33 illustrations. 351pp. 5⅜ x 8½. 21081-2 Pa. $8.95

THE MYTHS OF GREECE AND ROME, H. A. Guerber. A classic of mythology, generously illustrated, long prized for its simple, graphic, accurate retelling of the principal myths of Greece and Rome, and for its commentary on their origins and significance. With 64 illustrations by Michelangelo, Raphael, Titian, Rubens, Canova, Bernini and others. 480pp. 5⅜ x 8½. 27584-1 Pa. $9.95

PSYCHOLOGY OF MUSIC, Carl E. Seashore. Classic work discusses music as a medium from psychological viewpoint. Clear treatment of physical acoustics, auditory apparatus, sound perception, development of musical skills, nature of musical feeling, host of other topics. 88 figures. 408pp. 5⅜ x 8½. 21851-1 Pa. $10.95

THE PHILOSOPHY OF HISTORY, Georg W. Hegel. Great classic of Western thought develops concept that history is not chance but rational process, the evolution of freedom. 457pp. 5⅜ x 8½. 20112-0 Pa. $9.95

THE BOOK OF TEA, Kakuzo Okakura. Minor classic of the Orient: entertaining, charming explanation, interpretation of traditional Japanese culture in terms of tea ceremony. 94pp. 5⅜ x 8½. 20070-1 Pa. $3.95

LIFE IN ANCIENT EGYPT, Adolf Erman. Fullest, most thorough, detailed older account with much not in more recent books, domestic life, religion, magic, medicine, commerce, much more. Many illustrations reproduce tomb paintings, carvings, hieroglyphs, etc. 597pp. 5⅜ x 8½. 22632-8 Pa. $11.95

SUNDIALS, Their Theory and Construction, Albert Waugh. Far and away the best, most thorough coverage of ideas, mathematics concerned, types, construction, adjusting anywhere. Simple, nontechnical treatment allows even children to build several of these dials. Over 100 illustrations. 230pp. 5⅜ x 8½. 22947-5 Pa. $7.95

DYNAMICS OF FLUIDS IN POROUS MEDIA, Jacob Bear. For advanced students of ground water hydrology, soil mechanics and physics, drainage and irrigation engineering, and more. 335 illustrations. Exercises, with answers. 784pp. 6⅛ x 9¼. 65675-6 Pa. $19.95

SONGS OF EXPERIENCE: Facsimile Reproduction with 26 Plates in Full Color, William Blake. 26 full-color plates from a rare 1826 edition. Includes "The Tyger," "London," "Holy Thursday," and other poems. Printed text of poems. 48pp. 5¼ x 7. 24636-1 Pa. $4.95

OLD-TIME VIGNETTES IN FULL COLOR, Carol Belanger Grafton (ed.). Over 390 charming, often sentimental illustrations, selected from archives of Victorian graphics—pretty women posing, children playing, food, flowers, kittens and puppies, smiling cherubs, birds and butterflies, much more. All copyright-free. 48pp. 9¼ x 12¼. 27269-9 Pa. $5.95

PERSPECTIVE FOR ARTISTS, Rex Vicat Cole. Depth, perspective of sky and sea, shadows, much more, not usually covered. 391 diagrams, 81 reproductions of drawings and paintings. 279pp. 5⅜ x 8½. 22487-2 Pa. $6.95

DRAWING THE LIVING FIGURE, Joseph Sheppard. Innovative approach to artistic anatomy focuses on specifics of surface anatomy, rather than muscles and bones. Over 170 drawings of live models in front, back and side views, and in widely varying poses. Accompanying diagrams. 177 illustrations. Introduction. Index. 144pp. 8⅜ x11¼. 26723-7 Pa. $8.95

GOTHIC AND OLD ENGLISH ALPHABETS: 100 Complete Fonts, Dan X. Solo. Add power, elegance to posters, signs, other graphics with 100 stunning copyright-free alphabets: Blackstone, Dolbey, Germania, 97 more–including many lower-case, numerals, punctuation marks. 104pp. 8⅛ x 11. 24695-7 Pa. $8.95

HOW TO DO BEADWORK, Mary White. Fundamental book on craft from simple projects to five-bead chains and woven works. 106 illustrations. 142pp. 5⅜ x 8. 20697-1 Pa. $4.95

THE BOOK OF WOOD CARVING, Charles Marshall Sayers. Finest book for beginners discusses fundamentals and offers 34 designs. "Absolutely first rate . . . well thought out and well executed."–E. J. Tangerman. 118pp. 7¾ x 10⅝. 23654-4 Pa. $6.95

ILLUSTRATED CATALOG OF CIVIL WAR MILITARY GOODS: Union Army Weapons, Insignia, Uniform Accessories, and Other Equipment, Schuyler, Hartley, and Graham. Rare, profusely illustrated 1846 catalog includes Union Army uniform and dress regulations, arms and ammunition, coats, insignia, flags, swords, rifles, etc. 226 illustrations. 160pp. 9 x 12. 24939-5 Pa. $10.95

WOMEN'S FASHIONS OF THE EARLY 1900s: An Unabridged Republication of "New York Fashions, 1909," National Cloak & Suit Co. Rare catalog of mail-order fashions documents women's and children's clothing styles shortly after the turn of the century. Captions offer full descriptions, prices. Invaluable resource for fashion, costume historians. Approximately 725 illustrations. 128pp. 8⅜ x 11¼. 27276-1 Pa. $11.95

THE 1912 AND 1915 GUSTAV STICKLEY FURNITURE CATALOGS, Gustav Stickley. With over 200 detailed illustrations and descriptions, these two catalogs are essential reading and reference materials and identification guides for Stickley furniture. Captions cite materials, dimensions and prices. 112pp. 6½ x 9¼. 26676-1 Pa. $9.95

EARLY AMERICAN LOCOMOTIVES, John H. White, Jr. Finest locomotive engravings from early 19th century: historical (1804–74), main-line (after 1870), special, foreign, etc. 147 plates. 142pp. 11⅜ x 8¼. 22772-3 Pa. $10.95

THE TALL SHIPS OF TODAY IN PHOTOGRAPHS, Frank O. Braynard. Lavishly illustrated tribute to nearly 100 majestic contemporary sailing vessels: Amerigo Vespucci, Clearwater, Constitution, Eagle, Mayflower, Sea Cloud, Victory, many more. Authoritative captions provide statistics, background on each ship. 190 black-and-white photographs and illustrations. Introduction. 128pp. 8⅞ x 11¾. 27163-3 Pa. $13.95

EARLY NINETEENTH-CENTURY CRAFTS AND TRADES, Peter Stockham (ed.). Extremely rare 1807 volume describes to youngsters the crafts and trades of the day: brickmaker, weaver, dressmaker, bookbinder, ropemaker, saddler, many more. Quaint prose, charming illustrations for each craft. 20 black-and-white line illustrations. 192pp. 4⅝ x 6. 27293-1 Pa. $4.95

VICTORIAN FASHIONS AND COSTUMES FROM HARPER'S BAZAR, 1867–1898, Stella Blum (ed.). Day costumes, evening wear, sports clothes, shoes, hats, other accessories in over 1,000 detailed engravings. 320pp. 9⅜ x 12¼. 22990-4 Pa. $14.95

GUSTAV STICKLEY, THE CRAFTSMAN, Mary Ann Smith. Superb study surveys broad scope of Stickley's achievement, especially in architecture. Design philosophy, rise and fall of the Craftsman empire, descriptions and floor plans for many Craftsman houses, more. 86 black-and-white halftones. 31 line illustrations. Introduction 208pp. 6½ x 9¼. 27210-9 Pa. $9.95

THE LONG ISLAND RAIL ROAD IN EARLY PHOTOGRAPHS, Ron Ziel. Over 220 rare photos, informative text document origin (1844) and development of rail service on Long Island. Vintage views of early trains, locomotives, stations, passengers, crews, much more. Captions. 8⅞ x 11¾. 26301-0 Pa. $13.95

THE BOOK OF OLD SHIPS: From Egyptian Galleys to Clipper Ships, Henry B. Culver. Superb, authoritative history of sailing vessels, with 80 magnificent line illustrations. Galley, bark, caravel, longship, whaler, many more. Detailed, informative text on each vessel by noted naval historian. Introduction. 256pp. 5⅜ x 8½. 27332-6 Pa. $7.95

TEN BOOKS ON ARCHITECTURE, Vitruvius. The most important book ever written on architecture. Early Roman aesthetics, technology, classical orders, site selection, all other aspects. Morgan translation. 331pp. 5⅜ x 8½. 20645-9 Pa. $8.95

THE HUMAN FIGURE IN MOTION, Eadweard Muybridge. More than 4,500 stopped-action photos, in action series, showing undraped men, women, children jumping, lying down, throwing, sitting, wrestling, carrying, etc. 390pp. 7⅞ x 10⅝. 20204-6 Clothbd. $25.95

TREES OF THE EASTERN AND CENTRAL UNITED STATES AND CANADA, William M. Harlow. Best one-volume guide to 140 trees. Full descriptions, woodlore, range, etc. Over 600 illustrations. Handy size. 288pp. 4½ x 6⅜. 20395-6 Pa. $5.95

SONGS OF WESTERN BIRDS, Dr. Donald J. Borror. Complete song and call repertoire of 60 western species, including flycatchers, juncoes, cactus wrens, many more–includes fully illustrated booklet. Cassette and manual 99913-0 $8.95

GROWING AND USING HERBS AND SPICES, Milo Miloradovich. Versatile handbook provides all the information needed for cultivation and use of all the herbs and spices available in North America. 4 illustrations. Index. Glossary. 236pp. 5⅜ x 8½. 25058-X Pa. $6.95

BIG BOOK OF MAZES AND LABYRINTHS, Walter Shepherd. 50 mazes and labyrinths in all–classical, solid, ripple, and more–in one great volume. Perfect inexpensive puzzler for clever youngsters. Full solutions. 112pp. 8⅛ x 11. 22951-3 Pa. $4.95

PIANO TUNING, J. Cree Fischer. Clearest, best book for beginner, amateur. Simple repairs, raising dropped notes, tuning by easy method of flattened fifths. No previous skills needed. 4 illustrations. 201pp. 5⅜ x 8½. 23267-0 Pa. $6.95

A SOURCE BOOK IN THEATRICAL HISTORY, A. M. Nagler. Contemporary observers on acting, directing, make-up, costuming, stage props, machinery, scene design, from Ancient Greece to Chekhov. 611pp. 5⅜ x 8½. 20515-0 Pa. $12.95

THE COMPLETE NONSENSE OF EDWARD LEAR, Edward Lear. All nonsense limericks, zany alphabets, Owl and Pussycat, songs, nonsense botany, etc., illustrated by Lear. Total of 320pp. 5⅜ x 8½. (USO) 20167-8 Pa. $6.95

VICTORIAN PARLOUR POETRY: An Annotated Anthology, Michael R. Turner. 117 gems by Longfellow, Tennyson, Browning, many lesser-known poets. "The Village Blacksmith," "Curfew Must Not Ring Tonight," "Only a Baby Small," dozens more, often difficult to find elsewhere. Index of poets, titles, first lines. xxiii + 325pp. 5⅜ x 8¼. 27044-0 Pa. $8.95

DUBLINERS, James Joyce. Fifteen stories offer vivid, tightly focused observations of the lives of Dublin's poorer classes. At least one, "The Dead," is considered a masterpiece. Reprinted complete and unabridged from standard edition. 160pp. 5³⁄₁₆ x 8¼. 26870-5 Pa. $1.00

THE HAUNTED MONASTERY and THE CHINESE MAZE MURDERS, Robert van Gulik. Two full novels by van Gulik, set in 7th-century China, continue adventures of Judge Dee and his companions. An evil Taoist monastery, seemingly supernatural events; overgrown topiary maze hides strange crimes. 27 illustrations. 328pp. 5⅜ x 8½. 23502-5 Pa. $8.95

THE BOOK OF THE SACRED MAGIC OF ABRAMELIN THE MAGE, translated by S. MacGregor Mathers. Medieval manuscript of ceremonial magic. Basic document in Aleister Crowley, Golden Dawn groups. 268pp. 5⅜ x 8½. 23211-5 Pa. $8.95

NEW RUSSIAN-ENGLISH AND ENGLISH-RUSSIAN DICTIONARY, M. A. O'Brien. This is a remarkably handy Russian dictionary, containing a surprising amount of information, including over 70,000 entries. 366pp. 4½ x 6⅛. 20208-9 Pa. $9.95

HISTORIC HOMES OF THE AMERICAN PRESIDENTS, Second, Revised Edition, Irvin Haas. A traveler's guide to American Presidential homes, most open to the public, depicting and describing homes occupied by every American President from George Washington to George Bush. With visiting hours, admission charges, travel routes. 175 photographs. Index. 160pp. 8¼ x 11. 26751-2 Pa. $11.95

NEW YORK IN THE FORTIES, Andreas Feininger. 162 brilliant photographs by the well-known photographer, formerly with *Life* magazine. Commuters, shoppers, Times Square at night, much else from city at its peak. Captions by John von Hartz. 181pp. 9¼ x 10¾. 23585-8 Pa. $12.95

INDIAN SIGN LANGUAGE, William Tomkins. Over 525 signs developed by Sioux and other tribes. Written instructions and diagrams. Also 290 pictographs. 111pp. 6⅛ x 9¼. 22029-X Pa. $3.95

ANATOMY: A Complete Guide for Artists, Joseph Sheppard. A master of figure drawing shows artists how to render human anatomy convincingly. Over 460 illustrations. 224pp. 8⅜ x 11¼. 27279-6 Pa. $10.95

MEDIEVAL CALLIGRAPHY: Its History and Technique, Marc Drogin. Spirited history, comprehensive instruction manual covers 13 styles (ca. 4th century thru 15th). Excellent photographs; directions for duplicating medieval techniques with modern tools. 224pp. 8⅜ x 11¼. 26142-5 Pa. $11.95

DRIED FLOWERS: How to Prepare Them, Sarah Whitlock and Martha Rankin. Complete instructions on how to use silica gel, meal and borax, perlite aggregate, sand and borax, glycerine and water to create attractive permanent flower arrangements. 12 illustrations. 32pp. 5⅜ x 8½. 21802-3 Pa. $1.00

EASY-TO-MAKE BIRD FEEDERS FOR WOODWORKERS, Scott D. Campbell. Detailed, simple-to-use guide for designing, constructing, caring for and using feeders. Text, illustrations for 12 classic and contemporary designs. 96pp. 5⅜ x 8½. 25847-5 Pa. $2.95

SCOTTISH WONDER TALES FROM MYTH AND LEGEND, Donald A. Mackenzie. 16 lively tales tell of giants rumbling down mountainsides, of a magic wand that turns stone pillars into warriors, of gods and goddesses, evil hags, powerful forces and more. 240pp. 5⅜ x 8½. 29677-6 Pa. $6.95

THE HISTORY OF UNDERCLOTHES, C. Willett Cunnington and Phyllis Cunnington. Fascinating, well-documented survey covering six centuries of English undergarments, enhanced with over 100 illustrations: 12th-century laced-up bodice, footed long drawers (1795), 19th-century bustles, 19th-century corsets for men, Victorian "bust improvers," much more. 272pp. 5⅜ x 8¼. 27124-2 Pa. $9.95

ARTS AND CRAFTS FURNITURE: The Complete Brooks Catalog of 1912, Brooks Manufacturing Co. Photos and detailed descriptions of more than 150 now very collectible furniture designs from the Arts and Crafts movement depict davenports, settees, buffets, desks, tables, chairs, bedsteads, dressers and more, all built of solid, quarter-sawed oak. Invaluable for students and enthusiasts of antiques, Americana and the decorative arts. 80pp. 6½ x 9¼. 27471-3 Pa. $7.95

HOW WE INVENTED THE AIRPLANE: An Illustrated History, Orville Wright. Fascinating firsthand account covers early experiments, construction of planes and motors, first flights, much more. Introduction and commentary by Fred C. Kelly. 76 photographs. 96pp. 8¼ x 11. 25662-6 Pa. $8.95

THE ARTS OF THE SAILOR: Knotting, Splicing and Ropework, Hervey Garrett Smith. Indispensable shipboard reference covers tools, basic knots and useful hitches; handsewing and canvas work, more. Over 100 illustrations. Delightful reading for sea lovers. 256pp. 5⅜ x 8½. 26440-8 Pa. $7.95

FRANK LLOYD WRIGHT'S FALLINGWATER: The House and Its History, Second, Revised Edition, Donald Hoffmann. A total revision—both in text and illustrations—of the standard document on Fallingwater, the boldest, most personal architectural statement of Wright's mature years, updated with valuable new material from the recently opened Frank Lloyd Wright Archives. "Fascinating"–*The New York Times*. 116 illustrations. 128pp. 9¼ x 10¾. 27430-6 Pa. $11.95

AUTOBIOGRAPHY: The Story of My Experiments with Truth, Mohandas K. Gandhi. Boyhood, legal studies, purification, the growth of the Satyagraha (nonviolent protest) movement. Critical, inspiring work of the man responsible for the freedom of India. 480pp. 5⅜ x 8½. (USO)   24593-4 Pa. $8.95

CELTIC MYTHS AND LEGENDS, T. W. Rolleston. Masterful retelling of Irish and Welsh stories and tales. Cuchulain, King Arthur, Deirdre, the Grail, many more. First paperback edition. 58 full-page illustrations. 512pp. 5⅜ x 8½.   26507-2 Pa. $9.95

THE PRINCIPLES OF PSYCHOLOGY, William James. Famous long course complete, unabridged. Stream of thought, time perception, memory, experimental methods; great work decades ahead of its time. 94 figures. 1,391pp. 5⅜ x 8½. 2-vol. set.
Vol. I: 20381-6 Pa. $12.95
Vol. II: 20382-4 Pa. $12.95

THE WORLD AS WILL AND REPRESENTATION, Arthur Schopenhauer. Definitive English translation of Schopenhauer's life work, correcting more than 1,000 errors, omissions in earlier translations. Translated by E. F. J. Payne. Total of 1,269pp. 5⅜ x 8½. 2-vol. set.
Vol. 1: 21761-2 Pa. $11.95
Vol. 2: 21762-0 Pa. $11.95

MAGIC AND MYSTERY IN TIBET, Madame Alexandra David-Neel. Experiences among lamas, magicians, sages, sorcerers, Bonpa wizards. A true psychic discovery. 32 illustrations. 321pp. 5⅜ x 8½. (USO)   22682-4 Pa. $8.95

THE EGYPTIAN BOOK OF THE DEAD, E. A. Wallis Budge. Complete reproduction of Ani's papyrus, finest ever found. Full hieroglyphic text, interlinear transliteration, word-for-word translation, smooth translation. 533pp. 6½ x 9¼.
21866-X Pa. $10.95

MATHEMATICS FOR THE NONMATHEMATICIAN, Morris Kline. Detailed, college-level treatment of mathematics in cultural and historical context, with numerous exercises. Recommended Reading Lists. Tables. Numerous figures. 641pp. 5⅜ x 8½.
24823-2 Pa. $11.95

THEORY OF WING SECTIONS: Including a Summary of Airfoil Data, Ira H. Abbott and A. E. von Doenhoff. Concise compilation of subsonic aerodynamic characteristics of NACA wing sections, plus description of theory. 350pp. of tables. 693pp. 5⅜ x 8½.   60586-8 Pa. $14.95

THE RIME OF THE ANCIENT MARINER, Gustave Doré, S. T. Coleridge. Doré's finest work; 34 plates capture moods, subtleties of poem. Flawless full-size reproductions printed on facing pages with authoritative text of poem. "Beautiful. Simply beautiful."–*Publisher's Weekly.* 77pp. 9¼ x 12.   22305-1 Pa. $6.95

NORTH AMERICAN INDIAN DESIGNS FOR ARTISTS AND CRAFTSPEOPLE, Eva Wilson. Over 360 authentic copyright-free designs adapted from Navajo blankets, Hopi pottery, Sioux buffalo hides, more. Geometrics, symbolic figures, plant and animal motifs, etc. 128pp. 8⅜ x 11. (EUK)   25341-4 Pa. $8.95

SCULPTURE: Principles and Practice, Louis Slobodkin. Step-by-step approach to clay, plaster, metals, stone; classical and modern. 253 drawings, photos. 255pp. 8⅛ x 11.
22960-2 Pa. $10.95

PHOTOGRAPHIC SKETCHBOOK OF THE CIVIL WAR, Alexander Gardner. 100 photos taken on field during the Civil War. Famous shots of Manassas Harper's Ferry, Lincoln, Richmond, slave pens, etc. 244pp. 10⅝ x 8¼.   22731-6 Pa. $9.95

FIVE ACRES AND INDEPENDENCE, Maurice G. Kains. Great back-to-the-land classic explains basics of self-sufficient farming. The one book to get. 95 illustrations. 397pp. 5⅜ x 8½.   20974-1 Pa. $7.95

SONGS OF EASTERN BIRDS, Dr. Donald J. Borror. Songs and calls of 60 species most common to eastern U.S.: warblers, woodpeckers, flycatchers, thrushes, larks, many more in high-quality recording.   Cassette and manual 99912-2 $8.95

A MODERN HERBAL, Margaret Grieve. Much the fullest, most exact, most useful compilation of herbal material. Gigantic alphabetical encyclopedia, from aconite to zedoary, gives botanical information, medical properties, folklore, economic uses, much else. Indispensable to serious reader. 161 illustrations. 888pp. 6½ x 9¼. 2-vol. set. (USO)   Vol. I: 22798-7 Pa. $9.95
        Vol. II: 22799-5 Pa. $9.95

HIDDEN TREASURE MAZE BOOK, Dave Phillips. Solve 34 challenging mazes accompanied by heroic tales of adventure. Evil dragons, people-eating plants, blood-thirsty giants, many more dangerous adversaries lurk at every twist and turn. 34 mazes, stories, solutions. 48pp. 8¼ x 11.   24566-7 Pa. $2.95

LETTERS OF W. A. MOZART, Wolfgang A. Mozart. Remarkable letters show bawdy wit, humor, imagination, musical insights, contemporary musical world; includes some letters from Leopold Mozart. 276pp. 5⅜ x 8½.   22859-2 Pa. $7.95

BASIC PRINCIPLES OF CLASSICAL BALLET, Agrippina Vaganova. Great Russian theoretician, teacher explains methods for teaching classical ballet. 118 illustrations. 175pp. 5⅜ x 8½.   22036-2 Pa. $5.95

THE JUMPING FROG, Mark Twain. Revenge edition. The original story of The Celebrated Jumping Frog of Calaveras County, a hapless French translation, and Twain's hilarious "retranslation" from the French. 12 illustrations. 66pp. 5⅜ x 8½.   22686-7 Pa. $3.95

BEST REMEMBERED POEMS, Martin Gardner (ed.). The 126 poems in this superb collection of 19th- and 20th-century British and American verse range from Shelley's "To a Skylark" to the impassioned "Renascence" of Edna St. Vincent Millay and to Edward Lear's whimsical "The Owl and the Pussycat." 224pp. 5⅜ x 8½.
        27165-X Pa. $4.95

COMPLETE SONNETS, William Shakespeare. Over 150 exquisite poems deal with love, friendship, the tyranny of time, beauty's evanescence, death and other themes in language of remarkable power, precision and beauty. Glossary of archaic terms. 80pp. 5³⁄₁₆ x 8¼.   26686-9 Pa. $1.00

BODIES IN A BOOKSHOP, R. T. Campbell. Challenging mystery of blackmail and murder with ingenious plot and superbly drawn characters. In the best tradition of British suspense fiction. 192pp. 5⅜ x 8½.   24720-1 Pa. $6.95

THE WIT AND HUMOR OF OSCAR WILDE, Alvin Redman (ed.). More than 1,000 ripostes, paradoxes, wisecracks: Work is the curse of the drinking classes; I can resist everything except temptation; etc. 258pp. 5⅜ x 8½. 20602-5 Pa. $5.95

SHAKESPEARE LEXICON AND QUOTATION DICTIONARY, Alexander Schmidt. Full definitions, locations, shades of meaning in every word in plays and poems. More than 50,000 exact quotations. 1,485pp. 6½ x 9¼. 2-vol. set.
Vol. 1: 22726-X Pa. $16.95
Vol. 2: 22727-8 Pa. $16.95

SELECTED POEMS, Emily Dickinson. Over 100 best-known, best-loved poems by one of America's foremost poets, reprinted from authoritative early editions. No comparable edition at this price. Index of first lines. 64pp. 5$\frac{3}{16}$ x 8¼. 26466-1 Pa. $1.00

CELEBRATED CASES OF JUDGE DEE (DEE GOONG AN), translated by Robert van Gulik. Authentic 18th-century Chinese detective novel; Dee and associates solve three interlocked cases. Led to van Gulik's own stories with same characters. Extensive introduction. 9 illustrations. 237pp. 5⅜ x 8½. 23337-5 Pa. $6.95

THE MALLEUS MALEFICARUM OF KRAMER AND SPRENGER, translated by Montague Summers. Full text of most important witchhunter's "bible," used by both Catholics and Protestants. 278pp. 6⅝ x 10. 22802-9 Pa. $12.95

SPANISH STORIES/CUENTOS ESPAÑOLES: A Dual-Language Book, Angel Flores (ed.). Unique format offers 13 great stories in Spanish by Cervantes, Borges, others. Faithful English translations on facing pages. 352pp. 5⅜ x 8½. 25399-6 Pa. $8.95

THE CHICAGO WORLD'S FAIR OF 1893: A Photographic Record, Stanley Appelbaum (ed.). 128 rare photos show 200 buildings, Beaux-Arts architecture, Midway, original Ferris Wheel, Edison's kinetoscope, more. Architectural emphasis; full text. 116pp. 8¼ x 11. 23990-X Pa. $9.95

OLD QUEENS, N.Y., IN EARLY PHOTOGRAPHS, Vincent F. Seyfried and William Asadorian. Over 160 rare photographs of Maspeth, Jamaica, Jackson Heights, and other areas. Vintage views of DeWitt Clinton mansion, 1939 World's Fair and more. Captions. 192pp. 8⅞ x 11. 26358-4 Pa. $12.95

CAPTURED BY THE INDIANS: 15 Firsthand Accounts, 1750-1870, Frederick Drimmer. Astounding true historical accounts of grisly torture, bloody conflicts, relentless pursuits, miraculous escapes and more, by people who lived to tell the tale. 384pp. 5⅜ x 8½. 24901-8 Pa. $8.95

THE WORLD'S GREAT SPEECHES, Lewis Copeland and Lawrence W. Lamm (eds.). Vast collection of 278 speeches of Greeks to 1970. Powerful and effective models; unique look at history. 842pp. 5⅜ x 8½. 20468-5 Pa. $14.95

THE BOOK OF THE SWORD, Sir Richard F. Burton. Great Victorian scholar/adventurer's eloquent, erudite history of the "queen of weapons"–from prehistory to early Roman Empire. Evolution and development of early swords, variations (sabre, broadsword, cutlass, scimitar, etc.), much more. 336pp. 6⅛ x 9¼. 25434-8 Pa. $9.95

THE INFLUENCE OF SEA POWER UPON HISTORY, 1660–1783, A. T. Mahan. Influential classic of naval history and tactics still used as text in war colleges. First paperback edition. 4 maps. 24 battle plans. 640pp. 5⅜ x 8½. 25509-3 Pa. $12.95

THE STORY OF THE TITANIC AS TOLD BY ITS SURVIVORS, Jack Winocour (ed.). What it was really like. Panic, despair, shocking inefficiency, and a little heroism. More thrilling than any fictional account. 26 illustrations. 320pp. 5⅜ x 8½. 20610-6 Pa. $8.95

FAIRY AND FOLK TALES OF THE IRISH PEASANTRY, William Butler Yeats (ed.). Treasury of 64 tales from the twilight world of Celtic myth and legend: "The Soul Cages," "The Kildare Pooka," "King O'Toole and his Goose," many more. Introduction and Notes by W. B. Yeats. 352pp. 5⅜ x 8½. 26941-8 Pa. $8.95

BUDDHIST MAHAYANA TEXTS, E. B. Cowell and Others (eds.). Superb, accurate translations of basic documents in Mahayana Buddhism, highly important in history of religions. The Buddha-karita of Asvaghosha, Larger Sukhavativyuha, more. 448pp. 5⅜ x 8½. 25552-2 Pa. $9.95

ONE TWO THREE . . . INFINITY: Facts and Speculations of Science, George Gamow. Great physicist's fascinating, readable overview of contemporary science: number theory, relativity, fourth dimension, entropy, genes, atomic structure, much more. 128 illustrations. Index. 352pp. 5⅜ x 8½. 25664-2 Pa. $8.95

ENGINEERING IN HISTORY, Richard Shelton Kirby, et al. Broad, nontechnical survey of history's major technological advances: birth of Greek science, industrial revolution, electricity and applied science, 20th-century automation, much more. 181 illustrations. ". . . excellent . . ."–*Isis.* Bibliography. vii + 530pp. 5⅜ x 8¼. 26412-2 Pa. $14.95

DALÍ ON MODERN ART: The Cuckolds of Antiquated Modern Art, Salvador Dalí. Influential painter skewers modern art and its practitioners. Outrageous evaluations of Picasso, Cézanne, Turner, more. 15 renderings of paintings discussed. 44 calligraphic decorations by Dalí. 96pp. 5⅜ x 8½. (USO) 29220-7 Pa. $4.95

ANTIQUE PLAYING CARDS: A Pictorial History, Henry René D'Allemagne. Over 900 elaborate, decorative images from rare playing cards (14th–20th centuries): Bacchus, death, dancing dogs, hunting scenes, royal coats of arms, players cheating, much more. 96pp. 9¼ x 12¼. 29265-7 Pa. $11.95

MAKING FURNITURE MASTERPIECES: 30 Projects with Measured Drawings, Franklin H. Gottshall. Step-by-step instructions, illustrations for constructing handsome, useful pieces, among them a Sheraton desk, Chippendale chair, Spanish desk, Queen Anne table and a William and Mary dressing mirror. 224pp. 8⅛ x 11¼. 29338-6 Pa. $13.95

THE FOSSIL BOOK: A Record of Prehistoric Life, Patricia V. Rich et al. Profusely illustrated definitive guide covers everything from single-celled organisms and dinosaurs to birds and mammals and the interplay between climate and man. Over 1,500 illustrations. 760pp. 7½ x 10⅛. 29371-8 Pa. $29.95

Prices subject to change without notice.

Available at your book dealer or write for free catalog to Dept. GI, Dover Publications, Inc., 31 East 2nd St., Mineola, N.Y. 11501. Dover publishes more than 500 books each year on science, elementary and advanced mathematics, biology, music, art, literary history, social sciences and other areas.